Workbook to accompany

Prego!

Workbook to accompany

Prego!
An Invitation to Italian

Fifth Edition

Graziana Lazzarino
University of Colorado, Boulder

Andrea Dini
Hofstra University

Boston Burr Ridge, IL Dubuque, IA Madison, WI New York San Francisco St. Louis
Bangkok Bogotá Caracas Lisbon London Madrid
Mexico City Milan New Delhi Seoul Singapore Sydney Taipei Toronto

McGraw-Hill Higher Education
A Division of The ***McGraw-Hill*** *Companies*

This is an  book.

Workbook to accompany
Prego! An Invitation to Italian

Published by McGraw-Hill, an imprint of The McGraw-Hill Companies, Inc., 1221 Avenue of the Americas, New York, NY 10020.

2 3 4 5 6 7 8 9 0 QPD QPD 0 9 8 7 6 5 4 3 2 1

ISBN 0-07-243267-5

Vice president/Editor-in-chief: *Thalia Dorwick*
Sponsoring editor: *Leslie Hines*
Development editors: *Marissa Galliani-Sanavio* and *Lindsay Eufusia*
Marketing manager: *Nick Agnew*
Project manager: *David Sutton*
Senior Production Supervisor: *Pam Augspurger*
Compositor: *York Graphic Services, Inc.*
Typeface: *Palatino*
Printer: *Quebecor Printing Dubuque, Inc.*

Grateful acknowledgment is made for use of the following material:
Page 44, 49 © ALI Press Agency, Brussels; *50* Università degli Studi di Bergamo; *57* © ALI Press Agency, Brussels; *63 Grazia; 71, 74* Disegnatori Riuniti; *76 Grazia; 79* © ALI Press Agency, Brussels; *85 La Settimana Enigmistica; 93 Relax Enigmistica; 95 Grazia; 110 Panorama; 120, 121, 127* © ALI Press Agency, Brussels; *133* Disegnatori Riuniti; *135* © ALI Press Agency, Brussels; *142, 144 Relax Enigmistica; 155* Disegnatori Riuniti; *157, 158* © ALI Press Agency, Brussels; *165 L'Espresso; 169* © ALI Press Agency, Brussels; *170, 171, 176 Relax Enigmistica; 178 Oggi; 181* Disegnatori Riuniti; *182, 184, 185* © ALI Press Agency, Brussels; *190 Oggi; 200 Gioia; 204 Relax Enigmistica; 205 La Settimana Enigmistica; 208* © ALI Press Agency, Brussels; *209 La Settimana Enigmistica; 212 Panorama; 216* Disegnatori Riuniti; *222 Epoca; 224* © ALI Press Agency, Brussels; *226, 227 La Settimana Enigmistica; 230* Disegnatori Riuniti

http://www.mhhe.com

Contents

Preface

This *Workbook* is designed to accompany *Prego! An Invitation to Italian,* Fifth Edition. As in the fourth edition, the *Workbook* offers a variety of written exercises to reinforce the vocabulary and structures presented in the student text.

NEW FEATURES AND CHANGES IN THIS FIFTH EDITION

Lettura: These extended reading passages give students further insight into both traditional and changing Italian culture (from Sunday lunch with the in-laws to the evolution of TV programming from the 1960's to the present). The follow-up exercises check students' reading comprehension and often ask students to compare Italian lifestyle to their own. These cultural comparisons could serve as the basis for class discussion.

Prova-quiz: These review activities, now appearing in every third chapter starting in **Capitolo 3**, test students' understanding of key structures and vocabulary. They have been thoroughly updated to reflect changes in the fifth edition.

CHAPTER ORGANIZATION

The chapter sections follow the same sequence as the material in the student text.

The exercises in the **Capitolo preliminare**, under the headings *Saluti ed espressioni di cortesia, In classe, Alfabeto e suoni, Numeri da uno a cento, Calendario,* and *Parole simili,* reinforce the practical, functional material presented in the student text. The chapter concludes with the new **Lettura** section followed by the **Un po' di scrittura** and **Attualità** sections.

Capitoli 1 through **18** are organized as follows:

Vocabolario preliminare: All thematic chapter vocabulary is practiced in a rich and varied selection of exercises, including cloze paragraphs, dialogues, and crossword puzzles.

Grammatica: The three to six grammar points of each chapter in the student text appear under their own headings. They are reviewed and integrated with chapter vocabulary in both controlled and open-ended activities.

Proverbi e modi di dire: Boxes highlighting popular sayings appear one to three times a chapter.

Prova-quiz: Synthetic, efficient review activities follow the **Grammatica** section every third chapter.

Lettura: These insightful readings and accompanying exercises test reading comprehension and encourage cultural comparison analysis and discussions.

Un po' di scrittura: Students are invited to use their newly acquired skills to offer their personal views on cultural themes and issues.

Attualità: A rich selection of authentic materials, including advertisements, cartoons, surveys, and school brochures, brings students face-to-face with the everyday language of contemporary Italy. The accompanying exercises sharpen reading skills and encourage reflection and self-expression.

Answers to *Workbook* activities are in the *Instructor's Manual and Testing Program.* No answers are provided for open-ended activities, marked with the symbol ❖.

ACKNOWLEDGMENTS

The authors would like to thank Marissa Galliani-Sanavio, Leslie Hines, and Lindsay Eufusia for their creative input into the fifth edition, and Thalia Dorwick for supporting the entire project.

Name ______________________________

Date ______________________________

Class ______________________________

PRELIMINARE

A. Saluti ed espressioni di cortesia

A. Presentazioni (*Introductions*). Two students introduce themselves on the first day of class. Complete the brief dialogues.

DIALOGUE 1

Buon ____________[1]

Mi ____________[2] Chiara Martini.

____________[3] studentessa d'italiano.

Sono ____________[4] Firenze.

DIALOGUE 2

Buona ____________[1]

____________[2] chiamo Giampiero Crispolti.

Sono ____________[3] di psicologia.

____________[4] di Perugia.

❖ **B. E io, chi sono?** Now introduce yourself. Use the greetings you find most appropriate.

____

____

____

____

____

C. Saluti (*Greetings*). How do these people greet each other? Do they use the formal or familiar form of address? Complete the dialogues with the appropriate expressions.

DIALOGUE 1

SIG. BOSSI: ____________[1], signora, ____________ ____________?[2]

SIG.RA PIVETTI: Bene, ____________.[3] E ____________?[4]

SIG. BOSSI: Non ____________[5] male.

SIG.RA PIVETTI: ArrivederLa!

SIG. BOSSI: ____________![6]

DIALOGUE 2

CARLO: ____________,[1] Francesca!

FRANCESCA: Ciao, Carlo, come ____________?[2]

CARLO: Abbastanza ____________,[3] grazie. E ____________?[4]

FRANCESCA: Così ____________.[5]

CARLO: ____________,[6] Francesca!

FRANCESCA: ____________[7] presto!

D. Espressioni di cortesia. What would you say in the following situations?

1. You've just pushed someone accidentally.

   Scusi

2. You do not understand what someone has just said to you.

   Scusi

3. You are shaking hands with someone you've just met.

   piacere

4. Someone has just thanked you.

   prego

B. In classe

A. Espressioni, domande e istruzioni. Look back at the **In classe** section of your text, then give the appropriate expression, question, or instructions in Italian.

1. What do students say when they haven't understood?

   No, Non capisco

2. What do students say to find out how to spell **cappuccino** in Italian?

   Come si scrive

3. What do students say to find out what **primavera** means?

   cosa vuol dire

4. What do instructors say when they want students to listen?

   Ascoltate

5. What do instructors say when they want students to repeat something together?

   Repetete   Ripeta per favore

B. Ecco una classe. Using the words from the following list, write the names of objects found in a classroom on the lines provided on page 3. Consult the drawing if you need help.

un dizionario dictionary
un foglio di carta
un gesso chalk
una lavagna blackboard
un libro book
una mappa map
una matita pencil
un quaderno notebook
una sedia chair
un voto
un compito - homework

Name ______________________ Date ____________ Class ______________________

1. una lavagna
2. una ~~matita~~ gesso
3. ______________________
4. un quaderno
5. una matita
6. ______________________
7. una mappa
8. un dizionario
9. un libro
10. una sedia

C. Alfabeto e suoni

A. L'alfabeto italiano. Answer the following questions about the Italian alphabet.

1. What are the five letters the Italian alphabet uses in words of foreign origin?

   j k w x y

2. What letter in the Italian alphabet is never pronounced? h

B. Come si scrive? Spell the following names of famous Italians.

ESEMPIO: Gianni Versace → Gi, i, a, enne, enne, i, Vu, e, erre, esse, a, ci, e

1. Andrea Bocelli ______________________
2. Sophia Loren ______________________
3. Roberto Benigni ______________________
4. Dante Alighieri ______________________
5. Umberto Eco ______________________
6. Guglielmo Marconi ______________________

D. Numeri da uno a cento

A. Quanti (*How many*)? Write out the numbers given in parentheses.

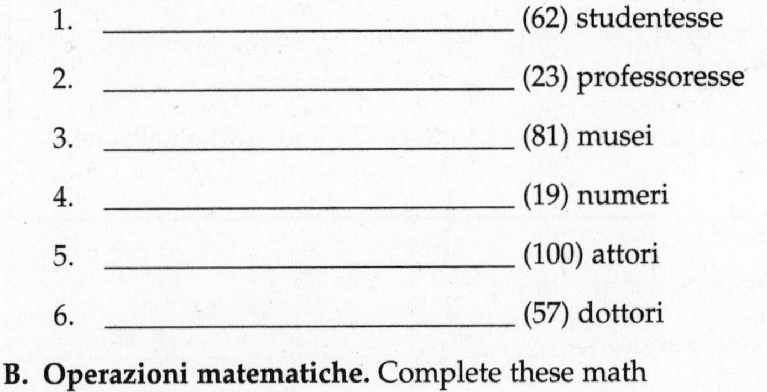

1. ______________________ (62) studentesse
2. ______________________ (23) professoresse
3. ______________________ (81) musei
4. ______________________ (19) numeri
5. ______________________ (100) attori
6. ______________________ (57) dottori

—...trentuno pecore,[a] signore; trentadue pecore, signore; trentatré pecore, signore...

[a]*sheep*

B. Operazioni matematiche. Complete these math problems. Write out all numbers.

1. tredici + ______________________ = ventiquattro
2. undici + ______________________ = sessantuno
3. due + ______________________ = settantacinque
4. quindici + ______________________ = quarantadue

5. venticinque + ______________________ = settantotto

6. sessanta – ______________________ = quarantotto

7. trenta – ______________________ = ventisette

8. cento – ______________________ = quindici

E. Calendario

A. Mesi e stagioni. Write the names of the seasons indicated by the dates. Then write the names of the corresponding four months. Some months are in two seasons. Remember that the day precedes the month in dates in Italian. The first season is done for you.

1. 21/12 → 19/3 *inverno*

   dicembre *febbraio*

   gennaio *marzo*

2. 20/3 → 20/6 ______________

3. 21/6 → 21/9 ______________

4. 22/9 → 20/12 ______________

PROVERBI E MODI DI DIRE

As in English, there is a rhyme in Italian for remembering how many days are in each month of the year. Read it several times, until you have memorized it.

Trenta giorni ha novembre, con aprile, giugno e settembre; di ventotto ce n'è uno, tutti gli altri ne hanno trentuno.

❖ **B. Anni, date di nascita.** Answer the following personal questions.

1. Quando sei nato/a (in quale giorno, mese e anno)? ______________

2. Quanti anni hai? ______________

3. Secondo te, quanti anni ha il professore o la professoressa d'italiano? ______________

Name ______________________ Date ____________ Class ______________________

C. Giorni della settimana. Here are the names of six of the days of the week, according to their origin. They are not in order. Can you recognize them?

1. il giorno della Luna ______________________
2. il giorno di Venere ______________________
3. il giorno di Saturno ______________________
4. il giorno di Marte ______________________
5. il giorno di Giove ______________________
6. il giorno di Mercurio ______________________

____

D. Calendario. Answer the following questions according to the calendar.

1. Che giorno della (*of the*) settimana è la Festa della donna, l'otto marzo? ______________________
2. Che giorno della settimana è la Festa del lavoro, il primo maggio? ______________________
3. Che giorno della settimana è la Festa della liberazione, il 25 aprile? ______________________
4. Che giorno della settimana è il capo d'anno, il primo gennaio? ______________________

GENNAIO						
L		2	9	16	23	30
M		3	10	17	24	31
M		4	11	18	25	
G		5	12	19	26	
V		6	13	20	27	
S		7	14	21	28	
D	1	8	15	22	29	

FEBBRAIO					
L		6	13	20	27
M		7	14	21	28
M	1	8	15	22	
G	2	9	16	23	
V	3	10	17	24	
S	4	11	18	25	
D	5	12	19	26	

MARZO					
L		6	13	20	27
M		7	14	21	28
M	1	8	15	22	29
G	2	9	16	23	30
V	3	10	17	24	31
S	4	11	18	25	
D	5	12	19	26	

APRILE					
L		3	10	17	24
M		4	11	18	25
M		5	12	19	26
G		6	13	20	27
V		7	14	21	28
S	1	8	15	22	29
D	2	9	16	23	30

MAGGIO					
L	1	8	15	22	29
M	2	9	16	23	30
M	3	10	17	24	31
G	4	11	18	25	
V	5	12	19	26	
S	6	13	20	27	
D	7	14	21	28	

GIUGNO					
L		5	12	19	26
M		6	13	20	27
M		7	14	21	28
G	1	8	15	22	29
V	2	9	16	23	30
S	3	10	17	24	
D	4	11	18	25	

LUGLIO						
L		3	10	17	24	31
M		4	11	18	25	
M		5	12	19	26	
G		6	13	20	27	
V		7	14	21	28	
S	1	8	15	22	29	
D	2	9	16	23	30	

AGOSTO					
L		7	14	21	28
M	1	8	15	22	29
M	2	9	16	23	30
G	3	10	17	24	31
V	4	11	18	25	
S	5	12	19	26	
D	6	13	20	27	

SETTEMBRE					
L		4	11	18	25
M		5	12	19	26
M		6	13	20	27
G		7	14	21	28
V	1	8	15	22	29
S	2	9	16	23	30
D	3	10	17	24	

OTTOBRE						
L		2	9	16	23	30
M		3	10	17	24	31
M		4	11	18	25	
G		5	12	19	26	
V		6	13	20	27	
S		7	14	21	28	
D	1	8	15	22	29	

NOVEMBRE					
L		6	13	20	27
M		7	14	21	28
M	1	8	15	22	29
G	2	9	16	23	30
V	3	10	17	24	
S	4	11	18	25	
D	5	12	19	26	

DICEMBRE					
L		4	11	18	25
M		5	12	19	26
M		6	13	20	27
G		7	14	21	28
V	1	8	15	22	29
S	2	9	16	23	30
D	3	10	17	24	31

F. Parole simili

A. Parole corrispondenti. Give the English equivalents for the following Italian words.

1. nazionale ______________________
2. informazione ______________________
3. opportunità ______________________
4. eccelente ______________________
5. coraggioso ______________________
6. attore ______________________

B. Indovina (*Guess*)**!** Write out the Italian cognates of these English words. Guess if you are not sure.

1. solution ______________________
2. science ______________________
3. capacity ______________________
4. international ______________________
5. curious ______________________
6. impossible ______________________

PROVERBI E MODI DI DIRE

Non c'è due senza tre.
Everything comes in threes. (Lit., There's no two without three.)

❖ **C. Qualità.** Using cognate adjectives, complete the following sentences. Use at least three adjectives for each and do not repeat any adjectives.

1. Io sono ______________________
2. La mia amica ideale è ______________________
3. Il presidente degli Stati Uniti è ______________________

LETTURA

A. Read this brief paragraph about an American who is interested in Italian. Then complete the chart based on the information in the paragraph.

Ciao! Mi chiamo Doug Sherwood. Sono americano, di Chicago, ma adesso[a] abito a[b] Torino, in via Po 2. Sono professore di musica e musicista. Le mie specialità sono la musica romantica e l'opera. Suono[c] il violino. Ho trentacinque anni. Sono un Leone! Sono nato il 20 di agosto. Sono serio, educato, generoso, impulsivo e romantico. La musica di Verdi e Puccini («La Traviata», «Otello», «Boheme», «Tosca») è la mia passione!

[a] *now*
[b] abito... *I live in*
[c] *I play*

Nome: ______________ Cognome: ______________

Nazionalità: ______________________

Residenza: ______________________

Indirizzo: ______________________

Professione: ______________________

Età: ______________________

Data di nascita (*Date of birth*): ______________________

Qualità: ______________________

❖ **B.** Following the model of Doug's paragraph in Exercise A, write a brief paragraph in which you tell your name and age, where you are from, where you live, what your profession is, and what you are like. Use another sheet of paper.

UN PO' DI SCRITTURA

❖ **Ciao! Buon giorno!** Write a brief conversation between two characters of your own choosing. They greet each other, introduce themselves, and say where they're from. Use your imagination! Write 5 or 6 lines. Use another sheet of paper.

Name ______________________ Date ____________ Class ____________________

ATTUALITÀ

Un profumo. Look over the following description of a new perfume, taken from the weekly magazine *Grazia.* It contains many words that are similar to English ones. Circle all the words you recognize, then answer the questions.

AROMI D'ORIENTE

Il fascino magico di una fragranza fatta di note esotiche. È Indian nights (nella foto) di Scherrer. Il suo bouquet è composto di essenze estratte da fiori, legni e frutti dell'India.

1. How many exact cognates did you find? ______________________________

   How many close cognates? ______________________________

2. What characteristics are singled out in the description?

   ____

❖ 3. Which characteristic seems most inviting to you?

   ____

Name ____________________

Date ____________________

Class ____________________

BENVENUTI A TUTTI!

VOCABOLARIO PRELIMINARE

A. In una stazione italiana. You have just arrived in Italy and are at a train station. There is a customer in line ahead of you. Complete his conversation with the clerk in a logical manner. Then answer the questions that follow.

CLIENTE: __________ __________.[1] Ho (*I have*) una prenotazione per due persone per Venezia.

IMPIEGATO: Che __________,[2] __________[3]?

CLIENTE: Walker.

IMPIEGATO: Ecco qui, due biglietti per Venezia.

CLIENTE: Ah, __________,[4] un'informazione. C'è ____ __________ __________[5] qui in stazione?

IMPIEGATO: No, ma c'è ____ __________[6] qui vicino, in Piazza Verdi.

CLIENTE: Grazie e __________.[7]

IMPIEGATO: __________[8]! Buona giornata.

1. Cognome del passeggero: ____________________
2. Destinazione: ____________________
3. C'è un ufficio cambi in stazione? ____________________
4. Dov'è una banca? ____________________

B. I mezzi di trasporto. Look at each drawing and write down the name of the means of transportation.

ESEMPIO:

un treno

1. __________ 2. __________ 3. __________

4. ________________ 5. ________________

C. Dove sono (*Where are they*)? Tell where the following people are. Follow the example.

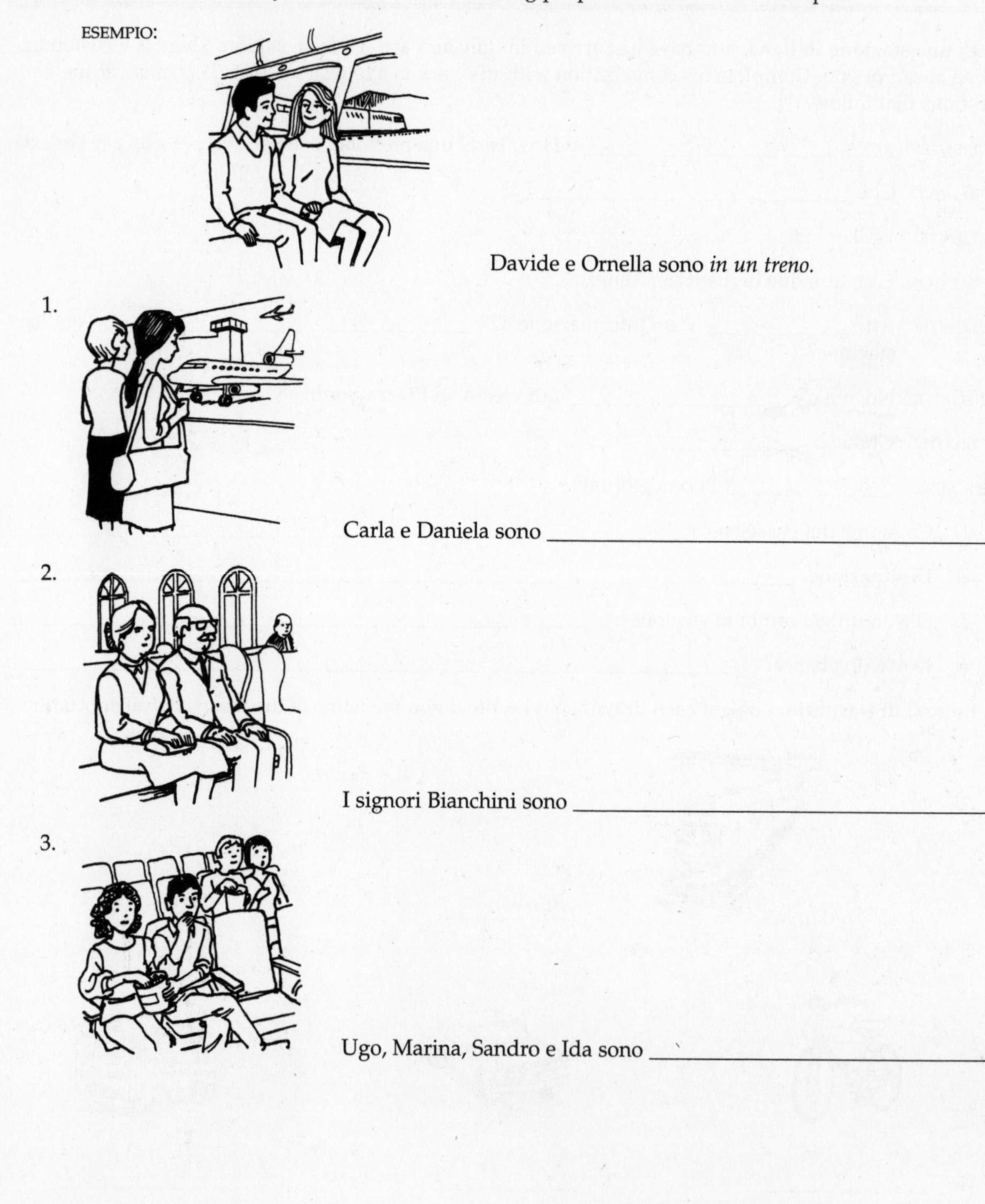

ESEMPIO: Davide e Ornella sono *in un treno.*

1. Carla e Daniela sono ________________________________.

2. I signori Bianchini sono ________________________________.

3. Ugo, Marina, Sandro e Ida sono ________________________________.

4.

Paolo e Francesca sono ______________________.

5.

Luigino e Mariella sono ______________________.

6.

Stefano e Sergio sono ______________________.

7.

Le signore sono ______________________.

8.

Grazia, Alberto, Lucia e Fabio sono ______________________.

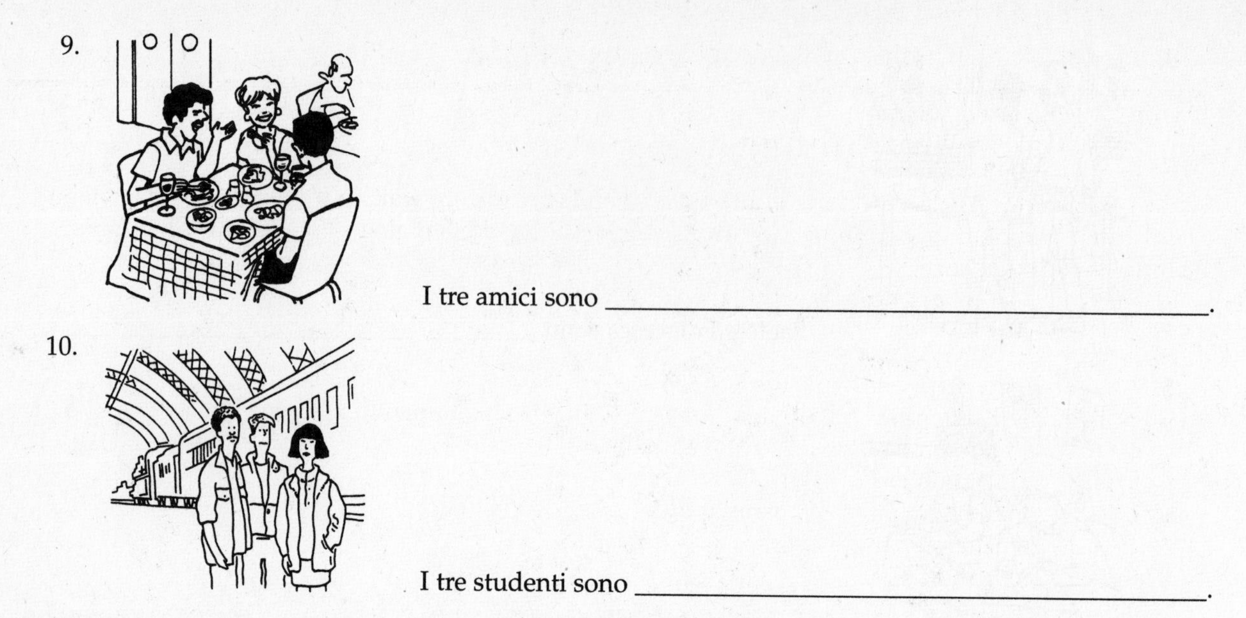

9. I tre amici sono ______________________________.

10. I tre studenti sono ______________________________.

D. Vicino o lontano? Antonio explains to Sara how to get to various places. Are his directions correct? Locate Antonio, Sara, and the places indicated on the map and judge for yourself! Then circle **vero** or **falso.**

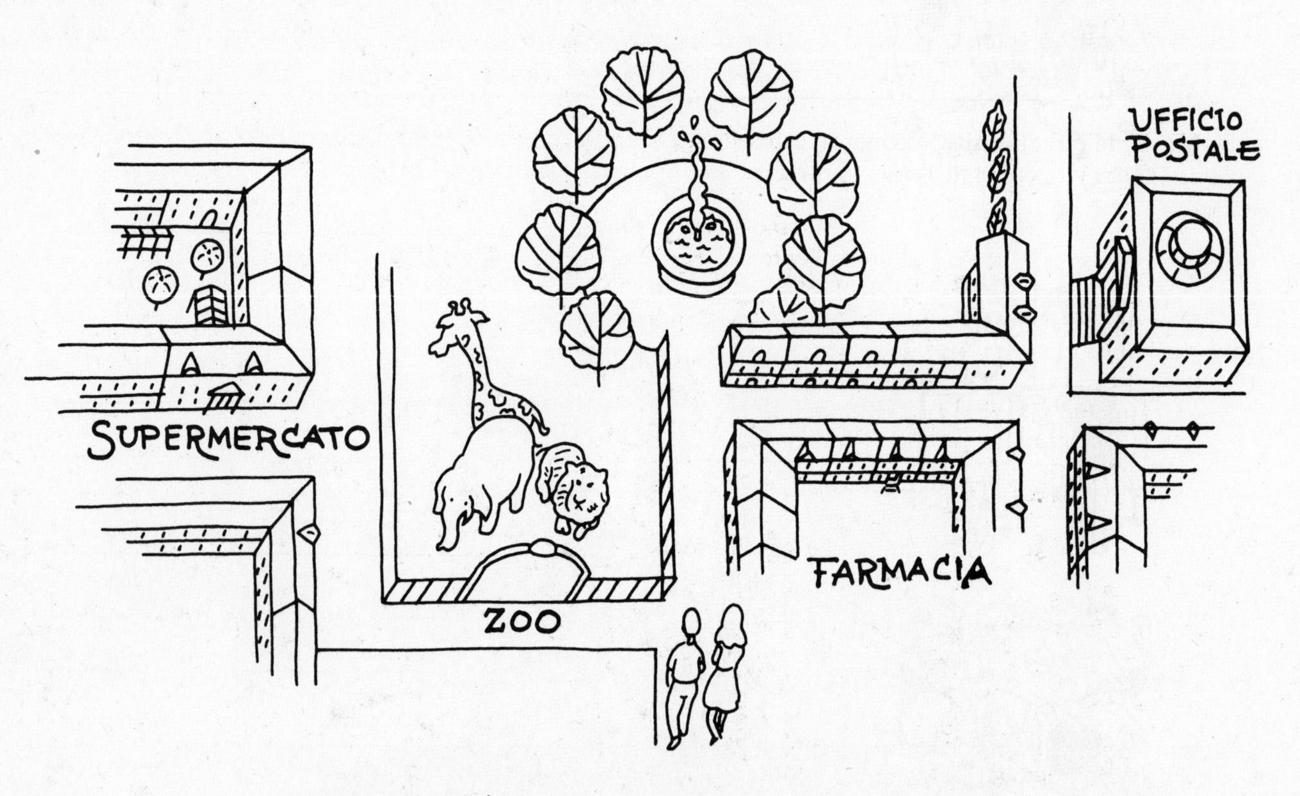

vero falso 1. Un supermercato? È qui vicino! Diritto, poi a sinistra, poi a destra, poi ancora a sinistra.

vero falso 2. Uno zoo? È qui vicino! Diritto, poi a destra.

vero falso 3. Un ufficio postale? Non è lontano! Diritto, poi a destra, poi a sinistra.

vero falso 4. Una farmacia? È proprio vicino! Diritto, poi a sinistra.

GRAMMATICA

A. Nomi: genere e numero

A. In una stazione. Alessandra, Irene, and Irene's son Leonardo are waiting for a train. It's past noon, and they are getting tired and hungry. What do they buy? Read the dialogue, then write what Irene bought for each person.

VENDITORE: Panini, banane, gelati, vino, aranciata, caffè, birra...
IRENE: Un caffè, Alessandra?
ALESSANDRA: Sì, grazie. E per Leonardo?
IRENE: Per Leonardo? Una banana e una bottiglia d'acqua minerale... Poi una birra, per me, e un caffè, per favore.
VENDITORE: Undicimila lire.
LEONARDO: Mamma, mamma, un panino!
IRENE: E anche un panino allora.
VENDITORE: Tredicimila lire.
IRENE: Ecco qui.
VENDITORE: Grazie e buon viaggio!

Irene: ______________________

Alessandra: ______________________

Leonardo: ______________________

B. Maschile o femminile? Leonardo can see the following objects and places from the train station. Divide them into two categories (masculine and feminine). Include the appropriate article (**un, uno, una...**).

Oggetti e luoghi: farmacia, studente, foto, stazione, ristorante, bar, cinema, caffè, auto, amico, treno, albergo, bici, moto, ospedale, via

MASCHILE:

____

____

____

FEMMINILE:

____

____

____

C. Ancora sul genere. Indicate the gender of the following nouns with *m* (masculine) or *f* (feminine).

1. _____ amico
2. _____ piazza
3. _____ ristorante
4. _____ gelato
5. _____ studente
6. _____ bicicletta
7. _____ automobile
8. _____ negozio
9. _____ treno
10. _____ moto

D. Singolari → plurali. Make the following singular nouns plural.

ESEMPIO: bicchiere → bicchieri

1. lira ____________________
2. stazione ____________________
3. dollaro ____________________
4. caffè ____________________
5. panino ____________________
6. birra ____________________
7. parente ____________________
8. signorina ____________________
9. ufficio ____________________
10. film ____________________

E. Plurali → singolari. Make the following plural nouns singular.

ESEMPIO: aeroporti → aeroporto

1. signore ____________________
2. professori ____________________
3. vini ____________________
4. aranciate ____________________
5. ragazzi ____________________
6. ragazze ____________________
7. università ____________________
8. lezioni ____________________

B. Articolo indeterminativo e **buono**

A. In un aeroporto. Fabio is leaving to visit his cousin, who lives in the United States. His friends Marco and Stefania are with him at the airport. Read the dialogue. Then make a list of what *you* would take along on such a trip.

MARCO: Allora, in partenza![a] Documenti? Biglietti? Soldi?
FABIO: Ho tutto,[b] ho tutto! Ecco qui: biglietto aereo, passaporto, carte di credito, dollari, indirizzo, numero di telefono, numero di telefono italiano per emergenze, mappa di Denver...
STEFANIA: E un sacco di[c] bagagli!
FABIO: Ma no, ho solo uno zaino, una borsa, un computer... e due valigie.
MARCO: «Solo»[d] due valigie, uno zaino, una borsa e un computer?
FABIO: Sono a Denver per due mesi, agosto e settembre. Ho bisogno di un sacco di cose...
MARCO: Buone vacanze allora! Ma un computer? Perché?
FABIO: Per studiare l'inglese...
STEFANIA: Ciao, Fabio, buon viaggio e buon divertimento!
FABIO: Grazie, a presto!

[a]Allora... *Well, you're off!*
[b]Ho... *I've got everything*
[c]un... *a ton of*
[d]*"Only"*

❖ Oggetti possibili per un viaggio in agosto e settembre:

____

____

B. Un, una... Fill in the blanks with the appropriate forms of the indefinite article.

ESEMPIO: *un* albergo e *una* banca

1. _____ professore e _____ professoressa
2. _____ stazione e _____ stadio
3. _____ aranciata e _____ caffè

4. _____ studente e _____ studentessa
5. _____ anno e _____ mese
6. _____ automobile e _____ treno
7. _____ zio e _____ zia
8. _____ cornetto (*croissant*) e _____ cappuccino

C. Uno, non due! Gabriella seems to be seeing double today. Make her phrases singular.

ESEMPIO: due stazioni → una stazione

1. due treni ______________________
2. due aeroplani ______________________
3. due automobili ______________________
4. due autobus ______________________
5. due biciclette ______________________
6. due zoo ______________________
7. due foto ______________________
8. due motociclette ______________________

PROVERBI E MODI DI DIRE

Il riso fa buon sangue.
Laughter is the best medicine (lit., makes good blood).

Nella botte piccola sta il vino buono.
Good things come in small packages.
(Lit., Good wine comes from a small cask.)

D. Una buon' idea. Rewrite the following phrases, adding the appropriate form of **buono.**

ESEMPIO: un cappuccino → un buon cappuccino

1. un amico ______________________
2. un'amica ______________________
3. una cioccolata ______________________
4. uno zio ______________________
5. un'automobile ______________________
6. un ospedale ______________________
7. uno stipendio ______________________
8. un vino ______________________

E. Che buono! Everything tastes good to you today. Use **che** plus the appropriate form of **buono** to express your appreciation.

ESEMPIO: pizza → Che buona pizza!

1. pasta ______________________________
2. cappuccino ______________________________
3. panino ______________________________
4. aranciata ______________________________
5. tè ______________________________
6. latte ______________________________
7. caffè ______________________________
8. gelato ______________________________

C. Presente di **avere** e pronomi soggetto

A. Io, tu... loro. Rewrite the following sentences, using the subject pronouns to give greater emphasis.

ESEMPIO: Abbiamo due libri. → Noi abbiamo due libri.

1. Hanno parenti in Italia. ______________________________
2. Avete amici? ______________________________
3. Ha un buon lavoro. ______________________________
4. Non hai dollari. ______________________________
5. Abbiamo un gatto. ______________________________
6. Carlo? Non ha un cane. ______________________________
7. Teresa? Non ha soldi. ______________________________
8. Non hanno una bicicletta. ______________________________

B. Chi (*Who*) **ha?** Complete each sentence with the correct form of the verb **avere.**

ESEMPIO: Io ____*ho*____ due lezioni.

1. Io e Marcella ______________ cugini in Australia.
2. Daniela ______________ una buona bicicletta?
3. Stefania e Caterina ______________ un appartamento.
4. ______________ un buon lavoro, tu e Valeria?
5. Io ______________ una macchina. Tu ______________ una motocicletta.
6. Voi ______________ dollari?

[a]di... *again*
[b]la... *low blood pressure*

C. Curiosa! Stefania wants to know what everybody else has! Answer and change the number of items from plural to singular as in the example.

ESEMPIO: Oggi Elena ha tre lezioni, e tu? → Io ho una lezione.

1. Ivana e Massimo hanno due gatti, e Daniele?

____

____

2. Carla ha due case, e voi?

____

____

3. Noi abbiamo quattro zii in Argentina, e loro?

____

____

4. Io ho due buoni amici, e tu?

____

____

5. Voi avete tre dollari, e Laura?

____

____

6. Tiziana ha due buoni libri, e tu?

____

____

D. Espressioni idiomatiche con **avere**

A. Bisogni e voglie (*Needs and wants*). Angelo and Silvia are at a train station in the summer, waiting for a train. Read the dialogue, then answer the questions.

ANGELO: Oh, che caldo. Non hai caldo, Silvia?
SILVIA: Un po', ma sto bene così...
ANGELO: E sete? Io ho proprio sete adesso. Hai voglia di una birra, di un tè freddo, di una Coca-Cola?
SILVIA: Mamma mia, Angelo, tu hai davvero sete[a]! Io no, grazie, sto bene così. Forse[b] ho voglia di un gelato.
ANGELO: Chissà se c'è un bar in questa stazione...
SILVIA: Sì, c'è, è vicino all'ufficio prenotazioni, ma non abbiamo tempo. Abbiamo bisogno di arrivare in orario[c] alla festa[d] e perciò abbiamo bisogno di prendere[e] l'Intercity tra[f] cinque minuti...
ANGELO: Hai ragione, non è una buona idea perché abbiamo fretta... Oh, ma guarda[g]! C'è un venditore qui sul binario[h]... Mi scusi, qui, per favore! Una birra, grazie!

[a]tu... *you really are thirsty*
[b]*Maybe*
[c]in... *on time* / [d]*party*
[e]percio... *therefore we have to catch* / [f]*in*
[g]*look* / [h]*platform*

How do Angelo and Silvia feel? Write one sentence about each of them.

Angelo: ______________________________

Silvia: ______________________________

❖ And what about you? Answer the following questions.

1. Come stai oggi? ______________________________
2. Di che cosa hai bisogno oggi? ______________________________
3. Hai fame? ______________________________
4. Hai sonno? ______________________________
5. Hai sete? ______________________________

B. Ho voglia di una pizza! Look at the drawings and complete each sentence with one of the following expressions.

Espressioni utili: avere... anni, avere fame, avere fretta, avere sete, avere sonno, avere voglia di

1. Oggi Marilena ______________________________
____

2. Francesco e Vincenzo ______________________________
____

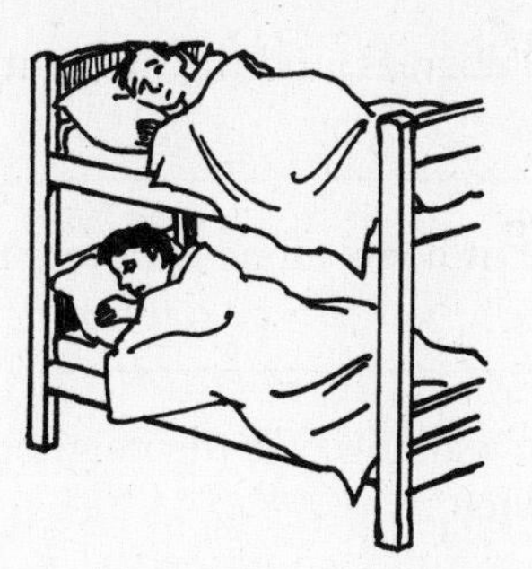

3. Noi ______________________________
____

4. Voi ______________________________
____

5. Il signor Cervaro ______________________
____

6. Stefania ______________________________
____

❖ **C. Io ho caldo, e tu?** Answer the following questions in complete sentences. You may answer either affirmatively or negatively. If your answer is affirmative, start with **Anche io** (**Anche tu,** etc.).

1. Vittorio e Susanna hanno caldo, e tu?

____

2. Laura ha freddo, e voi?

____

3. Io ho paura, e lei?

____

4. Noi abbiamo bisogno di aiuto, e tu?

____

D. Situazioni. Imagine that you're in the following situations. What would you say?

1. It has started to rain, and of course you left your umbrella (**ombrello**) at home. You go into a store and say:

____

2. The temperature has dropped to 15 degrees and you are out without a jacket.

____

3. It's 95 degrees, and the humidity is 90 percent.

___

4. You're at home alone and hear footsteps in the basement.

___

5. You're walking past the neighborhood café. The wonderful smells give you a great desire for a sandwich.

___

6. You got up this morning at six, and it is now midnight. You can barely keep your eyes open.

___

E. **Una nuova compagna di stanza.** You are interviewing a prospective roommate. Ask her . . .

1. how old she is. ___
2. if she has a cat or a dog. ___
3. if she has a car. ___
4. if she feels like having a coffee. ___
5. if she has allergies (**allergie**). ___

LETTURA

Una bella città e una bella regione...

Michele parla della (*speaks of*) sua città, Venezia.

Ciao, sono Michele e sono di Venezia. Ho ventuno anni e abito vicino a una piazza molto famosa, Piazza San Marco. Venezia è in Veneto, una regione del nord d'Italia. È una città molto antica, con monumenti famosi, musei, piazze e una atmosfera magica. Venezia è costruita[a] su una laguna ed è circondata[b] dall'acqua. A Venezia non ci sono macchine; ci sono invece i vaporetti[c] e le gondole, famose in tutto il mondo. In questa città abbiamo sempre molti turisti, soprattutto in estate. Venezia è bella in inverno, quando c'è la nebbia[d] e non c'è molta gente. È una città misteriosa, e quando c'è il Carnevale è ancora più[e] misteriosa. Amo molto Venezia e le sue isole, Burano, Murano, Torcello: a Burano le case sono di molti colori, Murano è famosa per la produzione del vetro[f] e Torcello ha una famosa chiesa con bellissimi mosaici. Il Veneto è poi una regione da visitare. A nord, vicino all'Austria, ci sono le Alpi e le Dolomiti, montagne affascinanti[g]; c'è Verona, la città di Romeo e Giulietta, con un grande anfiteatro romano; c'è Padova, la città di Sant'Antonio; e c'è anche il fiume[h] Brenta, famoso per le ville che sono lungo[i] i suoi canali.

[a] *built*
[b] *surrounded*
[c] *ferryboats*
[d] *fog*
[e] ancora... *even more*
[f] *glass*
[g] *fascinating*
[h] *river*
[i] *along*

1. Dov'è Venezia? ___
2. Caratteristiche di Venezia: ___

___

3. Cosa sono Burano, Murano e Torcello? ___

Name ______________________ Date ____________ Class ______________________

4. Perché sono famose? ______________________________

5. Bellezze (*Beautiful sites*) del Veneto: ______________________________

____

UN PO' DI SCRITTURA

❖ **Una letterina.** Write a short letter to your family in which you describe your new roommates. If you don't have any, just make some up! Write about 6 lines; use another sheet of paper.

ESEMPIO: Ho tre compagni di stanza! Abbiamo un appartamento proprio in centro. Marco ha vent'anni; ha un buon lavoro all'università. Alessia e Lorenza hanno diciotto anni; hanno un cane e un gatto. Non hanno un lavoro e hanno bisogno di soldi...

ATTUALITÀ

❖ **A. P come Perugia...** Julie has arrived in Umbria. She has decided to take a day trip to Bevagna, a small village not far from Assisi, to take pictures of the local medieval festival. She calls Barbara in Luino to let her know where she is.

JULIE: Ciao, Barbara! Sono a Bevagna!
BARBARA: Dove? Lavagna??
JULIE: No! B e v a g n a! **B** come Bologna, **E** come Empoli, **V** come Venezia...

Now imagine you are traveling through Italy. Choose three towns from the following list, **Città possibili,** and spell out their names the way Italians do, using the names of Italian cities. (If no name of an Italian city begins with a certain letter, the name of a foreign city or a common word is used.) Look over the following table.

A	come Ancona	**N**	come Napoli
B	come Bologna	**O**	come Otranto
C	come Cagliari	**P**	come Palermo
D	come Domodossola	**Q**	come Quaderno
E	come Empoli	**R**	come Roma
F	come Firenze	**S**	come Sassari
G	come Genova	**T**	come Torino
H	come Hotel	**U**	come Udine
I	come Imola	**V**	come Venezia
***J**	come Jolly	**W**	come Washington
†K	come Kaiser	**X**	come Xeres
L	come Livorno	**Y**	come York
M	come Milano	**Z**	come Zara

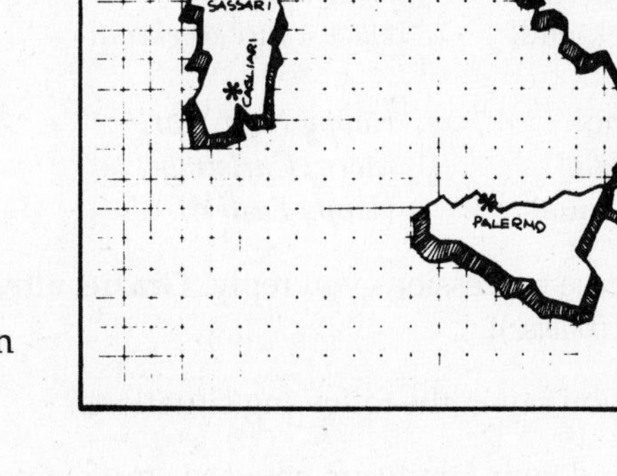

*The word **jolly** is used in Italian to designate the wild card in some card games. It is also the name of a well-known chain of hotels.
†**Kaiser** is the German word for *emperor.*

Città possibili: Fiesole, Piacenza, Jesi, Avellino, Eboli, Barletta, Milano, Ragusa, Nuoro, Ivrea, Asiago

ESEMPIO: S1: Ciao, Tatiana! Sono a Fiesole!
S2: Dove? Miesole??
S1: No, F i e s o l e! **F** come Firenze, **I** come Imola...

1. S1: ____________________
   S2: ____________________
   S1: ____________________
   ____
2. S1: ____________________
   S2: ____________________
   S1: ____________________
   ____
3. S1: ____________________
   S2: ____________________
   S1: ____________________
   ____

B. Buon viaggio! You say **Buon viaggio** (*Have a nice trip*)**!** to people who are going on a trip. When you are in Italy, you will hear **Buona giornata** (*Have a nice day*)**!** These are just two of the many expressions with the word **buono** that are used in Italian for special occasions.

Buon appetito!	*Enjoy your meal!*
Buon compleanno!	*Happy birthday!*
Buon divertimento!	*Have fun!*
Buona domenica!	*Have a nice Sunday!*
Buona fortuna!	*Good luck!*
Buona giornata!	*Have a good day!*
Buon lavoro!	*Enjoy your work!*
Buon viaggio!	*Have a nice trip!*
Buon week-end!	*Have a nice weekend!*
Buon Anno!	*Happy New Year!*
Buon Natale!	*Merry Christmas!*
Buona Pasqua!	*Happy Easter!*

To many of these expressions you reply: **Grazie, altrettanto** (*Thanks, the same to you*)**!** or simply **Altrettanto** (*Likewise*)**!**

What would you say in the following situations?

1. You and your family are about to start eating.

   ____

2. It's January 1.

   ____

3. Your friends are about to board a plane.

____

4. Your roommate is going to a party.

____

5. Your cousin turns twenty today.

____

6. Tomorrow is Saturday.

____

7. Your sister is heading to the office.

____

8. Your roommates are leaving for job interviews.

____

Capitolo

Name ______________________

Date ______________________

Class ______________________

2 LA CLASSE E I COMPAGNI

VOCABOLARIO PRELIMINARE

A. La classe e i compagni. Today is Enrico's first day of high school. Read the following passage and complete the descriptions that follow.

Oggi è il primo giorno di scuola, e io sono un po' nervoso... Sono in un'aula grande con venti studenti, venti banchi e venti sedie vecchie (anche la scuola è vecchia), una lavagna minuscola e un professore che[a] in questo momento scrive[b] sulla lavagna... Il professore è giovane ma molto serio... Ho già due compagni di banco. A destra una ragazza bassa e bionda, con occhi blu e occhiali, che si chiama Cinzia: una ragazza molto simpatica! A sinistra un ragazzo allegro che si chiama Emanuele. È bruno, con gli occhi marroni, robusto e sportivo. Io sono magro, piccolo, con capelli neri e occhi azzurri. Sono sportivo e molto energico. Vicino ad Emanuele c'è Simone e poi c'è Paola. Simone e Paola hanno i capelli biondi. I capelli di Paola sono lunghi e ricci, i capelli di Simone corti e lisci. Simone e Paola hanno gli occhi verdi e sono alti, ma Paola è magra e Simone è un po' grasso. Anche loro sono nervosi. Si vede bene![c]

[a]*who*
[b]*is writing*
[c]Si... *As one can well see!*

Descrizione dell'aula: ______________________

Numero di studenti: ______________________

Descrizione del professore: ______________________

Descrizione di Cinzia: ______________________

Descrizione di Emanuele: ______________________

Descrizione di Enrico: ______________________

Descrizione di Simone: ______________________

Descrizione di Paola: ______________________

B. Come sono? Describe these people, circling the appropriate adjectives.

1. una studentessa (bassa / allegra) e uno studente (vecchio / triste)

2. una donna (magra / antipatica) e una donna (grassa / vecchia)

3. una ragazza (alta / giovane) e un uomo (stupido / vecchio)

4. un ragazzo (bruno / biondo) e una ragazza (bruna / bionda)

5. un uomo (triste / basso) e una donna (alta / grassa)

C. Qualità! Give the opposite of the following adjectives.

1. giovane ________________
2. grasso ________________
3. allegro ________________
4. biondo ________________
5. grande ________________
6. lungo ________________
7. alto ________________
8. riccio ________________
9. simpatico ________________
10. onesto ________________
11. stressato ________________
12. responsabile ________________

D. Aggettivi di nazionalità. People from all over the world are attending an event at the campus International House. Give their nationalities.

1. John è un ragazzo di Filadelfia. È ________________.
2. Mireille è una studentessa di Parigi. È ________________.
3. Jackie è una ragazza di Toronto. È ________________.
4. Yuko è una bambina di Tokio. È ________________.
5. Walter è uno studente di Berlino. È ________________.
6. Deborah è una professoressa di Londra (*London*). È ________________.
7. José è un ragazzo di Acapulco. È ________________.
8. Andrei è un bambino di Mosca (*Moscow*). È ________________.
9. Miguel è un ragazzo di Madrid. È ________________.
10. Stefano è uno studente di Roma. È ________________.

E. Bandiere e colori! How many flags are you familiar with? Write as many colors as you can.

1. Di che colori è la bandiera americana?

____

2. Di che colori è la bandiera italiana?

____

❖ 3. Di che colori è la bandiera del tuo (*of your*) stato?

____

PROVERBI E MODI DI DIRE

Essere al verde.
*To be totally broke (lit., in the green).**

Rosso di sera, bel tempo si spera; rosso di mattina, il mal tempo s'avvicina.
Red sky at night, sailor's delight. Red sky in the morning, sailor's warning.
(Lit., With a red sunset, hope for good weather; with a red dawn, bad weather approaches.)

*Candles used to be painted green at the bottom; a candle that was **al verde** was almost totally consumed.

GRAMMATICA

A. Aggettivi

A. Ecco la foto di un amico... Pamela is showing her friend Valerio a picture of Andrea, an Italian friend of hers. Read the dialogue, then answer the questions that follow.

PAMELA: Ecco una foto di un mio amico, Andrea, di Madison, una città del Wisconsin.
VALERIO: È italiano o americano?
PAMELA: Andrea è italiano, di Firenze. È uno studente all'Università del Wisconsin, un bravo studente davvero. Lui studia[a] matematica ed è sempre molto serio, ma stressato e nervoso... Quando non studia è una persona divertente e allegra, pero[b]!

[a]*is studying*
[b]*however*

1. Di dov'è Andrea? Di che nazionalità? ______
2. Che tipo di studente è Andrea? ______
3. Com'è Andrea quando studia? ______
4. Che tipo di persona è Andrea quando non studia? ______

B. Italiani e francesi. Complete the following sentences, using the correct form of the adjective in italics.

1. Io ho un professore *italiano;* voi avete una professoressa ______?[1] Loro hanno un'automobile ______[2] e una bicicletta ______.[3] Io ho due amiche ______;[4] voi avete due amici ______?[5] Noi abbiamo uno zio ______[6] ed anche una zia ______.[7]
2. Ecco una parola *francese* in una ricetta (*recipe*) ______.[1] Voi avete un vino ______?[2] Noi abbiamo due automobili ______.[3] Ecco due camerieri ______.[4] Io ho due studentesse ______;[5] il professor Tozzi ha due studenti ______?[6]

C. Plurali. Make the following phrases plural.

1. esercizio facile ______
2. lezione difficile ______
3. appartamento caro ______
4. ragazza cinese ______
5. ragazzo irlandese ______
6. studente serio ______
7. studentessa brava ______

D. Singolari. Make the following phrases singular.

1. camerieri simpatici ______________________
2. studentesse intelligenti ______________________
3. dollari canadesi ______________________
4. piazze italiane ______________________
5. professori nervosi ______________________
6. bambine francesi ______________________
7. bambini carini ______________________

E. Femminili. Make the following phrases feminine.

1. un amico inglese ______________________
2. un professore allegro ______________________
3. un cugino divertente ______________________
4. un ragazzo triste ______________________
5. uno zio famoso ______________________
6. un cameriere gentile ______________________
7. un americano stressato ______________________
8. un italiano sensibile ______________________

F. Generoso... avaro. Rewrite the following phrases, giving the opposite of the adjective in italics.

1. una domanda *stupida* ______________________
2. una *buon'*idea ______________________
3. un uomo *simpatico* ______________________
4. due *grandi* chiese ______________________
5. due lezioni *difficili* ______________________
6. una *bella* foto ______________________
7. una *vecchia* signora ______________________
8. un *bravo* professore ______________________

G. Genova, una città poco conosciuta all' estero... Genova isn't well known abroad. Read the following passage and write the correct form of **molto** in the blanks.

Questa (*This*) è Genova, una città ________[1] famosa: la città di Cristoforo Colombo! È il capoluogo della Liguria. Genova è un porto ________[2] importante per il Mediterraneo, ma questa città ha anche ________[3] monumenti famosi, ________[4] musei e ________[5] chiese. Genova non è ________[6] conosciuta[b] (*known*). Purtroppo (*Unfortunately*) c'è anche ________[7] rumore (*noise, m.*) e ________[8] traffico. Insomma, non c'è ________[9] pace (*peace and quiet, f.*) nel centro storico.

❖ **H. Identikit.** Answer the questions to create a brief description of yourself.

1. Di che statura sei? ______________________________
2. Di che colore hai gli occhi? ______________________________
3. Di che colore hai i capelli? ______________________________
4. Come hai i capelli? ______________________________
5. Hai gli occhiali o le lenti a contatto? ______________________________

B. Presente di **essere**

A. Chi sono Simone, Emanuele e Roberto? Read the description of these three students, then complete the chart that follows.

Mi chiamo Simone e sono un italiano di Milano. Ho vent'anni e sono studente di economia alla Bocconi. Ho due compagni di casa. Uno si chiama Emanuele. Ha ventidue anni ed è molto sportivo e energico. Infatti è studente dell'ISEF, l'Istituto Superiore di Educazione Fisica. L'altro compagno si chiama Roberto e ha diciannove anni. È molto simpatico e divertente. È uno studente di veterinaria.

Età e professione di Simone: ______________________________

Età e professione di Emanuele: ______________________________

Com'è Emanuele? ______________________________

Età e professione di Roberto: ______________________________

Com'è Roberto? ______________________________

B. Siamo di... Complete the following sentences, using the correct form of **essere.**

1. Rosaria è di Roma. Io non ____________[1] di Roma. Loro due ____________[2] di Mantova. Anche noi ____________[3] di Mantova. Paolo ____________[4] di Padova. E tu, di dove ____________[5]? Voi ____________[6] di Verona.
2. Tu sei americana. E Davide, anche lui ____________[1] americano? Noi due ____________[2] americani, ma Luisa non ____________[3] americana: ____________[4] canadese. Anche Marianne e Philip ____________[5] canadesi.

C. Sei Luca? Franco is playing a game: he has been blindfolded and is trying to guess who his friends are by asking them questions about themselves. He doesn't seem to have any luck. Answer his questions negatively, as in the examples.

ESEMPIO: Sei biondo? → No, non sono biondo.
Siete biondi? → No, non siamo biondi.

1. Sei alta? ______________________________
2. Siete bruni? ______________________________
3. Sei giapponese? ______________________________

4. Siete bassi? ________________
5. Sei coreano? ________________
6. Siete magri? ________________

D. Non uno, ma due! Correct Silvia's statements—tell her there are two, not just one, of the things she sees.

ESEMPIO: C'è una stazione. → No, ci sono due stazioni!

1. C'è un aeroporto. ________________
2. C'è un cane. ________________
3. C'è una macchina. ________________
4. C'è uno studente. ________________
5. C'è una studentessa. ________________

C. Articolo determinativo e **bello**

A. Una lista per un cocktail party... You and a friend are writing down a list of items to buy for a cocktail party. Confirm your friend's choices, following the example. Use the definite article.

ESEMPIO: rum? → Il rum va bene!

1. vino bianco? ________________
2. birra? ________________
3. scotch? ________________
4. grappa? ________________
5. aranciata? ________________
6. acqua tonica? ________________

B. Ecco qui! Rewrite the following sentences, changing indefinite articles to definite articles.

ESEMPIO: Ecco un disco (*record*)! → Ecco il disco!

1. Ecco un professore! ________________
2. Ecco una professoressa! ________________
3. Ecco uno studente! ________________
4. Ecco un americano! ________________
5. Ecco un'americana! ________________
6. Ecco un ospedale! ________________
7. Ecco un supermercato! ________________
8. Ecco uno zoo! ________________

C. Caratteristiche psicologiche. Complete the paragraph using the appropriate definite articles.

_____[1] amico di Luisa è sempre stressato ma _____[2] amica di Franco è sempre calmissima. _____[3] madre di Giovanni è spesso (*often*) contenta ma _____[4] padre di Giovanni è spesso arrabbiato. _____[5] zio di Alberto è raramente (*rarely*) entusiasta ma _____[6] zia di Alberto è raramente depressa. _____[7] cugine di Marco sono molto spesso nervose ma _____[8] cugini di Marco sono sempre rilassati. _____[9] amici di Rosaria sono ospitali e generosi... Come sono _____[10] studenti di questa classe?

D. Categorie. To what categories do the following words belong? Create complete sentences, as in the example.

ESEMPIO: domenica → La domenica è un giorno.

Categorie: vini, formaggi (*cheese*), caffè, automobili, giorni

1. espresso ______________________________
2. Chianti (*m. sing.*) ______________________________
3. mozzarella ______________________________
4. sabato ______________________________
5. Fiat ______________________________
6. ricotta ______________________________
7. lunedì ______________________________
8. Alfa Romeo ______________________________

E. Che bello! Piero is showing you around his hometown, and you are quite impressed with all you see. Give the appropriate exclamations, using the correct form of **bello.**

ESEMPIO: casa → Che bella casa!

1. negozi ______________________________
2. piazza ______________________________
3. stadi ______________________________
4. università ______________________________
5. chiese ______________________________
6. zoo ______________________________
7. albergo ______________________________
8. stazione ______________________________

F. Gli amici di Mark. Mark is describing a photo of some American friends to Rosaria and Alberto. Complete the paragraph, circling the correct forms of the definite article and **bello.**

John ha (i / gli)[1] capelli biondi e (i / gli)[2] occhi azzurri. (La / Le)[3] ragazza di John, Meg, ha (bei / begli)[4] capelli rossi e (bei / begli)[5] occhi verdi. (I / Gli)[6] cugini di John sono quei ragazzi con (la / le)[7] motociclette nere. (L' / Lo)[8] amica di Meg è quella ragazza con quel bel sorriso. Questi sono (i / gli)[9] miei migliori amici!

D. Ancora sui plurali

A. Singolari e plurali. Make the following phrases plural. Say that there are two of every person or thing.

ESEMPIO: una magnifica toga → due magnifiche toghe

1. una valigia grigia ________________
2. un vecchio ristorante ________________
3. un negozio magnifico ________________
4. un'amica greca ________________
5. un amico simpatico ________________
6. un lungo viaggio ________________

B. Di tutto un po'. Make the following sentences plural.

ESEMPIO: Leggiamo (*We're reading*) un classico greco. → Leggiamo dei classici greci.

1. Il medico ha una figlia simpatica.

   ____

2. Il gatto è un animale domestico.

   ____

3. Ecco lo spago (*string*) per legare (*tie*) il pacco!

   ____

4. Abbiamo una valigia di buona marca (*brand*).

   ____

5. Abbiamo una collega apatica (*apathetic*).

   ____

PROVERBI E MODI DI DIRE

Al nemico che fugge, ponti d'oro.
Golden bridges to a fleeing enemy.

Troppi cuochi guastano il pranzo.
Too many cooks spoil the broth (lit., lunch).

LETTURA

Italiano a Perugia...

Parla Simone, uno studente italo-americano. Studia italiano in Italia quest'estate, a Perugia, all'Università per Stranieri.

La mia classe d'italiano è simpatica. Siamo venticinque studenti in un'aula grande con molte carte dell'Italia, banchi piccoli ma nuovi e una professoressa brava e entusiasta. Abbiamo molti libri per imparare[a] l'italiano, e gli studenti sono di molti stati del mondo. Ci sono americani, giapponesi, cinesi, tedeschi, spagnoli, greci, russi e polacchi. Il mio compagno di banco è un ragazzo di ventidue anni, Ivan. Lui è russo, di San Pietroburgo. È un ragazzo alto, robusto, biondo, con gli occhi azzurri. Parla[b] bene l'italiano ed è sempre molto gentile. L'altra compagna di banco è una ragazza spagnola, di Madrid, che si chiama Benita. Lei è piccola e magra, con i capelli bruni e lisci, e gli occhi neri. Ha ventisette anni, è molto seria e simpatica ed è molto contenta di imparare l'italiano. E io chi sono? Sono Simone, un italo-americano di New York. Ho parenti a Napoli e in Calabria, ma anche qui a Perugia: due zii e cinque cugini. E ho molti amici italiani: l'Università per Stranieri[c] è il posto ideale per fare amicizie.[d] Perugia è una città bella e interessante: ci sono molte piazze e monumenti, molte chiese e molti musei, e Assisi, con la sua Basilica di San Francesco, è vicina. D'estate c'è «Umbria Jazz», una manifestazione musicale importante. Mi piace[e] questa città!

[a] *learning*
[b] *He speaks*
[c] *Foreigners*
[d] fare... *making friends*
[e] Mi... *I like*

1. Caratteristiche della classe:

____

____

2. Nazioni degli studenti (esempio: studenti italiani = Italia):

____

____

3. Compagni di banco di Simone, descrizione fisica e del carattere (*personality*):

____

____

4. Chi è Simone? Perché è a Perugia?

____

____

5. Cosa c'è a Perugia? Perché è una città interessante?

____

____

UN PO' DI SCRITTURA

❖ **A. Amici, amiche.** Write a brief composition about some friends of yours, American or foreign. Write 8 or 10 lines; use another sheet of paper.

ESEMPIO: Ho due amici italiani, Simona e Francesco. Sono di Venezia, sono molto simpatici e generosi. Simona è bruna e ha gli occhi neri. Francesco...

❖ **B. Come sono?** Introduce yourself in a letter to a friend of a friend. Describe your appearance and your personality using expressions from the **Vocabolario preliminare** and the **Parole-extra** in your text. Write 8 or 10 lines; use another sheet of paper.

ESEMPIO: Mi chiamo Carla e sono di Pavia. Sono piccola, bruna, ho gli occhi...

ATTUALITÀ

❖ **Il partner ideale.** Here are the results of a poll on the ideal partner conducted by the center «La Metropoli», published by the daily newspaper *La Repubblica* and the weekly magazine *Anna*. These are the answers of 1,010 young people between the ages of 16 and 25. Read over the results, then give your own descriptions of **l'uomo ideale** and **la donna ideale.**

GIOVANI ANNI '90

Lui? Lo voglio ricco e famoso

Tramonta il mito dell'uomo tormentato. Oggi deve essere intraprendente e dinamico. Deve guadagnare bene. E loro, i ragazzi, che cosa si aspettano dalla donna della loro vita?

IL PARTNER DEVE ESSERE...

(in percentuale)	maschi	femmine
Bello/a	49	15
Gradevole	12	55
Muscoloso	6	26

L'uomo ideale
- Dolce e aggressivo
- Intraprendente
- Dinamico
- Sportivo
- Che sappia scherzare
- Muscoloso

La donna ideale
- Bella
- Decisa
- Avventurosa
- Che sappia stupire
- Comprensiva
- Coraggiosa

Espressioni utili: che sappia scherzare (*with a sense of humor*); che sappia stupire (*surprising*)

L'uomo ideale	La donna ideale
______________________	______________________
______________________	______________________
______________________	______________________
______________________	______________________
______________________	______________________
______________________	______________________
______________________	______________________
______________________	______________________
______________________	______________________

Capitolo

3

Name ______________________

Date ______________________

Class ______________________

MIA SORELLA STUDIA ALL'UNIVERSITÀ

VOCABOLARIO PRELIMINARE

A. Materie di studio... Read the following dialogue, then complete the chart with information from the dialogue.

VALERIO: Ciao, mi chiamo Valerio, e voi?
PRISCILLA: Priscilla, sono americana. Studio all'Università del Colorado.
ALIZA: Anch'io sono una studentessa dell'Università del Colorado.
VALERIO: Oh, siete del Colorado... Parenti?
PRISCILLA: Sì, Aliza è mia sorella...
VALERIO: Siete qui in Italia per studiare?
PRISCILLA: Sì, studio la storia dell'arte e la lingua italiana. Ma ho un interesse particolare per la storia e la filosofia del Rinascimento[a].
ALIZA: Io invece[b] studio storia moderna e contemporanea.
VALERIO: Che soggetto interessante!
ALIZA: Studio anche scienze politiche e economia.
VALERIO: Parlate già bene l'italiano![c] E poi siete nel posto giusto[d]. Firenze è la città del Rinascimento italiano.
PRISCILLA: E tu, Valerio, cosa studi[e]? Qual è la tua specializzazione?
VALERIO: Studio letteratura italiana contemporanea, ma ho passione anche per l'arte.

[a]*Renaissance*
[b]*on the other hand*
[c]Parlate... *You already speak Italian well!* / [d]nel... *in the right place*
[e]cosa... *what are you studying*

Materie di studio di Valerio: ______________________

Materie di studio di Priscilla: ______________________

Materie di studio di Aliza: ______________________

Perché Firenze è la città giusta per Priscilla e Aliza? ______________________

Chi sono Aliza e Priscilla? ______________________

B. Relazioni familiari. Provide the name of the family member defined.

1. È il fratello di mio padre: ______________________
2. È la sorella di mia madre: ______________________
3. È il figlio dei miei genitori: ______________________
4. È il padre di mio padre: ______________________
5. È la figlia dei miei nonni ed è anche uno dei miei genitori: ______________________
6. Sono figli dei miei zii: ______________________

❖ Now answer these questions about your family.

Hai un fratello? Come si chiama? Hai una sorella? Come si chiama? Quando sono nati? Quanti anni hanno? Hai molti parenti?

____

____

____

C. Associazioni. Match up the topics in the two columns.

A	B
1. _____ economia e commercio	a. il comportamento (*behavior*) del bambino
2. _____ lingue e letterature straniere	b. il linguaggio dei computer
3. _____ scienze politiche	c. i mass media e la società
4. _____ psicologia	d. le novelle cinesi
5. _____ informatica	e. il sistema monetario europeo
6. _____ sociologia	f. il parlamento inglese

D. Un piccolo cruciverba (*crossword puzzle*)**!**

ORIZZONTALI

2, 1 È la materia di Aristotele.
5, 1 I dottori studiano questa materia.
5, 10 Questi esami sono più frequenti in Italia.
9, 1 Gli studenti che studiano questa materia amano costruire (*love to build*).
15, 6 Giulio Cesare, Carlo Magno, Napoleone: in un corso di ______________ europea
17, 1 In quale (*which*) corso studiate la geometria e l'algebra?

VERTICALI

2, 2 Può (*It can*) essere fisica, nucleare o meccanica.
4, 13 Dante, Boccaccio, Shakespeare: in quale facoltà siete?
6, 7 storia, latino, fisica, biologia: sono ______________
8, 7 le origini dell'uomo e il suo comportamento: corso di ______________
11, 2 sinonimo di **legge;** gli avvocati studiano questa materia
13, 1 All'università gli studenti scelgono (*choose*) una ______________.
13, 10 Questi esami sono più frequenti negli Stati Uniti.

	1	2	3	4	5	6	7	8	9	10	11	12	13	14
1														
2	F	I	L	O	S	O	F	I	A	■				
3														
4														
5									■					
6						■		■						
7														
8													■	
9													■	
10														
11														
12		■		■										
13				L										
14				E		■								
15				T	■							■		
16				T							■			
17				E							■		■	
18				R										
19				E				■						

❖ **E. La mia (*My*) settimana all'università.** Complete the chart with your class schedule.

	lunedì	martedì	mercoledì	giovedì	venerdì	sabato
8.00						
9.00						
10.00						
11.00						
12.00						
1.00						
2.00						
3.00						
4.00						
—						

Now write a paragraph telling what your week is like. Use another sheet of paper.

Espressioni utili: al mattino (*in the morning*); al pomeriggio (*in the afternoon*); impegnato (*busy*); libero (*free*).

ESEMPIO: Il martedì e il giovedì ho un corso di antropologia al mattino e un corso di tennis al pomeriggio. Il lunedì e il mercoledì sono molto impegnata... Il venerdì sono libera tutto il giorno...

❖ **F. Domande personali.** Answer these questions about your academic interests, strengths, and weaknesses with the names of subjects.

1. Cosa studi questo semestre? ______________________
2. Cosa devi (*do you have to*) studiare? ______________________
3. In quale materia sei bravo/a? ______________________
4. In quale materia non sei bravo/a? ______________________
5. Qual è la tua (*your*) materia preferita di studio? ______________________
6. E qual è una materia noiosa? ______________________

GRAMMATICA

A. Presente dei verbi in -are

A. Che gruppo in gamba (*sharp*)! Marco talks about his college friends. Complete the paragraph with the correct verb endings.

Isabella studi_____[1] economia e commercio, lavor_____[2] part-time in una banca e parl_____[3] molto bene il tedesco. Monica e Sandro studi_____[4] lingue e letterature moderne, parl_____[5] bene il francese e lo spagnolo. Alla sera mangi_____[6] sempre in fretta perché lavor_____[7] per un giornale e non torn_____[8] mai (*never*) a casa per cena (*dinner*). Io abit_____[9] vicino all'università ma arriv_____[10] sempre in ritardo (*late*)! Frequent_____[11] la facoltà di ingegneria e impar_____[12] molto; i miei professori spieg_____[13] molto bene. Isabella, Monica, Sandro ed io siamo buoni amici; studi_____,[14] mangi_____,[15] e lavor_____[16] spesso insieme (*together*). Ogni (*Every*) sabato (noi) suon_____[17] in un club del centro e guadagniamo (*earn*) un po' di soldi!

B. Un professore che è un disastro... Complete the dialogue between Benedetta, Antonietta, and Giuseppina with the correct form of verbs from the list. Some verbs may be used more than once.

arrivare   cominciare   dimenticare   frequentare   imparare   parlare   ricordare   spiegare

BENEDETTA: Sono agitata, davvero! Il professore di biologia è un disastro: _____________________[1] malissimo e _____________________[2] le lezioni sempre in ritardo (*late*).

ANTONIETTA: Sì, non è una novità: _____________________[3] a lezione con circa (*about*) trenta minuti di ritardo ed è così noioso, _____________________[4] sempre nella stessa maniera. Non _____________________[5] mai che ha un orario d'ufficio (*office hours*) e _____________________[6] anche i compiti (*assignments*) degli studenti in classe.

GIUSEPPINA: Vero (*True*), con lui (noi) _____________________[7] poco! Perché non _____________________[8] di questo problema con la segretaria del Dipartimento?

C. Io e la mia famiglia. Complete the following description of a family with the correct form of verbs from the list. Some of the verbs may be used more than once.

abitare   amare   requentare   parlare   portare   telefonare   tornare

Io _____________________[1] la mia famiglia. Io e mia sorella _____________________[2] con mio padre e mia madre in una grande casa in centro città. Siamo una famiglia unita. Con noi _____________________[3] anche mia nonna. Quando mia sorella non è a casa perché _____________________[4] l'università in una città distante, i miei genitori _____________________[5] a lei molte volte al giorno per _____________________[6] con lei. Quando mia sorella _____________________[7] a casa il fine-settimana, _____________________[8] sempre un regalo per mia nonna.

D. Il mondo della scuola e il mondo del lavoro (*work*). Complete the sentences logically with the correct form of **-are** verbs. (Consult the lists in your textbook if you can't remember them all.)

1. Patrizia è una infermiera: ____________________ in un ospedale.
2. Sono professore d'italiano in una università americana: ____________________ lingua e letteratura italiana.
3. Voi siete studenti della facoltà di Medicina all'università: ____________________ anatomia.
4. Tu e Bruno siete musicisti: durante un concerto ____________________ il flauto e il clarinetto.
5. Noi siamo grandi capitalisti: ____________________ una bella Ferrari.
6. Sei uno studente con la memoria corta: ____________________ sempre tutto!
7. Angela è una studentessa: ____________________ il corso elementare di italiano.
8. Michele è un bravo ballerino: ____________________ il flamenco e il tango molto bene.
9. Luciano Pavarotti è un cantante d'opera: ____________________ al Met di New York e al Teatro alla Scala di Milano.
10. Sono il presidente di una grande banca: ____________________ molti soldi.

B. Dare, stare, andare e fare

A. Lezioni private. Anna has found a way to earn some money while at college. Everybody in the house has to tutor! Complete the paragraph with the correct forms of **dare.**

Io __________[1] lezioni di giapponese. Luca e Chiara __________[2] lezioni di musica. Tu __________[3] lezioni di chimica. Io e Luca __________[4] anche lezioni di matematica. Tu a Chiara __________[5] anche lezioni di filosofia. E Giusi? Lei __________[6] lezioni di fisica.

B. A un congresso. Now Anna is telling her friend Cristina how everybody is going to an important conference. Complete the paragraph with the correct forms of **andare.**

(Noi) Non __________[1] in aereo! Io __________[2] in treno; Luca e Chiara __________[3] in macchina; Giusi __________[4] in moto. E tu, Cristina, come __________[5]? Tu e Paolo __________[6] in pullman (*inter-city bus*)?

PROVERBI E MODI DI DIRE

Chi non fa, non falla.*
Those who do nothing make no mistakes.

Chi fa falla, e chi non fa sfarfalla.
Those who act, make mistakes; and those who do nothing really blunder.

*The verb **sbagliare,** not **fallare,** is currently used to mean *to make a mistake.*

C. Cosa facciamo stasera? Complete the following dialogue with the correct forms of **stare** and **fare.**

DANIELA: Ciao, Cinzia, come ______________[1]?

CINZIA: ______________[2] benissimo, grazie! Cosa ______________[3] stasera?

DANIELA: Mah! Io e Giorgio non ______________[4] niente di speciale, ______________[5] in casa con amici; (io) ______________[6] una bella spaghettata (*spaghetti dinner*). E voi, ______________[7] il solito (*usual*) giro in centro?

CINZIA: Probabilmente sì! A proposito (*By the way*), come ______________[8] i tuoi (*your*) amici di Bologna?

DANIELA: Loro ______________[9] bene; sono sempre molto energici, ______________[10] mille cose alla volta (*a thousand things at once*).

CINZIA: E la loro (*their*) bambina, Caterina, come ______________[11]?

DANIELA: Adesso ______________[12] meglio (*better*); va a scuola ed è contenta.

D. Breve conversazione. Complete the exchange by choosing the appropriate expression.

Espressioni utili: andate, andiamo, dai, insegnare, lavorare, studia, suonano

PAOLO: Dov'è mia sorella?

MONICA: Tua sorella ______________[1] in biblioteca con Marta. E voi, dove ______________[2]?

PAOLO: Patrizia ed io ______________[3] in libreria (*to the bookstore*) a comprare i libri per il corso di biologia. E tu, Monica, ______________[4] ancora (*still*) lezioni di fisica?

MONICA: Purtroppo no. ______________[5] fisica non è facile, e poi non ho molta pazienza. Preferisco (*I prefer*) ______________[6] in biblioteca!... Ecco tua sorella! Ma chi è quel ragazzo?

PAOLO: È un suo caro amico; ______________[7] il violino insieme (*together*).

E. Che noia! Imagine that you're attending a really boring lecture. Using another sheet of paper, write a note to pass to a friend in which you:

1. ask what he or she is going to do tonight. 2. ask if Gianni is giving a party. 3. ask if Marco and Adele are staying home. 4. suggest that you go eat at a pizzeria and then go to the movies. 5. ask if he and Manuela are taking the sociology orals on Monday. 6. tell him that it's really hot in the class and tell him it's only (**solo**) 11:15. 7. tell him that tomorrow you are going home by train. 8. ask him why he is not paying attention when the professor speaks!

❖ **F. Domande personali.** Answer the following personal questions.

1. Come vai a scuola? E al lavoro? Abiti lontano? Non ci sono mezzi pubblici? Il traffico è troppo intenso per la macchina?

   ____

   ____

2. Stai sempre attento/a in classe quando parla il professore o la professoressa? Fai una domanda quando hai difficoltà di comprensione? O stai zitto/a anche quando non capisci?

   ____

   ____

3. Quando dai l'esame finale di italiano? Dai molti scritti questo semestre?

   ____

   ____

4. Cosa fai questo fine settimana?

   ____

   ____

5. Stai a casa il sabato sera? O incontri gli amici?

   ____

   ____

6. Dai spesso feste o vai alle feste di amici?

   ____

   ____

C. Aggettivi possessivi

A. Di chi sono? Whose objects are these? Complete the sentences with the correct possessive adjective. Remember to include the definite article.

1. Tu compri (*are buying*) (*my*) _____ _____ macchina.
2. Noi facciamo (*our*) _____ _____ compiti.
3. Franco studia (*his*) _____ _____ lezioni.
4. Io vedo (*I see*) (*my*) _____ _____ compagni di classe.
5. Giulia invita (*her*) _____ _____ amici.
6. Dove abitano (*their*) _____ _____ fratelli?

B. Sì o no? Bettina wants to know what belongs to whom, so she asks you and the following people about everything she sees. Answer her questions affirmatively or negatively.

ESEMPIO: tu / chitarra →
—È la tua chitarra?
—Sì, è la mia chitarra.

1. io / scuola ______________________________

   No, ______________________________
2. tu / compiti ______________________________

   Sì, ______________________________
3. voi / matite ______________________________

   Sì, ______________________________
4. Luisa / bicicletta ______________________________

   No, ______________________________
5. Stefano / gatti ______________________________

   Sì, ______________________________
6. io e tu / quaderni (*notebooks*) ______________________________

   No, ______________________________

—La mia famiglia è molto originale...

C. Che lista lunga... Sonia is telling her friend Marco about a box she has found in her garage filled with many items belonging to her friends and family. Rephrase her statements using possessive adjectives.

Sonia:

Marco, la mia visita in garage è stata (*was*) una sorpresa... Ecco, finalmente, il libro di Paolo, lo zaino di Marisa, la penna dello zio Beppe, il block-notes di Irene, la borsa di Giovanni, gli occhiali che tu e Marisa usate sempre e ci sono anche le chiavi della nostra macchina, e c'è il cellulare di Francesco. Ma è incredibile!

Cosa c'è di Paolo in garage? *il suo libro*

1. E di Marisa? ______________________
2. E dello zio Beppe? ______________________
3. E di Irene? ______________________
4. E di Giovanni? ______________________
5. E di Marco e Marisa? ______________________
6. E di Sonia e Marco? ______________________
7. E di Francesco? ______________________

D. Possessivi con termini di parentela

A. Mini-dialoghi. Complete the following dialogues with the appropriate possessive adjective.

1. Beatriz e Jennifer parlano dei loro genitori.

BEATRIZ: E *tua* mamma, è italiana?

JENNIFER: Sì, ____________[1] mamma è italiana, ma ____________[2] papà è tedesco. E ____________[3] genitori, sono italiani?

BEATRIZ: No, ____________[4] genitori sono messicani.

2. Danila e Valeria, Mario e Cesare parlano dei loro cugini.

DANILA E VALERIA: Ciao, ragazzi (*guys*). Come stanno ____________[1] cugini? Sono proprio simpatici!

MARIO E CESARE: ____________[2] cugini stanno molto bene. E ____________[3] cugine?

DANILA E VALERIA: ____________[4] cugine stanno benissimo, grazie!

3. Loriana e Lisetta parlano della famiglia di Anna.

LORIANA: Come'è il marito di Anna?

LISETTA: ____________[1] marito? È simpaticissimo. Ha un grande senso dell'umorismo (*a great sense of humor*).

LORIANA: E hanno bambini, vero? Come sono?

LISETTA: ____________[2] bambini sono veramente carini, molto gentili e vivaci.

B. Chi arriva oggi? There are many arrivals in your neighborhood. Tell who is coming, as in the example.

ESEMPIO: a friend (*f.*) of mine →
Oggi arriva una mia amica.

1. a nephew of mine
____
2. two cousins of ours
____
3. two aunts of yours (*sing.*)
____
4. two sisters of yours (*pl.*)
____
5. a niece of theirs
____
6. a brother of hers
____

E. Questo e quello

A. Quello, non questo! Laura wants to decide everything today: whatever you say, she will say the opposite. Write what Laura says, according to the example.

ESEMPIO: Andiamo a questi bar? → No, a quei bar!

1. Invitiamo questo ragazzo? ______________________________
2. Prendiamo quest'automobile? ______________________________
3. Telefoniamo a queste amiche? ______________________________
4. Aspettiamo quest'autobus? ______________________________
5. Visitiamo questo zoo? ______________________________
6. Parliamo con questi studenti? ______________________________
7. Compriamo vestiti in questi negozi? ______________________________
8. Chiamiamo questi amici? ______________________________

B. Questa o quella per me pari sono? Complete the sentences with the correct form of **questo** or **quello.**

1. (Quella/Quello/Questo) moto funziona ancora (*still*).
2. (Questi/Quelli/Queste) professori sono eccellenti.
3. (Quel/Quella/Quell') amico non telefona mai.
4. (Quelle/Quei/Quegli) notti invernali sono lunghe.
5. (Questo/Questi/Questa) cinema non è buono.
6. (Quel/Quella/Quello) bar ha pochi clienti.

Name ______________________ Date ____________ Class ______________________

PROVA QUIZ

A. Ecco un esercizio! Fill in each blank with the appropriate form of the indefinite article.

ESEMPIO: Nadia ha *una* foto.

1. Ecco ______ chiesa gotica ed ecco ______ museo orientale.
2. Julie ha bisogno di ______ lezione di geografia sull'Italia.
3. La Bocconi è ______ università privata a Milano.
4. Barbara ha ______ zio, ______ zia e ______ cugino a New York.
5. C'è ______ stadio qui vicino? —Sì, dritto, poi a destra.
6. Julie, Barbara e Mauro sono in ______ caffè e bevono (*they're drinking*) ______ aranciata.

B. Anche lei. Complete each sentence with the appropriate form of **essere** + *adjective*.

ESEMPIO: Tu sei africano; anche lei è africana.

1. Tu sei irlandese; anche loro ______________________
2. Tu sei russa; anche lui ______________________
3. Tu sei inglese; anche Mary ______________________
4. Tu sei stanco; anche lui ______________________
5. Tu sei felice; anch'io ______________________

C. Io ricordo tutto! Describe what you and the following people do. Complete the sentences with the appropriate verb form.

1. Patrizia ______________ (lavorare) in un ospedale.
2. Io ______________ (insegnare) in questa scuola.
3. Voi ______________ (studiare) biologia.
4. Silvia e Bruno ______________ (suonare) il flauto.
5. Noi ______________ (guidare) una Alfa-Romeo rossa.
6. Tu ______________ (dimenticare) tutto!
7. Lei ______________ (frequentare) un corso di russo.
8. Michele ______________ (ballare) il twist.
9. Noi ______________ (cominciare) la lezione.
10. Io ______________ (cantare) spesso.

D. Traduzioni. Express in Italian. Use another sheet of paper.

1. I have a bicycle, you have a motorcycle, and she has a car.
2. They don't have an apartment. They have a house.
3. We have a good uncle; he is always in a hurry!
4. Peter has a job. He has a good job and a good salary.
5. Do you feel like having an ice cream?

LETTURA

Studiare in Italia*

Per gli studenti italiani la scuola comincia a sei anni, con la scuola elementare, che dura[a] cinque anni. Continua poi per altri tre fino ai[b] quattordici anni, con la scuola media. Scuola elementare e media formano la «scuola dell'obbligo.[c]» In questi otto anni gli studenti italiani studiano materie come la lingua italiana, la storia, la geografia, la matematica, le scienze, imparano il disegno[d] e fanno educazione fisica.

Dall'età di otto anni gli studenti cominciano lo studio di una lingua straniera, di solito l'inglese o il francese. Gli studenti italiani vanno a scuola sei giorni alla settimana, sabato incluso; possono scegliere[e] di studiare, per un'ora alla settimana, la religione cattolica. Gli esami sono orali e scritti: ci sono le «interrogazioni» orali ed i «compiti in classe» che sono esami scritti. Alla fine delle elementari e delle medie gli studenti devono superare degli esami finali complessivi.[f]

Dopo la scuola media, gli studenti hanno varie possibilità: il liceo (classico, scientifico, linguistico) e gli istituti tecnici o professionali. Queste scuole, chiamate superiori, durano cinque anni, fino ai diciannove anni, e sono divise[g] in un biennio (due anni) di materie generali e in un triennio (tre anni) di maggiore[h] specializzazione. Materie comuni per la scuola superiore sono italiano, storia, matematica, le scienze e la lingua straniera. Nel liceo classico, gli studenti studiano anche il latino, il greco antico, la filosofia; nel liceo scientifico, studiano la chimica, la fisica, la biologia.

Alla fine dei cinque anni gli studenti hanno l'«esame di maturità». Èn un esame lungo, complesso, con professori interni e esterni alla loro scuola: ci sono tre materie scritte e un orale sulle materie studiate nell'ultimo anno. L'esame di maturità è un esame che tutti gli studenti ricordano: è come un rito di passaggio all'età adulta.

Dopo questo esame, se gli studenti passano, e continuano a studiare, cominciano l'università. Se vanno a cercare un lavoro,[i] il diploma di maturità è sufficiente per molti tipi di lavoro.

[a]*lasts* / [b]fino... *up to*
[c]*mandatory*
[d]*drawing*
[e]possono... *they can choose*
[f]*comprehensive*
[g]*divided*
[h]*further*
[i]*job*

Write down three types or levels of school and related information, based on the **Lettura.**

	TIPO DI SCUOLA	DURATA	MATERIE FONDAMENTALI	TIPO DI ESAMI
1.				
2.				
3.				

❖ Now compare the Italian system with yours.

1. Quanti anni studiano gli studenti in questo paese (*country*)? ______
2. Quando comincia la scuola per gli studenti in questo paese? ______
3. Quali lingue straniere studiano gli studenti nei licei in questo paese? ______

*The Italian school system is currently under reform. The year 2000 general reform law has been approved, but its effects on elementary, middle, and secondary school education have yet to be finalized. The purpose of the reform law, however, is to make the educational systems of all the European Union nations similar.

4. Quali materie di base i professori dei licei in questo paese insegnano? Ci sono materie diverse da quelle (*different from*) dei licei italiani? ______________________

____

5. Ci sono esami orali, le «interrogazioni», nei licei in questo paese? ______________________

____

UN PO' DI SCRITTURA

❖ **A. Un ricordo** (*recollection*) **di scuola.** Taking your inspiration from this chapter's **Lettura,** write about your memories of an important event in your school career: the first day of school, your friends in junior high, your instructors in high school. Write as if you were at that moment in time. Write about 10 lines; use another sheet of paper.

Espressioni utili: il compagno / la compagna di classe (*classmate*), al liceo (*in high school*), il maestro / la maestra (*elementary school teacher*), alle Medie (*in junior high*), primo (*first, adj.*)

ESEMPIO: Sono le otto; suona la campana (*the bell rings*). Tutti arrivano in fretta! La nostra maestra aspetta gli studenti in classe. Ecco Fabrizio, il mio caro amico, in ritardo (*late*) come sempre...

❖ **B. Una lettera.** Write a letter to a friend and tell him or her your plans for the future. Write about 10 lines; use another sheet of paper.

Espressioni utili: avere intenzione di (*to plan to*), dopo (*after*), prima (*first, adv.*), poi (*then*)

ESEMPIO: Dopo l'università non ho intenzione di cercare (*look for*) subito (*immediately*) un lavoro. Prima faccio un viaggio in Europa. Poi...

ATTUALITÀ

❖ **Una scheda di iscrizione** (*application form*). Look over the following form from the **Università degli Studi di Bergamo** and fill it out with your own personal information.

Corsi di lingua e cultura italiana per stranieri

UNIVERSITÀ DEGLI STUDI DI BERGAMO

CORSO ESTIVO INTENSIVO DI LINGUA E CULTURA ITALIANA PER STRANIERI
SCHEDA DI ISCRIZIONE

1. Cognome ______________________________
Nome ______________________________
Secondo nome ______________________________
Sesso ______________________________
Luogo di nascita ______________________________
Data di nascita ______________________________
Nazionalità ______________________________
Prima lingua ______________________________

2. a. (*solo lavoratori*) (*only for working people*) ______________________________
Professione ______________________________
Titolo di studio (*Degree*) ______________________________

b. (*solo studenti*) ______________________________
Tipo di scuola frequentata ______________________________
____
Facoltà ______________________________

3. a. (*solo per chi ha già studiato l'italiano*) (*only for those who have already studied Italian*)
Quando ______________________________
Per quanto tempo (*For how long*) ______________________________
Dove ______________________________

b. Altre lingue conosciute ______________________________
A livello colloquiale ______________________________
A livello scolastico ______________________________
A livello professionale ______________________________

4. Lo studio dell'italiano è motivato da interessi: ______________________________
Professionali ______________________________
Artistici ______________________________
Musicali ______________________________
Letterari ______________________________
Scientifici ______________________________
Politico-economici ______________________________
Turistici ______________________________
Altri (*specificare*) ______________________________

5. È interessato
- al corso di tre settimane (5/23 luglio 2001)
- al corso di quattro settimane (5/30 luglio 2001)
- al corso di tre settimane (solo livello avanzato) dal 12 al 30 luglio 2001

6. Richiede la soluzione comprensiva di vitto e allogio (*Request for full room and board*)
Camera singola (*Single room*) ______________________________
Camera doppia (*Double room*) ______________________________

____
Firma (*Signature*)

Data ______________________________
Indirizzo ______________________________
Telefono/Fax n. ______________________________
Indirizzo di posta elettronica ______________________________

Capitolo 4

Name ______________________

Date ______________________

Class ______________________

FORZA AZZURRI!

VOCABOLARIO PRELIMINARE

A. Cosa fanno? Look at each drawing and complete the phrase with the appropriate verb. (Consult the lists in your textbook if you can't remember them all.)

ESEMPIO:

Gli studenti *disegnano*.

1. Gianni e Danilo ______________________.

2. Noi ______________________.

3. La signora Lina ______________________.

4. Tu e Giovanna ______________________.

5. Voi ______________________.

6. Tu ______________________.

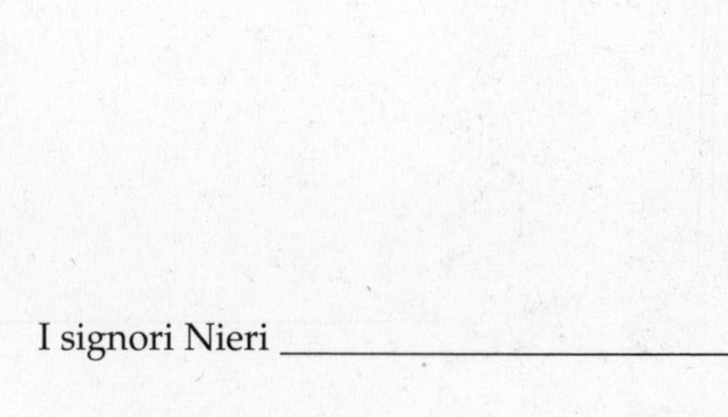

7. I signori Nieri ______________________.

8. Gina ______________________.

B. I programmi della giornata... Read the dialogue and describe each person's plans for the day.

LORENZO: Ciao, Rita, ciao, Alessandro! Cosa fate oggi?
ALESSANDRO: Vado a suonare la chitarra con Marcello e poi a fare un giro in bicicletta.
RITA: E mentre Alessandro impara la chitarra io vado a nuotare con Valeria e Vittoria. Poi andiamo a mangiare una pizza.
ALESSANDRO: E tu, Lorenzo, che programmi hai?
LORENZO: Mah, oggi non ho voglia di fare molto; voglio stare a casa e leggere un libro, o guardare un po' la televisione.
RITA: Sono sorpresa, sei sempre molto attivo, tu!

Atività di Alessandro: ______________________________

Attività di Rita: ______________________________

Attività di Lorenzo: ______________________________

C. Com'è il tempo? Look at each drawing and describe the weather. (Consult the lists in your textbook if you can't remember the weather verbs.)

1. ______________________ 2. ______________________

3. ______________________ 4. ______________________

5. ______________________

❖ **D. Mini-sondaggio** (*poll*)**.** Which of these activities do you do regularly, rarely, or never? Complete the chart, by writing an "X" in the appropriate column.

ATTIVITÀ	regolarmente	raramente	mai
1. andare a un concerto			
2. correre			
3. dipingere			
4. dormire			
5. fare aerobica			
6. fare un giro in moto			
7. guardare la TV			
8. leggere il giornale			
9. prendere lezioni di ballo			
10. pulire la casa			
11. scrivere lettere			
12. uscire con gli amici			

❖ **E. Mi piace...** (*I like...*) Tell what you like to do when you are in the following moods. Use the expression **Mi piace.**

ESEMPIO: stanco → Quando sono stanco/a mi piace dormire!

1. triste

____

____

2. allegro

____

____

3. nervoso

____

____

4. annoiato (*bored*)

____

____

5. di umore nero (*inv., in a terrible mood*)

____

____

GRAMMATICA

A. Presente dei verbi in **-ere** e **-ire**

A. Cosa preferisci? Complete the following dialogues using **preferire** + *infinito*.

ESEMPIO: S1: Io gioco a tennis, e tu?

S2: Io *preferisco giocare* a pallone.

1. S1: Io vado in biblioteca in macchina, e tu?

   S2: Io ____________ a piedi.

2. S1: Io parto stasera, e voi?

   S2: Noi ____________ domani.

3. S1: Io dormo in albergo, e Donata?

   S2: Donata ____________ in un ostello.

4. S1: Io ricevo la posta (*mail*) a casa, e voi?

   S2: Noi ____________ in ufficio.

5. S1: Io apro i regali (*presents*) stasera, e Piero?

   S2: Piero ____________ domani mattina.

6. S1: Io pago in lire, e loro?

   S2: Loro ____________ in dollari.

7. S1: Io scrivo poesie, e tu?

   S2: Io ____________ racconti.

8. S1: Io servo la cena in sala da pranzo (*dining room*), e voi?

   S2: Noi ____________ in terrazza.

B. Cosa fanno? Look at each drawing and tell what the various people are doing. (Consult the lists in your textbook for the appropriate verbs.)

ESEMPIO:

Prende un caffè.

1. ______________________ 2. ______________________

3. ______________________ 4. ______________________

C. Anch'io! Your friend Lucia is a little conceited. Point out that she isn't the only one who does certain things.

LUCIA: Io prendo lezioni di musica e di ballo!

TU: Anch'io ____![1]

LUCIA: Io seguo un corso di giapponese!

TU: Anche mio fratello ____![2]

LUCIA: Io ricevo sempre molti inviti (*invitations*)!

TU: Anche le mie sorelle ____![3]

LUCIA: Io servo sempre vino rosso con la carne!

TU: Anche mia zia ____![4]

LUCIA: Io leggo solo romanzi classici (*classic novels*)!

TU: Anch'io ____![5]

LUCIA: Io corro tutti i giorni!

TU: Anche noi ____![6]

D. Capire, finire o pulire? Complete the dialogues with the correct form of the verb.

1. S1: A queste conferenze (*lectures*) io non ____________________ mai niente (*anything*)!
   S2: Noi non ____________________ mai niente perché non siamo informati!
2. S1: Rita e Giorgio ____________________ di lavorare stasera. E tu, quando ____________________?
   S2: Anch'io ____________________ stasera, così possiamo partire tutti per le vacanze domani mattina.
3. S1: Voi non ____________________ mai la vostra camera! È un disastro!
   S2: Noi non abbiamo tempo! Perché non ____________________ tu la nostra camera?

—Attento a[a] dove metti i piedi.[b]

[a]Attento... *Watch*
[b]i... *your feet*

PROVERBI E MODI DI DIRE

Chi dorme non piglia pesci.
The early bird catches the worm. (Lit., He who sleeps doesn't catch any fish.)

Non destare il cane che dorme.
Let sleeping dogs lie. (Lit., Don't wake a sleeping dog.)

B. **Dire, uscire** e **venire; dovere, potere** e **volere**

A. Chi viene al concerto? Lorenza wants to know who is coming to the concert tonight. Complete the dialogue with the correct form of **venire.**

LORENZA: Cinzia, tu ______________[1] al concerto stasera?
CINZIA: Sì, ______________[2] con Paolo.
LORENZA: E voi, ______________[3] in macchina con Cinzia?
MASSIMO: No, noi ______________[4] con Anna e Mimmo.
LORENZA: Ma ______________[5] anche loro?
MASSIMO: Sì, stasera ______________[6] proprio tutti (*everyone, pl.*)!

B. Abitudini (*Habits*) **di famiglia.** Everyone in Simone's family leaves the house at a different time. Complete his story using the verb **uscire.**

Io ______________[1] di casa sempre presto la mattina: corro, compro il giornale, vado al bar a bere un cappuccino. Mio fratello invece ______________[2] di casa sempre tardi (*late*)! Non ha tempo di fare i suoi esercizi di yoga, non ha tempo di leggere il giornale e non fa mai colazione (*breakfast*). I miei genitori non ______________[3] mai prima delle (*before*) nove: ascoltano il notiziario (*news*) alla radio mentre bevono il caffè e poi vanno a fare un giro a piedi. Noi non ______________[4] mai di casa alla stessa ora! E tu, a che ora ______________[5] di casa la mattina?

C. Cosa dicono? Complete the dialogues with the correct form of **dire.**

1. s1: Cosa ______________ i giornali oggi?

   s2: ______________ sempre le stesse cose! Niente di speciale.
2. s1: Perché (tu) ______________ che il tuo passatempo preferito è la barca a vela? Non vai mai in barca!

   s2: Ma tu ______________ sempre la verità (*truth*)?
3. s1: Io ______________ che passeggiare è un'attività molto rilassante.

   s2: Io invece ______________ che dipingere è un'attività ancora più (*even more*) rilassante.
4. s1: Voi parlate troppo (*too much*) e non ______________ niente di interessante!

   s2: Almeno (*At least*) noi ______________ qualcosa (*something*)!

PROVERBI E MODI DI DIRE

Tra il dire e il fare c'è di mezzo il mare.
Easier said than done. (Lit., Between saying and doing there's the sea in the middle.)

Volere è potere.
Where there's a will, there's a way.

D. Caccia al verbo (*Verb hunting*)! Rossana and Giovanna want and need to do many things; they're not always able to, however. Complete the dialogue with the appropriate forms of **dovere, potere,** and **volere.**

ROSSANA: Sabato (io) ______________[1] andare alla manifestazione per la pace (*peace rally*), ma non so se ______________.[2] Forse ______________[3] stare a casa con mia sorella Monica perché la mamma lavora...

GIOVANNA: Io ho una soluzione! (Noi) ______________[4] portare Monica da Alessandra, così (lei) ______________[5] giocare con la figlia piccola di Alessandra.

ROSSANA: Ma anche Alessandra ______________[6] andare alla manifestazione!

GIOVANNA: Infatti! Così la nonna che sabato non ______________[7] cucinare perché il nonno ______________[8] andare al ristorante, fa la baby-sitter per Alessandra...

ROSSANA: Fantastico! ______________[9] subito telefonare alla signora Maria. (Io) ______________[10] sapere se lei è d'accordo (*agrees*).

E. Voglio, devo, posso... How often we say these words! Complete the sentences with the appropriate verb form and information of your choice.

ESEMPIO: Barbara e Danilo ___vogliono___ (volere) venire ___in America___.

1. Mauro ______________ (volere) prendere lezioni ______________.
2. Cristina ed io ______________ (dovere) andare ______________.
3. Oggi (io) ______________ (dovere) fare ______________.
4. Stasera (voi) ______________ (potere) venire ______________?
5. Luigi e Maria ______________ (volere) seguire un corso ______________.
6. (Io) ______________ (potere) fare un giro ______________?
7. (Tu) ______________ (volere) vedere ______________?
8. Angelo non ______________ (potere) suonare ______________.
9. (Noi) ______________ (volere) viaggiare ______________.
10. Domenica (tu) ______________ (dovere) giocare ______________?

◆ **F. Giorgio, aiutami** (*help me*)**!** Giorgio always has good advice for his friends. Pretend you are Giorgio and help out these people who find themselves in a bind. Be original!

ESEMPIO: Giorgio, il mio compagno di camera sta sempre al telefono. →
Il tuo compagno di camera deve comprare un telefono personale.

1. Giorgio, Rosaria è sempre stressata e non riesce a (*she can't*) dormire.

   ____

2. Giorgio, non ho soldi!

   ____

3. Giorgio, Maurizio ed io non sappiamo (*know how to*) cucinare.

   ____

4. Giorgio, Gina lavora in centro e non ha la macchina.

   ____

5. Giorgio, Margherita e Piero arrivano sempre in ritardo.

   ____

6. Giorgio, voglio imparare a cantare.

   ____

C. Pronomi di oggetto diretto

A. Gusti diversi. You and Gabriele are totally different. Complete the following statements about you and him with the appropriate direct object pronouns.

ESEMPIO: Lui ama i musei; io ___li___ odio (*hate*).

1. Lui ama la musica country; io _____ odio.
2. Lui ama i gelati al limone; io _____ odio.
3. Lui ama le sigarette; io _____ odio.
4. Lui ama gli sport; io _____ odio.
5. Lui ama l'estate; io _____ odio.
6. Lui ama le mostre (*exhibits*); io _____ odio.
7. Lui ama gli animali; io _____ odio.
8. Lui ama il risotto; io _____ odio.

B. Posso parlarti? Fill in the blank with the correct form of the direct object pronoun.

ESEMPIO: Vengo subito: potete aspettar_mi_ in cucina.

1. Lo chef è molto occupato adesso: non potete disturbar_____.
2. Giulio, sei libero stasera? Posso veder_____?
3. Ragazzi, sabato do una festa per il mio compleanno: posso invitar_____?
4. Mamma, ho visto una bellissima crostata di mele da Angelo: posso comprar_____?
5. Signora Gatto, finalmente le Sue figlie sono arrivate! Posso invitar_____ a cena?
6. Arriviamo tra (*in*) mezz'ora: potete aspettar_____ in pizzeria.
7. Se non hai voglia di fare gli gnocchi adesso, puoi preparar_____ più tardi (*later*).
8. Professore, ha un momento dopo la lezione? Posso veder_____?

D. L'ora

A. Che ora è? Look at the clocks and tell what time it is. Use the expressions **di mattina, del pomeriggio, di sera,** and **di notte** in your responses.

ESEMPIO:

È l'una del pomeriggio.

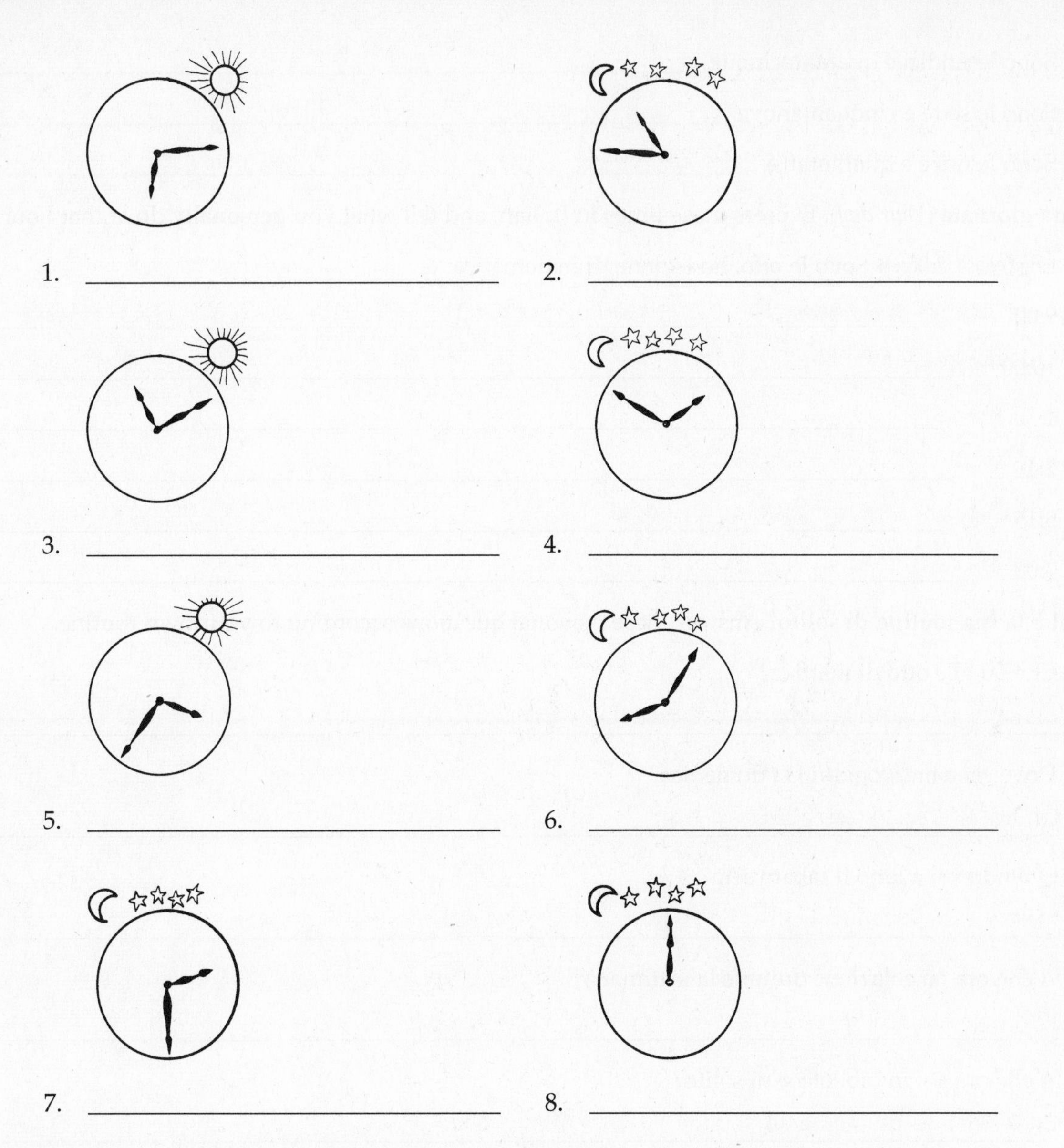

1. ______________________ 2. ______________________

3. ______________________ 4. ______________________

5. ______________________ 6. ______________________

7. ______________________ 8. ______________________

PROVERBI E MODI DI DIRE

Le ore del mattino hanno l'oro in bocca.
The morning hours are the most precious of the day (lit., have gold in their mouths).

Il tempo guarisce tutti i mali.
Time heals all wounds.

B. Ancora una volta! Rewrite these sentences, using an alternate time expression.

ESEMPIO: Sono le quattro e cinquanta. → Sono le cinque meno dieci.

1. Sono le tre e quindici. ______________________
2. Sono le otto e quaranta. ______________________
3. È l'una e trenta. ______________________

4. Sono le undici e quarantacinque. ______________________________

5. Sono le sette e cinquantanove. ______________________________

6. Sono le nove e quarantatré. ______________________________

❖ **C. La tua giornata** (*Your day*). Express these times in Italian, and tell what you personally do at that hour.

ESEMPIO: 8:00 → Sono le otto: ho lezione di matematica.

1. 9:00 ______________________________
2. 10:00 ______________________________
3. 1:30 ______________________________
4. 2:45 ______________________________
5. 5:15 ______________________________
6. 7:00 ______________________________

❖ **D. Qual è la tua routine di solito?** Answer these personal questions according to your own routine.

1. Che fai alle otto di mattina?

   ____

2. Dove sei a mezzogiorno la domenica?

   ____

3. Quando vai a letto il sabato sera?

   ____

4. A che ora fai colazione durante la settimana?

   ____

5. A che ora vai in biblioteca di solito?

   ____

6. Dove sei all'una di notte? Sei a casa o fuori?

   ____

LETTURA

La mia famiglia e il mio tempo libero

Ciao, mi chiamo Chiara e sono una bambina di undici anni. Abito in una città vicino a Firenze. Frequento la prima media, studio l'inglese e nel mio tempo libero vado a danza e gioco anche a tennis. Ascolto sempre la musica e ballo con mamma e papà quando hanno tempo. Sono figlia unica: non ho fratelli o sorelle, e ho solo una cugina. I miei genitori, Rossana e Fabrizio, hanno due fratelli: mio zio, il fratello di mio padre, si chiama Andrea e mia zia, la sorella di mia mamma, si chiama Antonella. Ho anche tre nonni: il padre di mio padre si chiama Giorgio, e la madre di mio padre Liria. Sono vecchi: hanno più di settant'anni. Mio nonno Mario, invece, è il papà della mamma. Purtroppo, la nonna non c'è più. È morta[a] prima della mia nascita.[b] Mia mamma ha quarant'anni adesso, non è più giovane, e non ho più[c] la speranza[d] di un fratellino o di una sorellina. C'è lo zio Andrea, che è sposato[e], e spero in un'altra cugina o in un cugino. Chissà![f] Ho molti amici, ma è sempre bello stare con la famiglia e vedere i parenti. La famiglia di origine di mia mamma è una famiglia molto numerosa: mia mamma non ricorda mai i nomi di tutti gli zii, le zie, i cugini: la nonna aveva[g] sei sorelle e un fratello.

Com'è la tua famiglia? Quante persone ci sono? Come sono i tuoi nonni?

[a]È... *She died* / [b]*birth*
[c]non... *I no longer have*
[d]*hope*
[e]*married* / [f]*Who knows!*
[g]*had*

❖ Now write a paragraph about your own family. Give some information about yourself and then write about your relatives. Use another sheet of paper.

UN PO' DI SCRITTURA

❖ **A. La mia serata tipica.** Describe your typical evening, giving times and activities. Write about 10 lines; use another sheet of paper.

ESEMPIO: Di solito studio fino alle (*until*) sei di sera, poi esco con gli amici. Andiamo al caffè Roma che è vicino a casa mia e facciamo programmi (*plans*) per la serata...

❖ **B. La mia giornata ideale.** Imagine that you have a wealth of free time. What are you going to do on your free day? Write about 12 lines; use another sheet of paper.

ESEMPIO: Oggi non devo studiare e non devo lavorare: posso finalmente fare tutto quello che (*everything that*) voglio! Per prima cosa (*First of all*), voglio andare a nuotare in piscina. Poi...

ATTUALITÀ

❖ **Da tutto il mondo** (*From all over the world*)! Here are two ads for au pairs published in the Italian magazine *Anna* with the addresses of two placement agencies. Write an ad according to the models.

Sabine Loesche.

"Au pair"... da tutto il mondo!

[a cura di Elda Urban]

Le ragazze più qualificate. Le agenzie più serie. Segnalazioni e indirizzi per dare un aiuto prezioso alla donna che lavora.

Candidata
Nome: Sabine Loesche
Data e luogo di nascita: 30 maggio 1975 Wernigerode
Nazionalità: tedesca
Periodo di soggiorno: da maggio per 6/12 mesi
Lingue conosciute: inglese, russo e un po' d'italiano
Esperienza: bambini da uno a sei anni
Hobbies: il giardinaggio, la musica, fare jogging. Ha la patente, ama gli animali.
È già stata in Italia per studiare l'italiano.

Agenzia
Au Pair International
Organizza soggiorni «alla pari» in collaborazione con diverse organizzazioni pubbliche o private di vari paesi europei.
Le ragazze vengono selezionate in base a una domanda, completa di referenze, certificati medici e foto. Sede: via S. Stefano 32 - 40125 Bologna, tel. 051/267575, fax 051/236594.

Candidata
Nome: Stephanie Busnot, nata a Flers il 22.10.1979
Nazionalità: francese.
Si offre come au pair per i mesi di luglio e agosto. Studentessa universitaria
Esperienze: bambini dai due ai 12 anni
Note: non fuma, ama cucinare e adora gli animali
Hobbies: jogging, ginnastica
Lingue: italiano (molto buono) e inglese
Formula di rapporto richiesta: **au-pair-plus** (36 ore settimanali = 6 ore x 6 giorni).

Agenzia
La Lampada di Aladino
La Lampada di Aladino fornisce un esauriente dossier di ogni potenziale ragazza au pair, corredato di referenze, certificato medico, foto, diplomi scolastici.
Per informazioni: La Lampada di Aladino s.n.c., via delle Abbadesse 48 - 20124 Milano tel. 02/6884325, fax 02/66804071. Sig.ra Chicca Bertoli.

CANDIDATA/O

Nome: ____________________

Data e luogo di nascita: ____________________

Nazionalità: ____________________

Periodo di soggiorno: ____________________

Lingue conosciute: ____________________

Esperienza: ____________________

Hobbies: ____________________

Capitolo

5

Name ______________________

Date ______________________

Class ______________________

PRENDIAMO UN CAFFÈ?

VOCABOLARIO PRELIMINARE

A. Cosa ordinano? Choose the drink from the list most suitable for each person described. (Use each drink only once.)

Le bevande: un aperitivo, un bicchiere di vino rosso, un cappuccino, una cioccolata calda con panna, una Coca-Cola, una spremuta d'arancia, un succo di carota, un tè caldo con miele, un tè freddo

ESEMPIO: Giampiero è un signore molto elegante; prima di cena prende sempre *un aperitivo*.

1. Daniela ha il raffreddore (*cold*) e ha bisogno di molta vitamina C. Prende ______________________.
2. A cena, in un ristorante italiano, Pietro prende ______________________.
3. I ragazzi mangiano il solito hamburger con le patatine fritte (*french fries*). Da bere prendono ______________________.
4. Il signor Pieri ha mal di gola (*a sore throat*). Prende ______________________.
5. Lidia e Paolo sciano da tre ore e hanno freddo! Prendono ______________________.
6. Fa molto caldo; Davide prende ______________________.
7. Francesca è vegetariana e mangia solo cibi (*foods*) naturali. Prende ______________________.
8. Sono le otto di mattina; i ragazzi prendono ______________________ con una pasta.

B. Al bar. Read the following dialogue between Andrea and Silvia. Then provide the information based on the dialogue.

ANDREA: Silvia... cosa prendi?
SILVIA: Una pasta va bene, grazie.
ANDREA: Non bevi niente? Un tè, o un caffè...
SILVIA: Un cappuccino allora, e anche un bicchiere di acqua minerale. Di solito non prendo niente nel pomeriggio, ma se insisti...
ANDREA: Un cappuccino? Ma il cappuccino è per la mattina!
SILVIA: No, non è vero, latte e caffè vanno sempre bene...
ANDREA: (*alla cassiera*) Allora... un succo di arancia, un cappuccino, un'acqua minerale e due paste.

Al banco.
IL BARISTA: Desiderano?
ANDREA: Un succo di arancia, ben fresco, un cappuccino, un'acqua minerale e due paste. Ecco lo scontrino.
IL BARISTA: Come vuole l'acqua?
SILVIA: Naturale, per favore.

Lo spuntino di Silvia: ______________________________

Lo spuntino di Andrea: ______________________________

❖ **C. E tu, cosa prendi di solito?** Check the column and the item that corresponds to your breakfast of choice. Then write two sentences, one beginning with **Di rado** (*Seldom*)... , the other with **Certe volte** (*At times*)... .

	DI RADO	CERTE VOLTE
un caffè (un espresso)	☐	☐
una brioche, un cornetto	☐	☐
un cappuccino	☐	☐
il latte	☐	☐
un tramezzino	☐	☐
una pasta	☐	☐
una bibita in lattina	☐	☐
i cereali	☐	☐
un succo di frutta	☐	☐
le uova strapazzate	☐	☐

1. ______________________________
2. ______________________________

❖ **D. Domande personali.** What do you drink at the following times or in the following situations?

1. alle otto di mattina

____

2. a cena

____

3. dopo attività sportive

____

4. quando studiate

____

5. con i salatini e le noccioline, quando guardate la TV

____

6. alle cinque del pomeriggio, con i biscotti

____

GRAMMATICA

A. Preposizioni articolate

A. Di chi sono queste cose? Indicate the owners of the following items, according to the example.

ESEMPIO: il sigaro / il dottore → Il sigaro è del dottore.

1. i biscotti / il bambino _______________
2. la brioche / lo zio _______________
3. i salatini / la nonna _______________
4. il burro, il pane e la marmellata / lo studente straniero _______________
5. le paste / le signore _______________
6. le bibite / gli studenti americani _______________

B. Di che cosa hanno paura? Tell what the following people need, want, or fear. Use **avere bisogno di, avere voglia di,** or **avere paura di** in your answer.

ESEMPIO: io / gli esami → Ho paura degli esami.

1. i bambini / il buio (*dark*)

____

2. noi / la bomba atomica

____

3. Anna / le vacanze

____

4. tu / il caffè macchiato

____

5. le persone ricche / le tasse (*taxes*)

6. lo zio Antonio / gli ospedali

7. Roberto / l'esame di matematica

8. io / ?

C. Da chi ricevono lettere? Tell from whom the following people receive letters.

ESEMPIO: Fabio / le amiche → Fabio riceve lettere dalle amiche.

1. la mamma / il papà

2. io e Grazia / la nonna

3. tu / la tua ragazza

4. i nonni / le zie

5. Francesca / gli amici

6. il signor Agnelli / l'avvocato (*lawyer*)

PROVERBI E MODI DI DIRE

Lontano dagli occhi, lontano dal cuore.
Out of sight, out of mind.

D. A che ora? Maria is a busy young woman. Based on the drawings, tell what she's doing and at what time.

ESEMPIO: Maria fa colazione alle sette.

1. 2. 3. 4.

5. 6. 7. 8.

1. ____
2. ____
3. ____
4. ____
5. ____
6. ____
7. ____
8. ____

E. Nel frigo di Maria. Maria's refrigerator is filled with all kinds of drinks. Complete the description of it with the preposition **di** + *article*. Then tell what drinks you have in your refrigerator.

1. Nel frigo di Maria ci sono ____________[1] acqua minerale, e ____________[2] bibite, c'è ____________[3] spremuta d'arancia, ci sono ____________[4] birre, c'è ____________[5] tè freddo e ____________[6] latte fresco.

❖ 2. Nel mio frigo ci sono ____

____

____

F. Dove? Complete the sentences with **preposizioni semplici** or **preposizioni articolate,** as necessary.

1. Dove mangiate? —Mangiamo ____________ cucina o ____________ sala da pranzo.
2. Da dove venite? —Veniamo ____________ biblioteca.
3. Dove andate? —Andiamo ____________ biblioteca.
4. Il libro ____________ professoressa è ____________ tavolo.
5. Francesca è molto diligente. Studia sempre ____________ 1.00 ____________ 9.00.
6. Valeria e Giacomo vanno ____________ufficio molto presto, ma escono ____________ufficio tardi.
7. Quando ho bisogno ____________ soldi, vado sempre ____________ banca.

B. Passato prossimo con **avere**

A. Che cosa fanno stasera e che cosa hanno fatto ieri sera? You and your friends don't like routines. What you do today is different from what you did yesterday. Complete the following sentences, using the **passato prossimo** of the italicized verb.

ESEMPIO: Stasera mangio al ristorante; ieri sera ___*ho mangiato*___ a casa.

1. Stasera *scrive* una poesia; ieri sera ________________ un racconto.
2. Stasera *finiamo* tardi; ieri sera ________________ presto.
3. Stasera *ho* amici a cena; ieri ________________ amici a pranzo.
4. Oggi *metto* il miele nel tè; ieri ________________ lo zucchero.
5. Oggi *cantiamo* in italiano; ieri ________________ in francese.
6. Stasera *leggete* il giornale; ieri sera ________________ un libro.
7. Oggi *prendono* l'autobus; ieri sera ________________ il treno.
8. Stasera *bevi* birra; ieri sera ________________ vino.
9. Oggi *pulisco* il garage; ieri ________________ la casa.
10. Oggi *dipingo* un ritratto (*portrait*); ieri ________________ un paesaggio (*landscape*).

B. Questa sera e ieri sera. Read the following paragraph, then rewrite it using the **passato prossimo.** Use another sheet of paper.

Questa sera io finisco il romanzo (*novel*) di Antonio Tabucchi e Marianna incomincia i racconti di Enrico Deaglio. Alle dieci io telefono a Federico e parliamo della riunione del Centro sociale; Marianna chiama Rossana e parlano della lezione di fotografia. Alle undici Marianna prepara la camomilla, alle undici e mezza leggiamo una rivista. A mezzanotte guardo un po' di televisione mentre Marianna prepara un panino. All'una ascoltiamo un po' di musica... Questa sera abbiamo un po' d'insonnia?

ESEMPIO: Ieri sera io ho finito il romanzo...

PROVERBI E MODI DI DIRE

Chi ha avuto ha avuto e chi ha dato ha dato.
What's done is done. (Lit., Those who've had have had and those who've given have given.)
Uomo avvisato, mezzo salvato.
Forewarned is forearmed. (Lit., An informed man is half saved.)

C. Cosa hai fatto ieri? Read the following dialogue between Tiziana and Sabrina.

TIZIANA: Cosa hai fatto ieri?
SABRINA: Più o meno le solite cose... Ho studiato per un esame d'italiano, ho mangiato al ristorante cinese, poi a casa ho letto il giornale, ho guardato la televisione, ho ascoltato un po' di musica, ho scritto un saggio al computer, ho fatto una doccia, ho giocato al computer e ho scritto due lettere...

❖ Now answer a few personal questions about your own routine yesterday.

1. Hai studiato?

____

2. Hai letto un libro?

____

3. Hai scritto al computer?

____

4. Hai mangiato al ristorante?

____

5. Hai fatto la doccia la mattina?

____

6. Hai bevuto un cappuccino a colazione?

____

7. Hai pulito la casa?

____

8. Hai fatto l'aerobica o degli esercizi fisici?

____

C. Passato prossimo con **essere**

A. Questa mattina e ieri mattina. Read the following paragraph, then rewrite it using the **passato prossimo.** Use another sheet of paper.

Questa mattina alle nove arriva Margherita e insieme andiamo a fare colazione al bar. Alle dieci lei va alla Stazione Centrale e alle dieci e mezza parte per Torino. Io vado all'università perché a mezzogiorno una professoressa americana viene a fare una conferenza (*lecture*) sul femminismo. Anche Mauro e Federico vengono alla conferenza ma non Gianni: è impegnato (*busy*) fino alle tre del pomeriggio.

ESEMPIO: Ieri mattina alle nove è arrivata Margherita...

—La televisione è arrivata anche da noi,[a] purtroppo...

[a]da... *in our area*

B. La serata di Cinzia e dei suoi amici. Read the dialogue and answer the questions that follow.

MARILENA: Cinzia, sei poi uscita di casa ieri sera? Sei andata al cinema con Romano e Lorella?

CINZIA: Sono stata a casa a studiare tutta la sera. Sono andati al cinema Paolo e Leonardo. Sono usciti alle nove. Invece Rita è venuta qui a casa, è arrivata alle nove e mezzo e siamo rimaste a casa a studiare. E i ragazzi sono tornati a mezzanotte passata. Paolo è andato subito a letto, e Leonardo è stato nello studio a giocare col computer per un po'.

1. Dove è stata Cinzia ieri sera? ______________________
2. Dove sono andati i ragazzi? ______________________
3. A che ora sono andati via? ______________________
4. Che cosa ha fatto Rita ieri sera? ______________________
5. Che cosa hanno fatto i ragazzi quando sono tornati? ______________________

____

C. La tua giornata ieri. Tell at what time you did these things yesterday.

ESEMPIO: uscire di casa → Ieri sono uscito/uscita di casa alle nove di mattina.

1. arrivare all'università

____

2. entrare in classe

____

3. andare in biblioteca

____

4. uscire con gli amici

____

5. tornare a casa

____

D. Viaggiare! Indicate where the people in Column A have been (Column B) and what sights they have seen (Column C). The first one has been done for you.

A PERSONE	B CITTÀ	C MONUMENTI
noi	Roma	la Statua della Libertà
Marco	Parigi	il Museo del Prado
gli zii	New York	il Teatro alla Scala
tu	Venezia	il Colosseo
voi	Madrid	il Ponte dei Sospiri
io	Milano	la Torre Eiffel

1. *Noi siamo stati a Roma e abbiamo visto il Colosseo.*
2. ______________________
3. ______________________

4. ____
5. ____
6. ____

E. *Essere* o *avere*? Complete the dialogue with the **passato prossimo** of the verbs.

MARIANNA: Federico, ______________________[1] (tu / chiedere) il conto al cameriere?

FEDERICO: Sì, ma lui ______________________[2] (andare) all'altro tavolo!

MARIANNA: ______________________[3] (tu / dire) che abbiamo fretta?

FEDERICO: Sì, ma lui ______________________[4] (rispondere) che tutti hanno fretta!

MARIANNA: Ma quel signore ______________________[5] (venire) dopo di noi!

FEDERICO: Sì, ma lui ______________________[6] (salutare, *to greet*) tutti. Deve essere un cliente abituale (*regular*)!

MARIANNA: Ecco, è la solita storia! Ma se io ______________________[7] (arrivare) prima e ______________________[8] (chiedere) il conto prima, voglio andare via prima!

FEDERICO: E allora andiamo!

CAMERIERE: Signori... un momento! ______________________[9] (io / preparare) il conto!

D. Conoscere e sapere

A. Sai fare questo esercizio? Complete the following sentences, using the appropriate form of **conoscere** or **sapere.**

1. Io non ______________ questa signora.
2. Tu ______________ giocare a tennis?
3. Voi ______________ perché cantano?
4. Enrico ______________ molti studenti stranieri.
5. Noi non ______________ cucinare.
6. Loro ______________ un buon ristorante.

B. Conosci l'Italia? Indicate whether you know the following people, places, or facts, and whether you have the following abilities.

ESEMPIO: San Francisco → Sì, conosco San Francisco. (*o* No, non conosco San Francisco.)
giocare a bridge → Sì, so giocare a bridge. (*o* No, non so giocare a bridge.)

1. un buon ristorante italiano ________________________________
2. parlare francese ________________________________
3. dove abita l'insegnante ________________________________
4. Giuseppe Tornatore ________________________________
5. chi è Isabella Rossellini ________________________________
6. fare il pesto ________________________________
7. delle ricette italiane ________________________________
8. ballare il tango ________________________________

PROVERBI E MODI DI DIRE

Chi sa fa e chi non sa insegna.
Those who know, do, and those who don't know, teach.

❖ **C. Non so...** Tell three things you don't know how to do.

ESEMPIO: Non so parlare russo.

1. ______________________
2. ______________________
3. ______________________

D. Non La conosco! There are many people you don't know. Complete the sentences, following the model of the cartoon caption.

—Lei chi è? Non La conosco!

1. Lui chi è? ______________________
2. Tu chi sei? ______________________
3. Voi chi siete? ______________________
4. Marta chi è? ______________________
5. Queste ragazze chi sono? ______________________
6. Questi ragazzi chi sono? ______________________
7. Lei, signora, chi è? ______________________
8. Lei, signore, chi è? ______________________

Name ______________________ Date __________ Class ______________

LETTURA

Il bar italiano

Dire «il bar», in italiano, non è come dire «bar» in lingua inglese. Il bar in Italia è un luogo dove le persone vanno a fare colazione la mattina, o dove passano del tempo, la sera con gli amici, a bere e a parlare. Al bar le persone possono anche bere alcolici, ma più spesso bevono un bel caffè forte, o vanno a prendere un gelato.

I bar italiani, nei centri storici o in periferia, spesso hanno tavolini all'aperto. Nelle sere d'estate gli italiani amano sedersi,[a] prendere un gelato o una bibita fredda e passare un po' di tempo in compagnia degli amici. Al bar spesso i bambini (e anche gli adulti) giocano a flipper,[b] a biliardino[c] o a carte.[d] Il bar è un luogo per parlare del calcio, per discutere di politica, qualche volta per vedere la televisione e per leggere il giornale. In un bar italiano spesso si trovano i giornali del giorno, che i clienti possono leggere. Il bar italiano è così molto diverso da quello americano, dove si va solo per bere alcolici, ascoltare musica o ballare.

I bar italiani sono affollati[e] soprattutto il sabato sera e la domenica, quando gli italiani vanno al bar a comprare le paste o il dolce, prima del pranzo con la famiglia. Di solito i bar italiani hanno una buona scelta di paste, torte, biscotti, caramelle[f] e cioccolato.

Il bar italiano è un luogo di incontro sociale anche per le persone che lavorano. Vanno al bar per fare colazione, per prendere un panino veloce durante la pausa del pranzo o per fare uno spuntino e per prendere un tè nel pomeriggio. Non esistono però prezzi speciali a seconda del giorno o dell'ora del giorno, come spesso succede negli Stati Uniti. In Italia, poi, non esiste una legge[g] che regola l'entrata nei bar. Anche i bambini possono entrare e anche i ragazzi di quattordici o quindici anni possono ordinare una birra.

[a] *to sit down*
[b] *pinball* / [c] *bar billiards* / [d] *cards*
[e] *crowded*
[f] *candies*
[g] *law*

Now make a list of the activities possible in Italian bars and bars in this country.

	ATTIVITÀ POSSIBILI AL BAR ITALIANO	ATTIVITÀ POSSIBILI AL BAR IN QUESTO PAESE
1.	______________________	______________________
2.	______________________	______________________
3.	______________________	______________________
4.	______________________	______________________
5.	______________________	______________________
6.	______________________	______________________

◆ According to the **Lettura**, what do Italians do in bars on Saturdays and Sundays? Is it different from what people in this country do in bars on Saturdays and Sundays? Write a paragraph. Use another sheet of paper.

UN PO' DI SCRITTURA

◆ **A. Il mio caffè preferito.** Describe your favorite coffee bar. Where is it? What is it like? What do you usually order? Who do you go there with? Use another sheet of paper.

ESEMPIO: Il mio bar preferito è un piccolo bar all'aperto in una vecchia piazza di Mantova. I tavolini sono vicino ad una fontana barocca, tra antichi palazzi (*buildings*) di pietra (*stone*) rossa...

❖ **B. Gente famosa.** Imagine that you are able to invite some famous personalities to your house. Who are they? What drinks do you serve them? What do you talk about? Use another sheet of paper.

ESEMPIO: Questa sera invito a casa mia per una piccola festa alcuni (*several*) amici: Nanni Moretti, regista (*film director*), Dacia Maraini, scrittrice (*writer*), Carlo Verdone, attore. Per Nanni voglio preparare un succo di pomodoro con ghiaccio e limone; per Dacia...

ATTUALITÀ

❖ **Un cocktail!** Here is the recipe for a very unique cocktail, published in the magazine *Grazia*. Many words are cognates. Read the recipe, then write your own recipe for an original drink. Compare it with those of your classmates.

cocktail alla rosa

Per una serata speciale provate a offrire ai vostri ospiti il cocktail alla rosa. Prendete gr. 70 di petali di rosa possibilmente colore avorio e arancio, dl. 7,5 di vino bianco e un decilitro di succo di limone. Mescolate il tutto in un recipiente e lasciate riposare, coperto, per mezz'ora in frigorifero. Filtrate e guarnite con alcuni petali di rosa. A questo punto aggiungete dl. 3,3 di champagne e servite il cocktail, naturalmente ben ghiacciato.

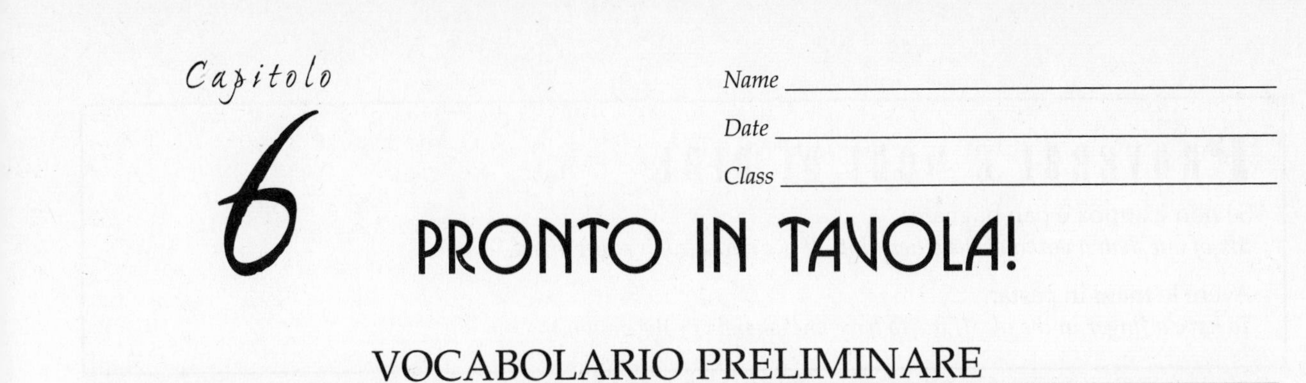

Capitolo 6

Name ______________________

Date ______________________

Class ______________________

PRONTO IN TAVOLA!

VOCABOLARIO PRELIMINARE

A. Un menu. La Forchetta d'Oro (*The Golden Fork*) è un buon ristorante ma c'è un problema: il computer ha avuto un corto circuito (*short circuit*) e il menu adesso è pieno di errori! Fa' le correzioni necessarie e aggiungi (*add*) i nomi delle categorie che mancano.

1. *Antipasti*
   Crostini
   Zuppa inglese
   Minestrone
   Macedonia

2. *Primi piatti*
   Polpette
   Salumi
   Risotto
   Tortellini alla panna

3. ______________________
   Crostata
   Zuppa inglese
   Torta al cioccolato
   Gelato

4. ______________________
   Arrosto di vitello
   Pesce
   Bistecca alla griglia
   Prosciutto e melone

5. *Contorni*
   Gnocchi al ragù
   Formaggio
   Verdura
   Insalata

❖ **B. Cosa preparo?** Stasera hai tre invitati (*guests*) a cena con dei gusti (*tastes*) molto particolari. Prepara un menu adatto (*suitable*) per tutti!

1. Marino mangia tutto eccetto (*except*) il pesce e la verdura cotta.
2. Daviana è a dieta: non mangia né (*neither*) carne rossa, né (*nor*) salumi, né dolci.
3. Franca è allergica al pomodoro; ama la carne al sangue e la pasta al dente.

MENU

Antipasto: ______________________

Primo: ______________________

Secondo: ______________________

Contorno: ______________________

Frutta: ______________________

Dolce: ______________________

PROVERBI E MODI DI DIRE

Se non è zuppa è pan bagnato.
Six of one, half a dozen of the other. (Lit., If it's not soup, it's wet bread.)

Avere le mani in pasta.
To have a finger in the pie. (Lit., To have one's hands in the dough.)

C. Che confusione! Sai trovare le seguenti parole ed espressioni nel giochetto?

Espressioni: al forno, alla carbonara, al sugo, fettuccine, in brodo, lasagne, pasta, ravioli, spaghetti

P	A	S	T	I	P	F	S	P	A	G	O	L
A	S	P	A	G	H	E	T	T	I	C	C	O
N	L	A	F	F	O	R	N	A	L	R	A	G
L	A	S	A	A	D	F	E	T	T	S	P	U
A	L	F	O	L	O	R	A	V	I	O	L	S
S	O	N	A	F	R	O	P	E	Q	U	R	L
A	R	A	N	O	B	R	A	C	A	L	L	A
G	U	O	N	R	N	I	S	T	U	C	C	G
N	O	N	O	N	I	S	T	C	C	I	N	R
E	Q	I	L	O	I	V	A	R	T	A	G	O
I	G	I	E	N	I	C	C	U	T	T	E	F

GRAMMATICA

A. Pronomi di oggetto indiretto*

A. Cosa mi dite? Completa le seguenti frasi con i pronomi di oggetto indiretto adeguati.

ESEMPIO: Signor Falzone, cosa ___Le___ posso offrire?

1. Domani è il compleanno di Valentina. Cosa ______ possiamo regalare?
2. Danilo, stasera mangiamo tutti a casa tua! Cosa ______ prepari?
3. Non trovo il mio libro di cucina; ______ puoi imprestare il tuo?
4. Ragazzi, non sapete niente (*nothing*)! Cosa ______ insegnano a scuola?
5. Mi dispiace (*I'm sorry*), Sonia, ma domani non posso dar______ la macchina: è ancora dal meccanico.
6. Non so cosa mandare a Simone per Natale; tu, cosa ______ mandi?
7. Io scrivo sempre ai nostri amici in California; perché tu non ______ scrivi mai?
8. Signora Lina, ha tempo? Ho bisogno di parlar______.

Prego!* uses the term **pronomi di oggetto indiretto so that students will recognize these pronouns as indirect object pronouns. In Italian, however, the correct term is **pronomi complemento indiretto.**

❖ **B. Situazioni.** Cosa fai nelle seguenti situazioni? Scegli una risposta o dai una tua risposta personale.

1. Sabato è il compleanno di una tua amica. Che cosa fai?
   a. Le telefono.
   b. Le mando un biglietto (*card*).
   c. Le compro un regalo (*gift*).
   d. ______________________________
2. Un amico ti chiede soldi. Che cosa fai?
   a. Gli dico che non ho soldi.
   b. Gli do tutti i soldi che ho.
   c. Gli dico di cercare un lavoro.
   d. ______________________________

C. Diretto o indiretto? Completa le seguenti frasi con le forme adeguate dei pronomi di oggetto diretto o indiretto.

1. Lei gli parla, ma lui non _____ ascolta.
2. Loro ci invitano sempre; noi non _____ invitiamo mai.
3. Se lo vedo, _____ saluto.
4. Per trovarla in casa, bisogna telefonar_____ prima.
5. Lui mi ama, ma io non _____ amo.
6. Quando _____ incontro, gli do sempre le tue notizie.

❖ **D. Una brutta notizia... o una bella notizia?** Segui il modello del fumetto (*cartoon*) per completare le frasi che seguono. Inventa una brutta o una bella notizia (hai perso le chiavi, hai scritto un libro e sei diventato famoso/diventata famosa...).

—Cari soci,[a] devo darvi una brutta notizia...

[a] *members*

1. Cara mamma, devo darti una ______________ notizia: ______________________________
   ____
2. Cari amici, devo ______________________________
   ____

3. Caro professore / Cara professoressa, devo ______

______

4. Caro Presidente, devo ______

______

B. Accordo del participio passato nel passato prossimo

A. Sì o no? Rispondi alle seguenti domande. Usa i pronomi di oggetto diretto.

ESEMPIO: Hai studiato la lezione? → Sì, l'ho studiata. (*o* No, non l'ho studiata.)

1. Hai imparato le parole? ______
2. Hai preso l'autobus? ______
3. Hai lasciato la mancia? ______
4. Hai comprato i gelati? ______
5. Hai scritto le lettere? ______
6. Hai letto l'oroscopo? ______
7. Hai fatto le fotografie? ______
8. Hai mangiato le paste? ______
9. Hai suonato la chitarra? ______
10. Hai visto i ragazzi? ______
11. Hai dato la festa? ______
12. Hai capito questa lezione? ______

B. Velocemente! Sei veloce e finisci tutto in poco tempo. Di' che hai già completato i seguenti lavori.

ESEMPIO: Quando pulisci il garage? → L'ho già pulito.

1. Quando scrivi la lettera? ______
2. Quando lavi i piatti? ______
3. Quando paghi le tasse? ______
4. Quando compri il dizionario? ______
5. Quando prendi la medicina? ______
6. Quando impari le **Parole da ricordare**? ______

C. Un giro in Sicilia. Completa il seguente dialogo con l'ausiliare adeguato.

PAT: Ciao, Mike! Ben tornato! Dove __________ passato (**passare** = *to spend*) le vacanze?

MIKE: Le __________ passate in Sicilia.

PAT: __________ viaggiato da solo (*alone*)?

MIKE: No, __________ andato con un gruppo.

PAT: Quanti giorni __________ stati a Palermo?

MIKE: Una settimana. Poi __________ fatto il giro (*tour*) dell'isola in pullman (*bus*).

C. Piacere

A. Piace o non piace? Guarda i disegni e di' se alla gente piacciono o non piacciono le varie cose.

ESEMPIO:

gli spettatori (*spectators*) / l'opera →
Agli spettatori piace l'opera.

1. i ragazzi / la pizza con le acciughe (*anchovies*) ______________________

____

2. Marco / andare in bici ______________________

____

3. Giovanna / fare i compiti di fisica ______________________________

____

4. gli studenti / dare gli esami ______________________________

____

5. il gatto / le salsicce ______________________________

____

6. la signora Marzotti / le perle ______________________________

____

B. Ti piace il minestrone? Esprimi le seguenti idee nella forma adeguata.

ESEMPIO: Come dici che ti piace ballare? → Mi piace ballare.

1. Come domandi a delle amiche se a loro piacciono gli gnocchi? ________________
2. Come dici che non ti piacciono gli spinaci? ________________
3. Come domandi a un amico se gli piace il risotto? ________________
4. Come domandi a una turista se le piace Roma? ________________
5. Come dici che ti piacciono gli spaghetti alla carbonara? ________________
6. Come domandi a un gruppo di bambini se gli piace giocare al pallone? ________________
7. Come domandi a un professore se gli piace cucinare? ________________
8. Come domandi a una professoressa se le piace insegnare alle otto? ________________

C. Non mi è piaciuto! Sei appena tornato/tornata dalla Trattoria del Pescatore, che ti è stata raccomandata da un'amica. Ora lei vuole sapere se hai provato certi piatti. Rispondi di sì, e di' se ogni piatto ti è piaciuto o no.

ESEMPIO: Hai provato il coniglio (*rabbit*) con la polenta? →
Sì, ma non mi è piaciuto. (Sì, mi è piaciuto moltissimo!)

1. Hai provato le lasagne alla bolognese?
____
2. Hai provato gli spaghetti alla carbonara?
____
3. Hai provato la cotoletta alla milanese?
____
4. Hai provato il tiramisù?
____
5. Hai provato i crostini con i fegatini (*livers*) di pollo?
____

D. L'amico / L'amica ideale. Crea dei dialoghi tra te e un amico. Rispondi alle domande anche per il tuo amico. Se dai risposte negative, proponi (*propose*) un'alternativa.

ESEMPIO: la musica classica →
—Ti piace la musica classica?
—Sì, mi piace la musica classica. (No, non mi piace la musica classica, ma mi piacciono gli U2.)

1. i film stranieri

____

____

2. andare in discoteca

____

____

3. le macchine italiane

____

____

4. lo spumante (*champagne*)

____

____

5. le poesie di Maya Angelou

____

____

❖ **E. Mi sai dire cosa ti piace?** Conosci tante persone particolari. A loro non piace questo o quello e ti chiedi cosa è che gli piace. Segui l'esempio e completa le seguenti frasi. Devi usare la fantasia e fingere di chiacchierare.

ESEMPIO: a un amico / un'amica che vive in città →
Non ti piace lo smog, non ti piace il rumore (*noise*), non ti piace la confusione...
Mi sai dire, allora, cosa ti piace nella vita?

1. al tuo compagno / alla tua compagna di stanza:

Non ti _______________, non ti _______________, non ti _______________... Mi _______________ dire, allora, cosa _______ piace nella vita?

2. ai tuoi genitori:

Non vi _______________, non vi _______________, non vi _______________... Mi _______________ dire, allora, cosa _______ piace nella vita?

3. all'insegnante d'italiano:

Non Le _______________, non Le _______________, non Le _______________... Mi _______________ dire, allora, cosa _______ piace nella vita?

4. ai tuoi vicini di casa (*neighbors*):

Non vi ________________________, non vi ________________________, non vi ________________________... Mi ____________ dire, allora, cosa ________ piace nella vita?

D. Interrogativi

A. Quante domande! Amelia si è trasferita a Bari e ha degli amici nuovi. Suo fratello Fabio le fa tante domande. Completa il loro dialogo. Usa gli interrogativi adeguati.

Interrogativi: che cosa, come, con chi, dove, quando

FABIO: ____________[1] sono i tuoi nuovi amici di Bari?

AMELIA: Sono molto simpatici!

FABIO: ____________[2] andate di solito (*usually*) il sabato sera?

AMELIA: Di solito andiamo al cinema o a teatro.

FABIO: ____________[3] esci stasera?

AMELIA: Stasera esco con Caterina, la mia nuova collega d'ufficio.

FABIO: ____________[4] avete intenzione di fare?

AMELIA: Andiamo a passeggiare sul lungomare (*sea front*). È una bellissima serata!

FABIO: ____________[5] torni a casa a trovarci (*to visit*)?

AMELIA: Probabilmente il mese prossimo.

FABIO: Allora, a presto!

—Quale dei[a] due posso usare, mamma?

[a]*of the*

B. Test velocissimo! Completa le frasi. Scegli l'interrogativo giusto.

1. (Chi / Che) viene a teatro con me sabato sera?
2. (Quale / Che cosa) giornale preferisci? *La Repubblica* o *Il Corriere della Sera?*
3. (Perché / Dove) non prendiamo l'autobus qui (*here*)?

4. (Qual / Cosa) è il tuo passatempo preferito?
5. (A chi / Di chi) scrivi lettere di solito?
6. (Di chi / Con chi) sono questi dischi?
7. (Che / Dove) rivista stai leggendo?
8. (Quanto / Quanti) ragazzi vengono in bici?

PROVA-QUIZ

A. La conosci? Leo vuole conoscere meglio Lella, l'amica di Marisa. Completa il dialogo con le espressioni adeguate.

Espressioni: cena, conosci, la, le, mi, piace, so, telefono

LEO: ______________[1] bene Lella?

MARISA: Sì, ______________[2] conosco molto bene; frequentiamo un corso di cucina insieme.

LEO: Ma allora è vero che le ______________[3] cucinare! Quando la vedi ancora?

MARISA: Mah! Penso di invitarla a ______________[4] domani.

LEO: Se ______________[5] dai il suo indirizzo (*address*), posso dar______________[6] un passaggio (*ride*) io!

MARISA: ______________[7] che vive con i suoi (*her parents*) ma non ricordo l'indirizzo. Quando le ______________[8] stasera, le chiedo dove abita e... se ha bisogno di un passaggio!

B. Domande, domande... C'è qualcuno di nuovo al Centro sociale e Giovanna vuole sapere tutto su di lui (*about him*). Completa il dialogo con gli interrogativi adeguati.

GIOVANNA: ______________[1] è quel ragazzo nuovo?

GIORGIO: Un amico di Luisa.

GIOVANNA: ______________[2] si chiama?

GIORGIO: Hassan.

GIOVANNA: ______________[3] viene?

GIORGIO: Da Tunisi.

GIOVANNA: ______________[4] è qui?

GIORGIO: Per lavorare al Centro sociale.

GIOVANNA: ______________[5] tempo ha a disposizione (*available*)?

GIORGIO: Quattro ore, il sabato e la domenica.

GIOVANNA: ______________[6] vuole incominciare?

GIORGIO: Questa settimana.

GIOVANNA: ______________[7] preferisce fare?

GIORGIO: Senti, Giovanna, ______________[8] non fai le tue domande direttamente ad Hassan?

C. Al bar. Completa il seguente paragrafo con le preposizioni semplici o preposizioni articolate adeguate.

Quando vado ____________[1] bar, di solito prendo qualcosa (*something*) ____________[2] banco. ____________[3] otto di mattina prendo un cappuccino ____________[4] una brioche. ____________[5] mezzogiorno prendo un panino, un'acqua minerale e un caffè. ____________[6] acqua minerale metto ____________[7] limone; ____________[8] caffè metto ____________[9] latte e ____________[10] zucchero. ____________[11] sette di sera prendo un aperitivo ____________[12] le olive e ____________[13] mezzanotte, dopo il cinema, una camomilla calda. ____________[14] camomilla metto sempre ____________[15] miele: aiuta (*it helps*) a dormire!

D. Un appuntamento. Luca e Matteo fanno programmi per la serata. Completa il loro dialogo con le forme adeguate di **dire, uscire** e **venire.**

LUCA: Matteo, cosa ____________[1] se stasera andiamo a casa di Luigi?

MATTEO: Io ____________[2] che va bene! Ma lui cosa ____________?[3]

LUCA: Lui è contento perché ha l'influenza e da due giorni non ____________[4] di casa.

MATTEO: ____________[5] anche Rossana?

LUCA: No, Rossana e Giovanna questa sera ____________[6] insieme.

MATTEO: Dove vanno?

LUCA: Vanno al Piccolo Teatro a vedere Margherita. (Loro) ____________[7] che è molto emozionata e ha bisogno di sostegno (*support*).

MATTEO: Anche la vita (*life*) delle attrici ha i suoi problemi!

E. Traduzioni. Traduci in italiano. Scrivi su un tuo foglio.

1. s1: You never call Federico! He always calls you!
   s2: It isn't true! I call him every week.
   s1: And you never write to Giovanna!
   s2: I write to her every month!

2. s1: Nina tells me that you don't like cookbooks.
   s2: I don't like to cook but I like to read cookbooks!

3. s1: Are you going to invite us to dinner? What are you going to prepare for us?
   s2: I'm very sorry. I can't invite you to dinner tonight, but I'll prepare fresh gnocchi for you tomorrow!

4. s1: Hello. Can I speak to Cinzia?
   s2: I'm sorry, she isn't in. She left the house ten minutes ago.
   s1: When is she coming back?
   s2: In (**Tra**) an hour.

5. I'm Marco. I'm an Italian student. I study at the University of Rome. I speak Italian and English. I love (**Amo**) all sports. I go skiing whenever (**ogni volta che**) I can. I love to drive but I hate (**odio**) to fly. I'm afraid of planes! I want to visit New York in September. How am I going to New York? By boat (**In nave**)!

LETTURA

Il pranzo della domenica

Roberto ci parla del ruolo del pranzo della domenica nella sua famiglia.

Il pranzo della domenica è un pranzo importante, di solito, nelle famiglie italiane. È stato sempre il pranzo centrale nella vita della mia famiglia, ed è un pranzo importante anche in casa dei genitori di mia moglie, dove abito adesso.

In casa di mia moglie, durante questa estate calda, cominciamo sempre il pranzo domenicale con un antipasto di prosciutto e melone, un bel melone maturo, delizioso. A casa mia, invece, mia madre ha sempre cominciato il pranzo della domenica con i crostini, in autunno, inverno, estate o primavera: sulla tavola, solo crostini. Qui nella mia nuova casa, i crostini invece non si mangiano mai. Ci sono di solito delle verdure miste, e in inverno dei salumi.

Il primo anche qui è obbligatorio: pasta al sugo, tagliatelle, o fettuccine, o spaghetti o gnocchi di patate col sugo di carne, sempre con tanto formaggio parmigiano. La pasta è sempre la protagonista di questi pranzi. In certe occasioni, quando ci sono ospiti, si preparano anche due o tre tipi di pasta, con tipi diversi di sugo. Naturalmente, l'antipasto e il primo, come il secondo, vengono sempre accompagnati dal vino, rosso con i sughi di carne, bianco con le carni bianche o con il pesce. Mi piace molto il pesce, che però con i genitori di mia moglie non mangio mai.

Anche il secondo, poi, è sostanzioso[a]: o la bistecca e le salsicce[b] alla griglia, o la bistecca e il coniglio arrosto, o la bistecca e il pollo alla griglia e sempre, invariabilmente, un bel contorno di patate arrosto e l'insalata mista. Dai miei genitori, invece, ho quasi sempre mangiato pollo: pollo arrosto, alla griglia, farcito[c]... Dopo la carne arrivano i formaggi, e poi la frutta fresca, e poi, finalmente, il dolce, col caffè che è l'ultima cosa che beviamo a pranzo. Qui mia moglie preferisce le crostate di frutta. La mia famiglia ha sempre preferito il tiramisù o il gelato. Adesso il gelato lo compro fuori, ma non è un grande problema! Il pranzo della domenica è insomma semplice per gli ingredienti, ma ricco per l'abbondanza. Ed è di solito formale per l'aspetto: noi siamo vestiti bene e la tavola è ben apparecchiata con la tovaglia[d] più bella e i piatti di porcellana.

[a]*filling* / [b]*sausages*

[c]*stuffed*

[d]*tablecloth*

Che tipo di piatti mangia Roberto nella sua nuova casa la domenica? Quali piatti invece non mangia più (*anymore*)? Fa' una lista, secondo le portate (*courses*).

PIATTI CHE ROBERTO MANGIA	PIATTI CHE ROBERTO NON MANGIA PIÙ
___________________	___________________
___________________	___________________
___________________	___________________
___________________	___________________
___________________	___________________

❖ E tu, cosa mangi la domenica? I tuoi pranzi sono elaborati? Scrivi il menu tipico del pranzo domenicale della tua famiglia, per categorie, se possibile (antipasto, primo, secondo, contorni, formaggi, frutta, dolce). Scrivi anche quali sono le bevande che accompagnano i cibi. Scrivi su un tuo foglio.

UN PO' DI SCRITTURA

❖ **A. Una cena importante.** Hai mai preparato una cena o un pranzo importante? Se sì, descrivi il menu nei dettagli e spiega per chi l'hai preparato, se hai servito vino, dove hai mangiato e se agli invitati è piaciuto tutto. Se non hai mai preparato una cena o un pranzo importante, inventa una descrizione. Scrivi una pagina. Scrivi su un tuo foglio.

ESEMPIO: L'estate scorsa ho preparato una cena speciale per venti amici. Ho cucinato tutto il giorno. Ho incominciato con un antipasto misto... Abbiamo mangiato in giardino...

❖ **B. Parliamo di cucina!** Conosci la cucina di altri paesi? Ti interessa conoscere le abitudini (*habits*) culinarie di altri paesi? Perché sì o perché no? È importante sapere come mangiano gli altri? Scrivi una pagina in cui (*which*) rispondi a queste domande. Scrivi su un tuo foglio.

ESEMPIO: Ho molti amici francesi, quindi (*thus*) conosco abbastanza bene la cucina francese. I piatti che loro preparano sono diversi da quelli che (*the ones that*) troviamo nei ristoranti francesi qui negli Stati Uniti...

ATTUALITÀ

Dove andiamo a mangiare? Dai un'occhiata a questo elenco di ristoranti, poi scegli quello adatto alle seguenti persone.

Giggetto er pescatore - via Sant'Elia 13 Firenze - tel. 87.93.11/87.99.29 - riposo domenica - ferie dal 12 al 31 agosto - AEx, Visa, Din, CartaSì, Eurocard - cani ammessi (in giardino) - prenotazione necessaria - coperti 250 - aria condizionata no - tavoli all'aperto sì - orari cucina 12,30-15/19,30-23.
Prezzo: 60 mila.
Specialità: pesce fresco, pesce al forno alla Giggetto, linguine all'aragosta.

Perilli - via Piemonte 53/c Pisa - tel. 46.35.06/46.46.26 - riposo lunedì - ferie dal 6 al 25 agosto - AEx, Visa, Din, CartaSì, Eurocard - cani ammessi - prenotazione consigliabile - coperti 200 - aria condizionata no - travoli all'aperto sì - orari cucina 12,30-15/20-23.
Prezzo; 60 mila.
Specialità: risotto con aragoste.

Il dito e la luna - via dei Sabelli 47 Lucca - tel. 49.40.726 - riposo domenica e lunedì - ferie agosto - cani non ammessi - prenotazione consigliabile - coperti 85 - aria condizionata no - tavoli all'aperto no - orari cucina solo sera 20-23,30.
Prezzo: 20/30 mila.
Specialità: pasta alla Norma, risotto alle fragole, scaloppine con salsa di ortiche.

Nuova Fiorentina - via A. Brofferio 43/51 Montecatini Terme - tel. 38.00.03 - riposo lunedì tutto il giorno e martedì a pranzo - ferie dal 13 al 29 agosto - cani non ammessi - prenotazione non necessaria - coperti 200 - aria condizionata no - tavoli all'aperto sì - orari cucina 12,30-15/19,30-0,45.
Prezzo: 35 mila.
Specialità: pizzeria forno a legna, carne alla brace, cucina all toscana.

Ambasciata d'Abruzzo - via Pietro Tacchini 26 Montecatini Terme - tel. 87.82.56/87.49.64 - riposo domenica - ferie dal 6 agosto al 3 settembre - AEx, Visa, Din, CartaSì, Eurocard, Airplus - cani non ammessi - prenotazione necessaria - coperti 120 - aria condizionta sì - tavoli all'aperto sì - orari cucina 12-15,30/19-23.
Prezzo: 35 mila.
Specialità: ravioli funghi e spinaci, cinghiale all'agrodolce, piatti freddi.

Ropiè - via di S. Francesco a Ripa 104 Sesto Fiorentino - tel. 58.00.694 - riposo domenica e lunedì - non chiude per ferie - AEx - cani non ammessi - prenotazione no - coperti 30-35 - aria condizionata sì - tavoli all'aperto no - orario cucina (solo sera) 20,30-24 (su prenotazione anche pranzo).
Prezzo: 35/45 mila.
Specialità: risotto al basilico, salmone in salsa bianca.

Il Pulcino ballerino - via degli Equi 68 Firenze - tel. 49.03.01 - riposo lunedì - ferie dal 6 al 16 agosto - cani ammessi - prenotazione consigliabile - coperti 70 - aria condizionata no - tavoli all'aperto no - orario cucina solo sera 20-24.
Prezzo: 20/25 mila.
Specialità: sedanini alla rucola, pasta con fagioli e gamberi, carni, verdure e formaggi cotti sulla pietra rovente.

1. La signora Mincuzzi: vuole mangiare il risotto. È domenica.

____

2. I signori Bruni: hanno un cane. Vogliono spendere poco.

____

3. I Muti: hanno una famiglia numerosa e i bambini vogliono mangiare la pizza.

____

4. Daniela: soffre di (*she suffers from*) allergie e ha bisogno dell'aria condizionata. Adora i ravioli.

____

5. Franco e Gina: è mezzanotte e mezzo e non hanno ancora mangiato.

____

Capitolo

7

Name ______________________

Date ______________________

Class ______________________

FARE BELLA FIGURA

VOCABOLARIO PRELIMINARE

A. Le attività di ogni giorno. Guarda i disegni e descrivi la mattina tipica di Francesca.

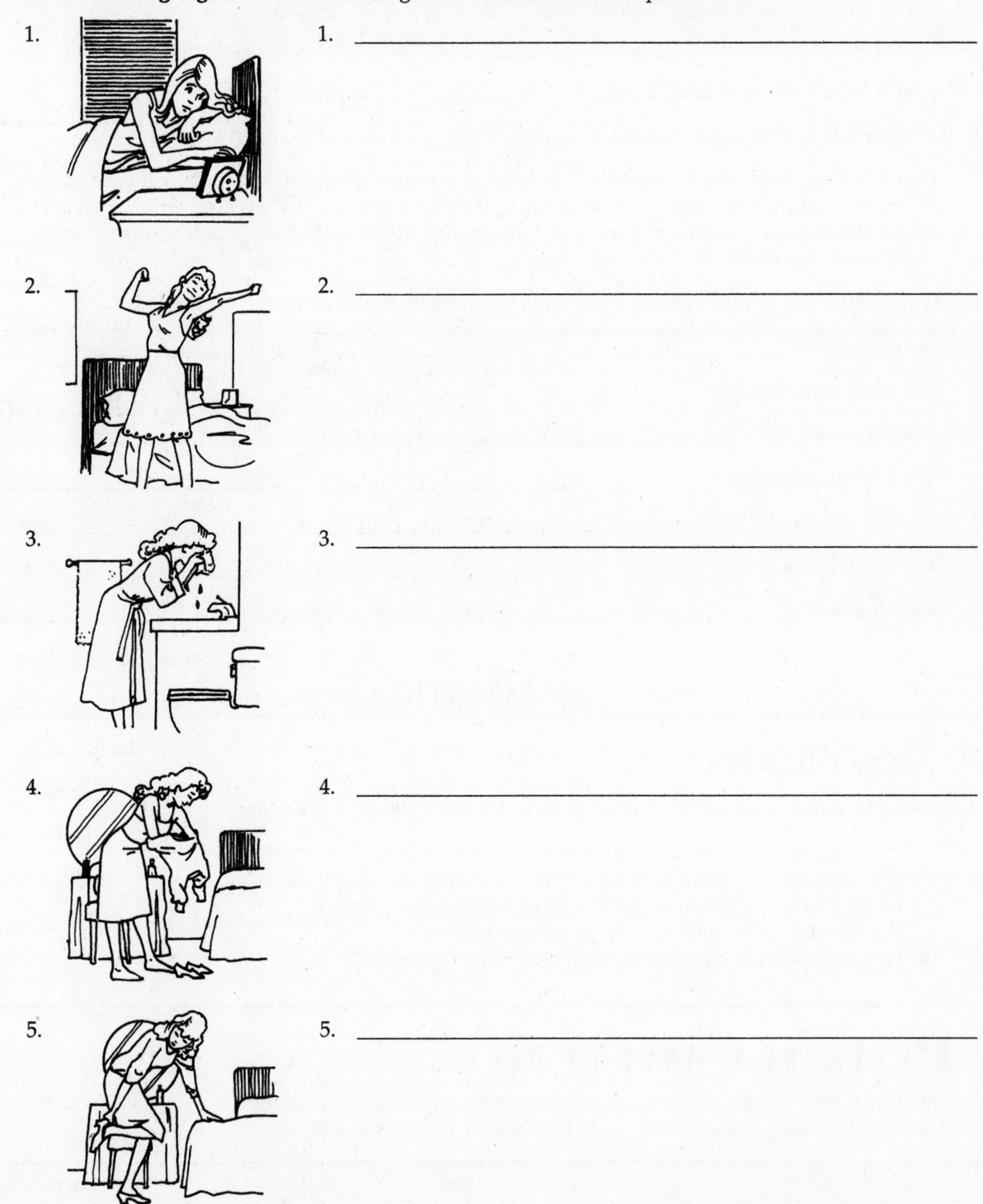

1. ______________________
2. ______________________
3. ______________________
4. ______________________
5. ______________________

B. Laurearsi o diplomarsi? Completa le frasi con i verbi seguenti: **chiamarsi, diplomarsi, fermarsi, laurearsi, sentirsi, specializzarsi, sposarsi.**

ESEMPIO: Ugo e Vittoria si ___*sposano*___ se trovano una casa.

1. Io mi ____________ Valentina. Tu come ti ____________?
2. Andate dal dottore quando non vi ____________ bene?
3. Maria frequenta l'università. Vuole prima ____________ in medicina, e poi ____________ in cardiologia.
4. Gli studenti italiani si ____________ alla fine del liceo. Poi vanno all'università.
5. Paola ha bisogno di soldi; deve ____________ in banca.

C. Le lamentele (*complaints*) **di Tiziana.** Completa il paragrafo scegliendo i verbi adatti.

Tiziana si lamenta di tutto! Si (arrabbia / diverte)[1] se fa troppo caldo e se fa troppo freddo. Se gli amici si (divertono / lavano)[2] al cinema o in discoteca, lei si (veste / annoia).[3] Tiziana si (ricorda / accontenta)[4] sempre dei momenti infelici, ma si (ricorda / dimentica)[5] dei momenti felici. E poiché (*since*) non ha imparato ad (accontentarsi / annoiarsi),[6] ogni sera si (addormenta / sveglia)[7] di cattivo umore.

❖ **D. Ancora sulla vita di tutti i giorni.** Descrivi la tua giornata tipica, secondo i suggerimenti.

Quando mi alzo ____________

Alle 10.00 di mattina ____________

A mezzogiorno ____________

Alle 3.00 del pomeriggio ____________

Alle 7.00 di sera ____________

Alle 10.30 di sera ____________

A mezzanotte ____________

GRAMMATICA

A. Verbi riflessivi

A. Riflessivo o no? Completa le seguenti frasi. Scegli una delle espressioni date tra parentesi.

1. Prima di uscire io (sveglio / mi sveglio) i bambini e preparo la colazione.
2. Noi (laviamo / ci laviamo) le mani prima di mangiare.
3. Lei (si chiama / chiama) il marito e gli dice di comprare il pane.
4. Lui (sbaglia / si sbaglia) sempre gli esercizi più facili.
5. Loro (organizzano / si organizzano) bene prima di partire.

PROVERBI E MODI DI DIRE

Chi s'aiuta, Dio l'aiuta.
God helps those who help themselves.

Fidarsi è bene, non fidarsi è meglio.
To trust is good, not to trust is better.

B. Nel passato. Completa le seguenti frasi con il passato prossimo del verbo tra parentesi.

1. Noi ______________________ (svegliarsi) alle 6.00, poi ______________________ (alzarsi) e ______________________ (fare colazione).
2. Luciano ______________________ (fermarsi) a mangiare un panino al bar della stazione.
3. Dopo la telefonata (*phone call*) di Marina, ______________________ (vestirsi / voi) in fretta e ______________________ (uscire).
4. Perché ______________________ (annoiarsi / tu) ieri sera? Tutti gli altri ______________________ (divertirsi) molto.
5. ______________________ (Laurearsi / noi) in quattro anni.
6. ______________________ (Sposarsi / io) dopo la laurea.

—Vedo che oggi si sente meglio,[a] Rossi!

[a]*better*

C. È sempre la stessa vita! Oggi Massimo ha fatto le stesse cose che fa tutti i giorni. Riscrivi ciascuna (*each*) frase al passato prossimo.

ESEMPIO: Massimo si alza alle otto. → Si è alzato alle otto.

1. Va in bagno per una doccia.

   ____

2. Si asciuga.

   ____

3. Si lava i denti.

   ____

4. Si fa la barba.

   ____

5. Si guarda allo specchio e si pettina.

   ____

6. Si mette le lenti a contatto.

   ____

7. Si veste.

____

8. Esce di casa alle otto per prendere l'autobus.

____

❖ **D. La mia vita.** Ora racconta la tua giornata tipica. Usa il passato prossimo.

ESEMPIO: Ieri mi sono svegliata alle otto...

____

____

____

____

____

____

____

B. Costruzione reciproca

A. Aiutarsi. Completa le frasi con la costruzione reciproca.

ESEMPIO: Ilaria e le amiche *si vedono* spesso.

1. Quando gli italiani ____________ (incontrarsi), ____________ (abbracciarsi) e ____________ (baciarsi).
2. Per Natale, io e i miei amici ____________ (farsi) dei regali.
3. Che cosa ____________ (dirsi / voi) quando ____________ (salutarsi)?
4. Marina e Daniele ____________ (scriversi) e ____________ (telefonarsi) spesso.
5. Noi ____________ (conoscersi) da molto tempo, e ____________ (capirsi) molto bene.
6. Voi ____________ (aiutarsi) quando siete in difficoltà?

B. La storia di Paolo e Francesca. Racconta a Valeria la storia d'amore di due amici tuoi, secondo i suggerimenti.

ESEMPIO: conoscersi / l'anno scorso → Si sono conosciuti l'anno scorso.

1. incontrarsi / in un bar

____

2. vedersi / all'università

____

3. rivedersi (*to see each other again*) / due giorni dopo?

____

4. telefonarsi / ogni giorno

____

5. baciarsi / dopo un mese

____

6. sposarsi / dopo un anno

____

PROVERBI E MODI DI DIRE

Gli estremi si toccano.
Extremes meet.

—Allora ci vediamo fra cinque minuti, il tempo per mettere in ordine[a] la mia camera!

[a]*order*

C. Presente + da + espressioni di tempo

A. Da quanto tempo? Usa le informazioni date per fare delle domande e poi rispondere. Comincia con **da quanto tempo.**

ESEMPIO: Eric / suonare la chitarra / due anni →
Da quanto tempo suona la chitarra Eric? Da due anni.

1. Nicoletta / uscire con Mauro / quattro anni

____

2. voi / scrivere racconti / molti anni

____

3. Mario e Renata / vivere in Svizzera / cinque anni

____

4. tu / aspettare / mezz'ora

____

5. io / non pulire il frigo / un mese

____

6. Leo / prendere lezioni di musica / molto tempo

____

❖ **B. Domande per te.** Di' da quanto tempo fai le seguenti cose.

ESEMPIO: Da quanto tempo scrivi queste frasi? → Scrivo queste frasi da (cinque minuti).

1. Da quanto tempo sei qui?

____

2. Da quanto tempo corri (giochi a tennis, nuoti)?

____

3. Da quanto tempo leggi riviste e giornali?

____

4. Da quanto tempo frequenti lo stesso bar?

____

5. Da quanto tempo non esci di casa?

____

6. Da quanto tempo studi chimica (informatica, storia)?

____

D. Avverbi

A. Facilmente! Cambia i seguenti aggettivi in avverbi.

ESEMPIO: splendido → splendidamente

1. chiaro _______________
2. particolare _______________
3. affettuoso _______________
4. fortunato _______________
5. intelligente _______________
6. probabile _______________
7. intero _______________

8. gentile ______________________
9. speciale ______________________
10. vero ______________________

❖ **B. Personalmente.** Completa le seguenti frasi secondo le tue preferenze. Scegli uno degli avverbi tra parentesi.

1. Preferisco i film che finiscono (tragicamente / felicemente / comicamente).
2. Non mi piacciono le persone che arrivano (presto / tardi / inaspettatamente [*unexpectedly*]).
3. Sono d'accordo con i miei genitori (completamente / parzialmente / raramente).
4. Di solito io faccio le cose (impulsivamente / meditatamente / consapevolmente [*consciously*]).
5. Mi piacciono le persone che mi rispondono (gentilmente / pacatamente [*calmly*] / aggressivamente).
6. Spero di vivere il resto dei miei giorni (comodamente [*comfortably*] / tranquillamente / pericolosamente).

E. Numeri superiori a 100

A. Prezzi italiani. Carlo e Cristina si trasferiscono (*are moving*) in un appartamento nuovo, e devono comprare molte cose. Guarda l'elenco delle spese e scrivi in lettere (*write out*) il prezzo di ogni articolo.

1. uno stereo: 2.000.000 L. ______________________
2. un frigo: 700.000 L. ______________________
3. un televisore: 800.000 L. ______________________
4. una lavatrice (*washer*): 635.000 L. ______________________
5. un divano (*couch*): 2.200.000 L. ______________________
6. un aspirapolvere (*vacuum cleaner*): 550.000 L. ______________________
7. un letto: 900.000 L. ______________________
8. un servizio di piatti (*set of dishes*): 250.000 L. ______________________

B. Prezzi americani. Ora di' quanto costano approssimativamente i seguenti articoli. Scrivi i prezzi, in lettere, in italiano.

1. un lettore (*player*) di compact disc ______________________
2. un computer ______________________
3. una giacca di pelle (*leather jacket*) ______________________
4. un monolocale (*studio apartment*) ______________________
5. una motocicletta ______________________

C. Operazioni matematiche. Scrivi in lettere le seguenti operazioni matematiche e le loro risposte.

Espressioni utili: più (+), meno (−), diviso (÷), per (×), fa/uguale (=)

1. $150 \times 10 =$

____

____

2. 2.650.000 − 2.560.000 =

____

____

3. 323 + 702 =

____

____

4. 3.000.000 ÷ 600.000 =

____

____

LETTURA

La vita di tutti i giorni...

Stefania ci racconta la sua routine quotidiana.

Cosa faccio io tutti i giorni? Le stesse cose, più o meno... Ho proprio una vita monotona. Quando mi alzo non faccio colazione, perché preferisco fare colazione al bar. Mi sveglio presto, verso le sei, ma mi alzo dopo mezz'ora, perché voglio fare con calma ed essere di buon umore. Quando mi alzo vado in bagno, mi lavo con una bella doccia fredda, poi mi asciugo[a] e mi vesto con cura e guardo il telegiornale in televisione, e poi esco per andare all'università. Certo, prima di vestirmi mi sono guardata bene allo specchio, mi sono pettinata i capelli e messa il trucco[b]. I vestiti non sono un problema, la sera prima li stiro[c] sempre, e così sono pronti la mattina. Insomma, sono ben organizzata.

Alle dieci dopo la prima ora di lezione, di solito, faccio una pausa per andare a prendere un cappuccino o un caffè. Massimo (il mio ragazzo) e io ci incontriamo al bar, lui lavora vicino all'università. Ci abbracciamo, ci baciamo e ci raccontiamo le nostre cose per almeno mezz'ora.

Dalle undici a mezzogiorno ho ancora lezione e a mezzogiorno vado a mangiare un panino. Massimo e io ci telefoniamo per parlare un po'. Dopo vado a lezione fino alle tre e alle tre vado in biblioteca, fino alle cinque o alle sei. Alle sette torno a casa e ceno, e poi Massimo e io ci incontriamo per andare al cinema o per guardare la televisione. Se non vedo Massimo, esco subito dopo cena per andare in palestra, dove corro, faccio l'aerobica o nuoto. Verso le dieci e mezzo di sera torno a casa e studio fino a mezzanotte. Vado quindi a letto, dormo per sei ore e il mattino dopo di nuovo la stessa vita... Solo il sabato e la domenica sono diversi, sono i giorni in cui posso rilassarmi e cambiare i programmi.

[a]*mi . . . I dry off*
[b]*makeup* / [c]*I iron*

Cosa fa Stefania?

1. Tra le sei e le dieci: ____

____

2. Tra le undici e le sette: ____

____

3. Dopo cena fino all'ora di dormire: ______________________________

____

4. Il sabato e la domenica: ______________________________

____

❖ E tu, hai un tipo di giornata simile a quella di Stefania? Cosa fai a certe ore del giorno e della sera?

Alle sei di mattina ______________________________

Mi sveglio ______________________________

Mi alzo ______________________________

Poi ______________________________

Esco di casa ______________________________

Per pranzo ______________________________

Per cena ______________________________

Nel pomeriggio ______________________________

La sera ______________________________

Il sabato e la domenica ______________________________

UN PO' DI SCRITTURA

❖ **A. Giornate in famiglia.** Com'è la giornata dei membri della tua famiglia? Quando si divertono, si annoiano, si arrabbiano, si lamentano? Scegli un membro della tua famiglia e scrivi una breve composizione. Scrivi su un tuo foglio.

ESEMPIO: Mio fratello si alza sempre tardi. Si lava, si veste, non si fa la barba e poi corre al lavoro. Di solito si dimentica qualcosa (*something*): le chiavi, gli occhiali, la cartella dei documenti (*briefcase*)...

❖ **B. Usanze** (*Habits*) **fantastiche.** Scrivi un piccolo racconto. Crea un personaggio immaginario: Chi è? Cosa fa? Quali sono le sue caratteristiche? Come passa il tempo? Scrivi su un tuo foglio.

ESEMPIO: Valentina è una ragazza del 2042. Non si veste certo come vestivano i suoi nonni nel 2000 e non si diverte con le stesse cose...

ATTUALITÀ

Ecco una pubblicità pubblicata sul settimanale (*weekly magazine*) *Panorama.* Guarda il disegno e leggi le due frasi, poi descrivi cosa succede (*is happening*) nella vignetta (*cartoon*) e spiega che cosa promette la pubblicità. Ti sembra una pubblicità efficace o no? Perché? Scrivi un paragrafo. Scrivi su un tuo foglio.

ALLA SICUREZZA DELLA CASA, COME A QUELLA DEL VIAGGIO,
CI PENSA EUROPASSISTANCE.

Name ______________________

Date ______________________

Class ______________________

C'ERA UNA VOLTA

VOCABOLARIO PRELIMINARE

A. Piccole conversazioni. Completa con la forma adatta delle seguenti parole: **l'attore; la colonna sonora; il cronista; il giornalista; l'intervista; pubblicare; la redattrice; la redazione; la recensione; la stampa.**

1. s1: Hai letto la ____________________[1] dell'ultimo film di Moretti?

   s2: Sì, diceva che gli ____________________[2] sono stati bravissimi e che la ____________________[3] era eccezionale: anch'io ho pensato che la musica era perfetta.

2. s1: Stefano è un ____________________[1] della *Repubblica,* ma è stanco di occuparsi di cronaca nera. Preferisce fare ____________________[2] a personaggi famosi.

   s2: Voglio fargli conoscere la mia ____________________.[3] Al mio giornale cercano un ____________________[4] per la sezione spettacoli.

3. s1: Non mi piace la ____________________[1] americana. Non ____________________[2] abbastanza notizie di politica estera.

   s2: Non tutti i giornali americani sono uguali. Ci sono anche quelli che hanno una buona ____________________[3] per l'estero.

B. Che significa? Spiega il significato dei seguenti verbi con un sinonimo o con una piccola frase in italiano.

ESEMPIO: mandare in onda → trasmettere

1. doppiare: ______________________________
2. girare: ______________________________
3. produrre: ______________________________
4. recensire: ______________________________
5. trasmettere: ______________________________

C. Televisione o cinema. Leggi il dialogo e poi rispondi alle domande.

ROSSANA: Hai letto la recensione del film di Benigni? Vuoi andare a vederlo?
FABRIZIO: C'è una partita di calcio sulla Rai, gioca l'Italia!
ROSSANA: Sempre televisione, televisione, televisione...
FABRIZIO: Io la televisione la vedo per gli sport, e per il telegiornale. I giornali li leggo raramente, preferisco le riviste, o i settimanali. La recensione dove l'hai letta?
ROSSANA: L'ho letta su *La Repubblica* di oggi. Perché non andiamo al cinema stasera?
FABRIZIO: Gioca l'Italia, come ti ho detto...

ROSSANA: Ma che insistenza! Vuoi vedere la partita, eh? Sai che hanno inventato il videoregistratore? Perché non registri la partita e vieni al cinema?

FABRIZIO: Sei tu insistente! La partita è affascinante perché è una trasmissione in diretta, non voglio vederla col videoregistratore.

ROSSANA: Va bene, allora vado al cinema da sola.

1. Che cosa danno sulla Rai che Fabrizio vuole vedere? ______________________________

____

2. Cosa vede Fabrizio di solito? ______________________________

____

3. Cosa legge Fabrizio? ______________________________

____

4. Che idea ha Rossana sulla partita? ______________________________

____

5. Come risponde Fabrizio? ______________________________

____

D. Fuori posto. Trova la parola che sembra fuori posto e spiega perché.

ESEMPIO: lo schermo, stampare, il quotidiano →
Lo schermo è la parola fuori posto, perché non riguarda i giornali.

1. il produttore, le notizie, l'attrice

____

2. doppiare, girare, pubblicare

____

3. il settimanale, il mensile, la produttrice

____

4. la trasmissione, lo schermo, il quotidiano

____

GRAMMATICA

A. Imperfetto

A. Ora e prima. Riscrivi le seguenti frasi. Di' che prima avevi...

ESEMPIO: Ora non ho fame. → Prima avevo fame.

1. Ora non ho sete. ______________________________
2. Ora non abbiamo paura. ______________________________
3. Ora non hanno fretta. ______________________________
4. Ora non hai freddo. ______________________________

5. Ora non avete caldo. ______________________

6. Ora non ha sonno. ______________________

B. Un cantante del passato. Chi era Elvis? Completa il brano con i verbi all'imperfetto.

abitare amare avere cantare essere prendere scrivere suonare

Elvis Presley ______________[1] un cantante americano molto famoso. Lui ______________[2] le sue canzoni, ______________[3] la chitarra e ______________[4] per i giovani negli anni 50, 60 e 70. Durante l'ultima parte della sua vita ______________[5] a Las Vegas e ______________[6] molte droghe. Elvis ______________[7] molti problemi, ma i suoi ammiratori lo ______________[8].

C. Una passeggiata. Le seguenti sono le tue frasi dette ieri durante una passeggiata. Racconta le tue impressioni sulla passeggiata di ieri. Usa l'imperfetto.

ESEMPIO: Non fa freddo → Non faceva freddo.

1. Non piove, fa bello!

   ____

2. Sono le quattro del pomeriggio.

   ____

3. C'è molta gente per le vie.

   ____

4. I bambini ritornano a casa da scuola.

   ____

5. Le persone guardano le vetrine (*shop windows*).

   ____

6. Molti turisti entrano ed escono da chiese e musei.

   ____

D. Da bambino/a (*When you were a child*)... A Marina piace sapere come erano gli altri da giovani. Completa le sue domande e rispondi con frasi complete. Usa l'imperfetto.

1. Come ______________ (essere) da piccolo/a?

   ____

2. ______________ (Giocare) tutto il giorno quando ______________ (essere) piccolo/a?

   ____

3. Dove ______________ (abitare) quando ______________ (avere) otto anni?

   ____

4. Ti ______________________ (piacere) andare a scuola?

____

5. Che cosa ______________________ (preferire) mangiare?

____

6. Che cosa ______________________ (bere) a colazione?

____

7. ______________________ (Dire) molte bugie?

____

8. Chi ti ______________________ (raccontare) le favole la sera?

____

9. ______________________ (Sapere) scrivere a cinque anni?

____

10. ______________________ (Potere) uscire quando ______________________ (volere)?

____

11. A che ora ______________________ (dovere) andare a letto?

____

12. Quando ______________________ (fare) i compiti?

____

B. Imperfetto e passato prossimo

A. Quella volta, invece... Completa le seguenti frasi con le forme adeguate dell'imperfetto o del passato prossimo. Aggiungi nuove informazioni.

ESEMPIO: Di solito compravo carne; ieri, invece, ho comprato pesce.

1. Di solito prendevo l'aereo; quel giorno, invece, ______________________

____

2. Di solito ______________________; quella domenica, invece, ci siamo alzati a mezzogiorno.

3. Di solito non parlavamo mai; quella volta, invece, ______________________

____

4. Di solito ______________________; ieri, invece, sei andato a teatro.

____

5. Di solito le regalavate un libro; quell'anno, invece, ______________________

____

6. Di solito Paolo ______________________; ieri, invece, mi ha detto «Ciao!»
7. Di solito facevo la doccia la sera; lunedì, invece, ______________________

____

8. Di solito ______________________; ieri, invece, non ha piovuto.

B. Pigrone (*Lazybones*)**!** Guido è un pigrone e si diverte sempre mentre tu ed i vostri compagni di casa studiate o lavorate. Spiega come il suo comportamento ieri vi dava fastidio.

1. Ieri mi sono arrabbiata perché mentre io ______________ (studiare), lui ______________ (ascoltare) dischi.
2. Ieri Luigi si è arrabbiato perché mentre ______________ (pulire) il bagno, Guido non ______________ (fare) nulla (*anything*).
3. Ieri Francesca si è arrabbiata, perché mentre ______________ (fare) una traduzione, Guido ______________ (cantare) l'opera.
4. Ieri voi vi siete arrabbiati perché mentre ______________ (guardare) la TV, Guido ______________ (parlare) a voce alta (*loud*).
5. Ieri ti sei arrabbiato perché mentre tu ______________ (preparare) i panini, Guido li ______________ (mangiare).

C. Trapassato

A. Perché erano tristi o allegri? Cosa era successo che ha fatto sentire tristi o allegre le seguenti persone? Costruisci delle frasi con la forma adeguata del trapassato.

ESEMPIO: Francesca era scontenta... (perdere le chiavi di casa) →
Francesca era scontenta perché aveva perduto le chiavi di casa.

1. Valeria era contenta... (imparare a guidare l'automobile)

____

2. Gabriella e Paolo erano scontenti... (non potere trovare lavoro)

____

3. Claudio era contento... (uscire con Marcella)

____

4. Eravamo contenti... (dormire bene)

____

5. Eravate scontenti... (non andare al cinema)

____

6. Eri contento... (sognare di avere molti soldi)

____

7. Erano scontenti (non fare bene gli esercizi di grammatica)

____

8. Ero contento... (ricevere una lettera da Alberto)

____

❖ **B. L'anno prima.** Completa le seguenti frasi con le forme adeguate del trapassato e aggiungi delle informazioni nuove.

ESEMPIO: L'anno scorso sono andati in Sicilia. L'anno prima... → L'anno prima erano andati in Sardegna.

1. Ieri mi sono alzato alle sei. Il giorno prima...

____

2. L'anno scorso siamo state a New York. L'anno prima...

____

3. Ieri Gina è andata al cinema. Il giorno prima...

____

4. L'anno scorso ho trovato un orologio. L'anno prima...

____

5. Ieri avete comprato pesce. Il giorno prima...

____

6. L'anno scorso è nata la sua sorellina. L'anno prima...

____

C. Sapevi che... ? È da tanto che Marta non parla con gli amici. La sua amica le racconta le ultime novità (*latest news*). Comincia ogni frase con **Sapevi che...** .

ESEMPIO: Rosanna si è laureata → Sapevi che Rosanna si era laureata?

1. Stefano ha comprato una Mercedes.

____

2. Ha avuto un incidente (*accident*).

____

3. È andato all'ospedale.

____

4. È uscito dall'ospedale dopo una settimana.

____

5. Marina ha trovato un buon lavoro.

____

6. Si è sposata con Roberto.

   ____

7. Hanno comprato una casa a Roma.

   ____

◆ **D. Domande per te.** Rispondi alle seguenti domande con frasi complete.

1. Avevi già imparato a scrivere prima di andare a scuola?

   ____

2. Avevi già studiato l'italiano prima di incominciare l'università?

   ____

3. Ti sei già laureato/laureata a sedici anni?

   ____

4. Si era già sposata a ventun anni tua madre?

   ____

D. Suffissi

A. Letterina o letterona? Guarda i disegni e scrivi la risposta ad ogni domanda.

ESEMPIO:

Cristina ha ricevuto una letterina? →
No, ha ricevuto una letterona.

1. Claudio è un ragazzino?

   ____

2. Mariella ha dei piedoni?

   ____

3. I ragazzi hanno fatto delle pizzacce?

___

4. Plutone ha un nasone?

___

PROVERBI E MODI DI DIRE

La gatta frettolosa fece i gattini ciechi.
Haste makes waste. (*Lit., The hasty cat had blind kittens.*)

B. La favola di Hansel e Gretel. Riscrivi il seguente testo senza i suffissi. Scrivi su un tuo foglio.

Hansel e Gretel erano due bambini piccini piccini. Loro abitavano in un boschetto con il loro papá e la loro mamma. Un bel giorno, mentre camminavano per il boschetto hanno perso la strada. Dopo molte ore, sono arrivati a una casetta con un giardinetto piccolo e grazioso. La casetta era tutta di cioccolato, ma ci abitava una vecchia e brutta stregaccia. Questa stregaccia era molto cattiva, e voleva prepararsi un bel pranzetto con Hansel e Gretel. Fortunatamente, i genitori dei bambini sono arrivati in tempo a salvarli dalla pentola... Loro hanno mandato via la stregaccia e hanno riportato Hansel e Gretel a casa loro. E, da quel giorno, tutti vissero felici e contenti.

LETTURA

La televisione del passato...

Leggi cosa racconta Alberto, un professionista di 38 anni, sulla televisione italiana di quando era bambino. Poi rispondi alle domande.

Il sabato sera, da bambino, guardavo «Canzonissima», e mi addormentavo al tavolo della sala da pranzo[a], mentre ancora i cantanti cantavano le loro canzoni d'amore. «Canzonissima» era una trasmissione popolare, l'appuntamento immancabile[b] col varietà, che gli italiani amavano e ancora oggi amano molto. Canzoni, balletti, ballerine, umorismo, qualche gioco: due ore di allegria per chi passa la serata a casa a guardare la televisione. La serata del sabato davanti al piccolo schermo era per molti —compresa la mia famiglia— un rituale che non doveva essere disturbato. Dico «era» perché oggi le cose sono un po' cambiate: ci sono più televisori in una stessa casa, videoregistratori, computer. Provate ad immaginare, per un momento, se potete (ma sono certo che è difficile), una serata senza telecomando[c], pochi canali televisivi (in Italia, fino al 1980, i canali erano solo due, con una programmazione abbastanza povera) e soprattutto senza il videoregistratore e senza il computer, con le sue chat rooms dell'Internet. In più, immaginate di avere un solo televisore per casa: e le lotte[d] per vedere i programmi favoriti. Il sabato, almeno, su «Canzonissima» non c'era discussione. La domenica era un'altra cosa, con le partite, «tutto il calcio minuto per minuto» alla televisione e un padre appassionatissimo[e] di questo sport. Per me, che non amavo il calcio, era una vera tortura. Mia nonna andava a curare il giardino, mia sorella studiava e mia madre faceva le faccende[f], mentre mio padre guardava la televisione e ascoltava la radio per sapere i risultati di tutte le partite. Il lunedì leggeva le pagine sportive dei quotidiani e cominciava ad aspettare le partite della prossima domenica. Anche una canzone degli anni '60 ricordava i problemi familiari causati dalla passione per il «pallone»: «Perché la

[a]*sala... dining room*
[b]*not to be missed*
[c]*remote control*
[d]*arguments*
[e]*passionately fond*
[f]*housework*

domenica mi lasci sempre sola, per andare a vedere la partita di pallone?», cantava infatti Rita Pavone, nota cantante dell'epoca. Putroppo, papà, invece di andare allo stadio, guardava la partita a casa, alla televisione. Accadeva[g] così che noi della famiglia non potevamo sfuggire al tifo[h] e soffrivamo[i] con lui se la sua squadra perdeva e gioiavamo[j] quando vinceva.

[g]*It happened*
[h]sfuggire... *get away from the fan* / [i]*we suffered*
[j]*we were overjoyed*

1. Come è cambiata la situazione per la televisione tra gli anni '60 e '70 e oggi, secondo il racconto?

   ____

2. Cos'era «Canzonissima»? Perché era famosa?

   ____

3. Cosa faceva la famiglia di Alberto la domenica?

   ____

4. Quali erano le trasmissione preferite dal padre di Alberto?

   ____

❖ 5. E tu, ricordi delle trasmissioni che preferivi nella tua infanzia?

   ____

❖ 6. Guardi la televisione? Cosa guardi in televisione, che genere (*genre*) di trasmissioni?

   ____

UN PO' DI SCRITTURA

❖ **A. Storie di famiglie.** Hai letto un libro o visto un film che parlava di una famiglia? Com'era la famiglia rappresentata? Quali erano gli elementi positivi e quelli negativi della loro vita familiare? Scrivi una pagina. Scrivi su un tuo foglio.

ESEMPIO: Uno dei classici della letteratura italiana, *Il giardino dei Finzi-Contini* di Giorgio Bassani, racconta la storia di una famiglia ebrea (*Jewish*) durante il fascismo. La protagonista si chiamava Micòl e abitava con i genitori, la nonna e il fratello a Ferrara...

❖ **B. Favole nuove.** Scrivi una breve favola con i personaggi tradizionali delle fiabe (la matrigna [*stepmother*], il mago [*wizard*], Biancaneve [*Snow White*] o Cenerentola [*Cinderella*]) ma... con qualche variante. Divertiti! Scrivi una pagina. Scrivi su un tuo foglio.

ESEMPIO: C'era una volta una matrigna buonissima che adorava la sua figliastra Cenerentola e non sopportava (*couldn't stand*) le sue figlie egoiste e prepotenti (*domineering*)...

ATTUALITÀ

A. Cosa dice Umberto Eco? Guarda i risultati del sondaggio di *Panorama* nella pagina 110 e rispondi alle seguenti domande.

1. Gli italiani ascoltano i critici prima di scegliere un film?

   _____ spesso

   _____ mai

   _____ talvolta (*at times*)

PRIMI. *Umberto Eco e Lietta Tornabuoni.*

Libri, cinema, musica, teatro: ecco gli arbitri del gusto. Vince Eco, ma c'è anche Costanzo.

di SANDRA PETRIGNANI

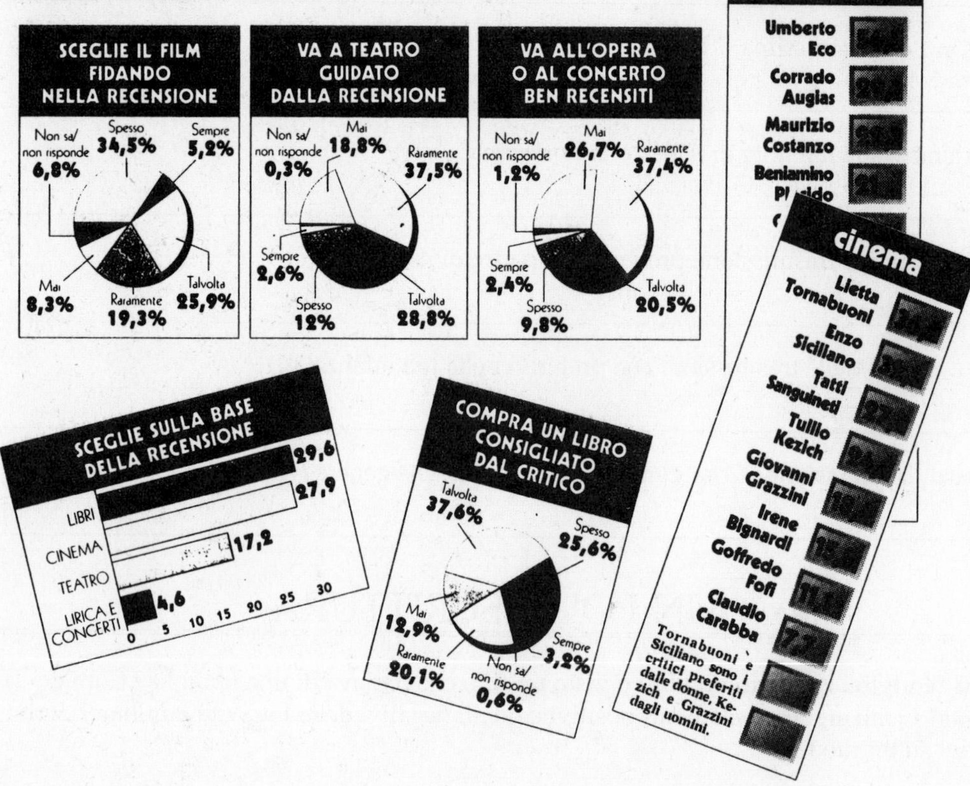

2. Il parere (*opinion*) del critico è importante per vendere libri?

   _____ sempre

   _____ raramente

   _____ talvolta

3. La critica (*review*) è importante per l'opera e i concerti?

   _____ mai

   _____ sempre

   _____ raramente

4. Chi è Umberto Eco?

   _____ un attore

   _____ un critico di libri

   _____ un musicista

5. Chi sono Lietta Tornabuoni e Goffredo Fofi?

 ____ cantanti d'opera

 ____ pianisti

 ____ critici cinematografici

❖ **B. Tu e i critici.** Per te, è importante o no il parere del critico? Scrivi una pagina in cui rispondi alle seguenti domande. Scrivi su un tuo foglio.

1. Leggi la critica prima di vedere un film?
2. Guardi il voto della critica per scegliere un film?
3. Ignori la critica e scegli a seconda (*according to*) degli attori o del regista?
4. Guardi la pubblicità sui giornali?
5. Leggi la recensione prima di leggere un libro?
6. Ascolti il parere degli amici su libri, film e spettacoli?

Capitolo 9 COME TI SENTI?

Name ______________________________

Date ______________________________

Class ______________________________

VOCABOLARIO PRELIMINARE

A. Come ti senti? Come vedi, i personaggi nei disegni non si sentono bene. Di cosa soffrono?

ESEMPIO: Il signore soffre di mal di cuore.

1. Il ragazzo ______________________________

2. L'uomo ______________________________

3. La donna ______________________________

4. Il giovane ______________________________

5. La signora ______________________________

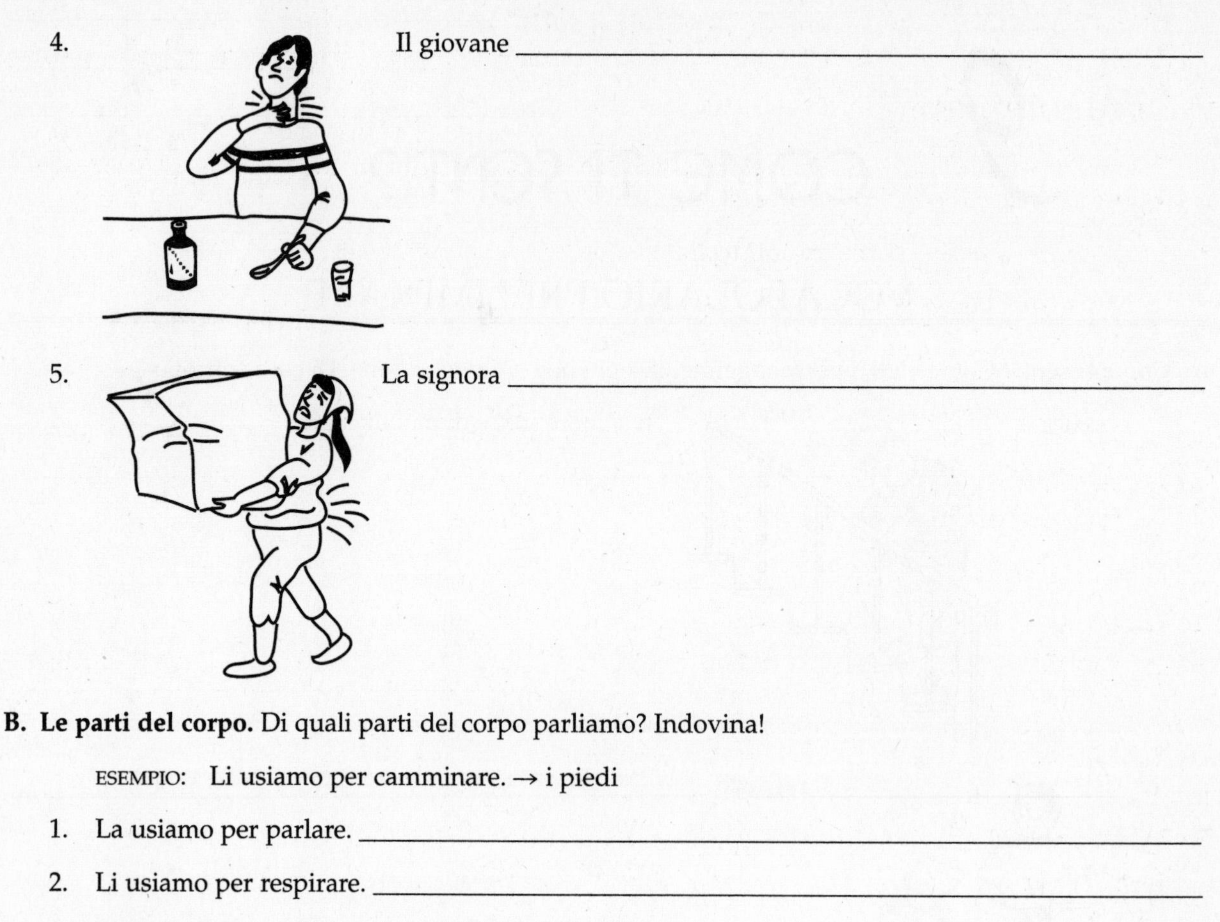

B. Le parti del corpo. Di quali parti del corpo parliamo? Indovina!

ESEMPIO: Li usiamo per camminare. → i piedi

1. La usiamo per parlare. ______________________________
2. Li usiamo per respirare. ______________________________
3. Fa male quando abbiamo il raffreddore o l'influenza. ______________________________
4. Fanno male se mangiamo molti dolci. ______________________________
5. Le usiamo per scrivere. ______________________________
6. Lo mandiamo ai nostri innamorati per San Valentino. ______________________________
7. Le usiamo per nuotare. ______________________________
8. Con essi (*them*) vediamo il mondo. ______________________________

❖ **C. Domande per te.** Rispondi alle seguenti domande.

1. Ti sei mai rotto/rotta una gamba? Se sì, come e quando?

   ____

2. Quando sei stato malato/stata malata l'ultima volta? Sei andato/andata dal dottore per guarire?

   ____

3. Hai mai il mal di testa, o il mal di denti? Quando?

   ____

4. Sei mai andato/andata all'ospedale? Perché?

   ____

Name ______________________ Date ____________ Class ______________________

GRAMMATICA

A. Pronomi tonici

A. Con noi o con lei? I tuoi amici non si ricordano con chi si allenano oggi. Devi informarli. Sostituisci le parole tra parentesi con i pronomi tonici adeguati.

ESEMPIO: Puoi allenarti con noi? (con Laura) → No, devo allenarmi con lei.

1. Puoi fare ginnastica con noi? (con Marco)

   ____

2. Posso giocare il doppio (*doubles*) con te? (con Paola e Leo)

   ____

3. Può pattinare con loro? (con me e Luca)

   ____

4. Possiamo correre con lui? (con Silvia)

   ____

5. Possono nuotare con Mirella? (con te e Alberto)

   ____

B. Per me o per te? Abbina (*Match*) le risposte della colonna B con le domande della colonna A.

A

1. _____ Il caffè è per te?
2. _____ Parlate di me?
3. _____ Com'è Sandro?
4. _____ Perché hanno invitato solo noi?
5. _____ Dove ci troviamo stasera? Da voi?
6. _____ Questa lettera è per la signora Lina?
7. _____ È più importante la salute o il lavoro?
8. _____ Chiara e Gianna lavorano da sole?

B

a. Sì, da noi.
b. Sì, preferiscono fare da sé.
c. Sì, è per lei.
d. Secondo me, la salute.
e. È pieno (*full*) di sé.
f. Sì, parliamo proprio di te.
g. Non so, di solito invitano anche loro.
h. No, non è per me.

C. Da voi o da loro? Completa le seguenti frasi con i pronomi tonici adeguati. Aggiungi le preposizioni dove è necessario.

ESEMPIO: I signori Brunetti abitano al quinto piano (*fifth floor*), io abito al sesto (*on the sixth*); loro abitano sotto ___di me___.

1. Buon compleanno, Alessia! Questi sci nuovi sono per ____________!
2. Non ho proprio voglia di uscire con Bianca e Michele: parlano sempre di ____________!
3. Se Massimo deve allenarsi domani, vieni senza ____________.
4. Non posso assolutamente perdere; tutta la squadra conta su ____________.

5. Eccovi finalmente! Cercavo proprio ____________!
6. Partiamo tutti da casa nostra: venite da ____________ alle otto.
7. Non ho visto Paola e Daniela perché sono partite prima ____________.

B. Comparativi

A. Comparativi. Guarda i disegni e rispondi alle domande con frasi complete.

ESEMPIO: 

Chi è più alto, Franco o Gustavo? → Gustavo è più alto di Franco.

1. 

Chi è più veloce, Nella o Mara?
____

2. Per il signor Rossi, è più facile nuotare o sciare?
____

3. 

Chi è più forte, Gregorio o Michele?
____

4. Per Gianna, cosa è più faticoso: il ciclismo o il footing?

____

5. Chi fa più ginnastica, Stefania o Roberto?

STEFANIA

ROBERTO

____

B. Sei più bravo di me? Leggi le descrizioni delle seguenti persone e cose e scrivi delle frasi con il comparativo.

ESEMPIO: Marisa ha 28 anni. Grazia ha 34 anni. → Marisa è più giovane di Grazia.

1. Maria è alta 1,65 m. Giuliana è alta 1,70 m.

____

2. Francesco pesa (*weighs*) 100 kg. Marco pesa 89 kg.

____

3. Per Cristina è facile pattinare. Per Cristina è difficile nuotare.

____

4. Simone si allena molto. Anche Chiara si allena molto.

____

5. Il baseball è poco faticoso. Il calcio è molto faticoso.

____

6. L'alimentazione è importante. Anche lo sport è importante.

____

C. Ancora comparativi. Completa le frasi con **di, che** o **di quel che.**

ESEMPIO: Ho partecipato a più ___*di*___ dieci maratone.

1. Giovanni è meno energico ____________ Ugo.
2. Claudia mangia più carne ____________ Marcella.
3. I nostri giocatori bevono più acqua ____________ aranciata.
4. I tuoi amici giocano più a calcio ____________ a baseball.
5. Paola è più simpatica ____________ credi.
6. Fa più freddo a Milano ____________ a Roma.

7. Per Luisa è più divertente nuotare ______________ correre.

8. Tuo fratello è meno noioso ______________ te.

9. Mia sorella ha più amici ______________ amiche.

10. Mia madre ha ricevuto più lettere da me ______________ dai miei fratelli.

D. Lisa, Antonella, Gianni e Marina, chi ha più, chi ha meno... Paragona adesso queste quattro persone a seconda dell'altezza, del peso, degli hobby (qui il nuoto), del lavoro, dello stipendio e delle spese che hanno fatto ieri. Scrivi sei frasi e cerca di essere piuttosto preciso. (Usa **più, meno, tanto... quanto.**)

ESEMPIO: Marina è più grande di Lisa, Antonella e Gianni, Gianni è più grande di Lisa e Antonella, Lisa è più grande di Antonella ma meno grande di Gianni.

	LISA segretaria	ANTONELLA studentessa	GIANNI guardia notturna (*night watchman*)	MARINA insegnante
ETÀ	23	21	28	38
ALTEZZA	1,73 m	1,65 m	1,73 m	1,58 m
PESO	64 kg	52 kg	90 kg	48 kg
NUOTO	2 volte alla settimana	il giovedì	—	il mercoledì e il venerdì
LAVORO	tutti i pomeriggi	—	il martedì sera e il sabato	dal lunedì al venerdì dalle 8 alle 15
STIPENDIO MENSILE	1.800.00 £	—	2.500.000 £	2.300.000 £
IERI HANNO COMPRATO	3 dischi 2 libri	1 disco	—	5 libri 2 dischi

1. ____

____

2. ____

____

3. ____

____

4. ____

____

5. ____

____

6. ____

____

C. Superlativi relativi

A. Un tipo entusiasta. Cambia le seguenti frasi in modo da dimostrare (*show*) entusiasmo per la tua città. Usa il superlativo relativo. Usa espressioni come **della città, della regione e del paese.**

ESEMPIO: È una bella chiesa. → È la chiesa più bella del mondo (*world*).

1. È un grande stadio. ______________________________
2. È un albergo moderno. ______________________________
3. È un museo famoso. ______________________________
4. È un buon ristorante. ______________________________
5. È un bel teatro. ______________________________
6. È un viale lungo. ______________________________

❖ **B. Il più o il meno di tutti?** Cosa pensi dei seguenti sport e atleti? Completa le frasi secondo il tuo parere.

ESEMPIO: Di tutti gli sport, il golf →
Di tutti gli sport, il golf *è il più (il meno) interessante!*

1. Di tutti gli sport, il canottaggio (*rowing*) ______________________________!
2. Di tutti gli atleti di atletica leggera, Carl Lewis ______________________________!
3. Di tutti i tennisti, André Agassi ______________________________!
4. Di tutte le pattinatrici (*skaters*), Michelle Kwan ______________________________!
5. Di tutte le partite, quelle di football ______________________________!

❖ **C. Domande per te.** Rispondi alle seguenti domande. Esprimi la tua opinione personale. Scrivi frasi complete!

1. Secondo te, qual è l'attore più bravo di tutti? E l'attrice più brava di tutte?

____

____

2. Qual è stato il film meno interessante dell'anno? Perché?

____

____

3. Qual è lo sport più popolare nel tuo paese? E lo sport meno popolare?

____

____

4. Qual è il posto (*place*) più interessante di questa città? Perché?

____

____

5. E il ristorante meno costoso della città? Cosa mangi quando vai lì (*there*)? Quanto spendi?

____

____

—Attento, questo è l'ostacolo più pericoloso!

D. Comparativi e superlativi irregolari

A. Meglio o migliore? Completa le seguenti frasi. Usa **meglio** o **migliore/i.**

ESEMPIO: Nessuno cucina meglio di me.

1. Abbiamo mangiato nei ______________ ristoranti.
2. Quando studi ______________ tu? Di notte o di giorno?
3. C'è un tenore che canta ______________ di Luciano Pavarotti? —Sì, Plácido Domingo!
4. Abbiamo usato la stessa macchina fotografica, ma le sue foto sono ______________ delle mie.
5. Hanno risposto ______________ di quel che credevo.
6. L'esame di Nicoletta è stato il ______________ di tutti.
7. Ieri notte ho dormito ______________ perché non c'era più vento (*wind*).

Name ______________________ Date ____________ Class ______________________

PROVERBI E MODI DI DIRE

Meglio un asino vivo che un dottore morto.
Better a live ass than a dead scholar.

Meglio un uovo oggi che una gallina domani.
A bird in the hand is worth two in the bush. (Lit., Better an egg today than a hen tomorrow.)

❖ **B. I buoni propositi** (*intentions*). Di' due cose che devi fare di più e due cose che devi fare di meno.

ESEMPIO: Devo camminare di più.
Devo fumare di meno.

1. ______________________
2. ______________________
3. ______________________
4. ______________________

❖ **C. Una volta era meglio...** Erano fatte meglio le cose nel passato? Segui il modello del fumetto e scrivi quattro frasi che descrivono le cose o le situazioni che erano migliori. Comincia con **Una volta...**

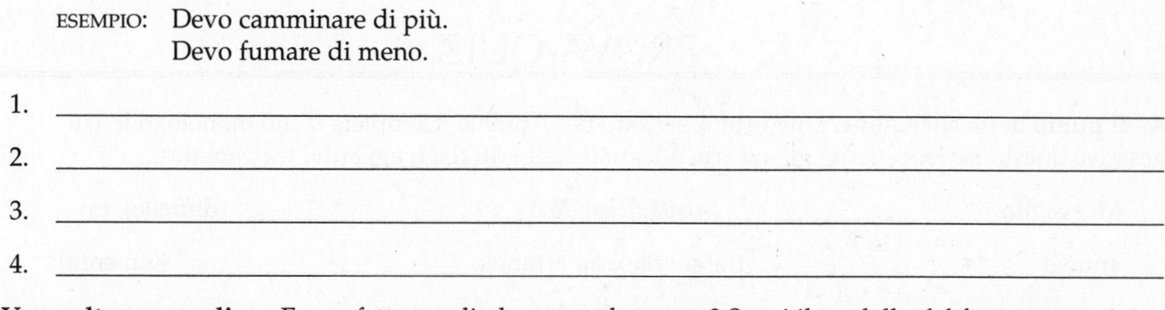

—Una volta gli animali sopportavano[a] meglio il freddo.

[a]*used to tolerate*

1. ______________________
2. ______________________
3. ______________________
4. ______________________

D. Bene o male? Completa le frasi con la forma corretta di: **migliore, peggiore, meglio** o **peggio.**

1. Secondo me, Michael Jackson canta ______________ (*better*) di Prince.
2. No, secondo me, Prince è ______________ (*better*) di Michael Jackson!
3. Pensate che i vini della California siano ______________ (*better*) di quelli italiani?

4. In Italia non cambia nulla: il nuovo governo è ______________ (*worse*) di quello di prima.
5. Mi piace cucinare: cucino ______________ (*better*) di mia madre.
6. Qual è ______________ (*the best*) squadra di football in America?
7. Qual è ______________ (*the worst*) squadra di calcio in Italia?
8. Il formaggio del Wisconsin è ______________ (*the best*) del mondo!
9. Federico Fellini e Michelangelo Antonioni sono ______________ (*the best*) registi italiani.
10. Oggi sto ______________ (*worse*) di ieri.

PROVA-QUIZ

A. Il punto della situazione. È un brutto periodo per Antonio. Completa il suo monologo in cui descrive questo periodo. Scrivi gli avverbi adeguati suggeriti dagli aggettivi tra parentesi.

Mi sveglio ____________________[1] (triste); mi alzo ____________________[2] (difficile); mi annoio ____________________[3] (frequente); mi arrabbio ____________________[4] (violento); mi diverto ____________________[5] (raro); mi addormento ____________________[6] (innaspettato)... Mi sono forse preso un esaurimento nervoso (*nervous breakdown*)?

B. Cronaca di un amore. Completa la seguente storia con le forme adeguate dell'imperfetto o del passato prossimo dei verbi dati tra parentesi.

La mia prima fidanzata ____________________[1] (essere) Laura. ____________________[2] (Essere) simpatica, divertente e comprensiva. ____________________[3] (Studiare) architettura e ____________________[4] (lavorare) sui suoi progetti tutto il giorno. Intanto io ____________________[5] (divertirmi) con gli amici, non ____________________[6] (dare) mai gli esami e ____________________[7] (perdere) tempo. Un giorno lei ____________________[8] (laurearsi) e ____________________[9] (aprire) uno studio con Tommaso, un collega. Io la ____________________[10] (prendere in giro, *to make fun of*) perché ____________________[11] (stare) sempre in ufficio a lavorare, sempre a lavorare, con quel suo stupido collega...

L'anno scorso Laura ____________________[12] (partire) per un viaggio di lavoro con Tommaso. (Loro) ____________________[13] (andare) a Lisbona e, quando ____________________[14] (tornare), ____________________[15] (sposarsi). Secondo me, quei due non ____________________[16] (imparare) a divertirsi!

C. Due fratelli. Leggi la storia di Antonio e Leo. Completa il brano con le espressioni adeguate.

Espressioni: che, meglio, meno velocemente, migliore, minore, più, ottimo, poco, tanto quanto

Antonio si allena ____________________[1] Leo ma corre ____________________[2] di lui. È un bravo giocatore ma non è il ____________________[3] della squadra; preferisce divertirsi più ____________________[4] correre ma sa che l'allenatore conta su di lui e allora cerca di dare il

________.[5] Leo è un suo ________[6] amico, è il

________[7] dei suoi fratelli ed è il ________[8] energico della famiglia.

Escono ________[9] insieme perché studiano in due città diverse ma si capiscono molto.

D. Dov'eri? Laura vuole sapere dove era andata e cosa faceva ieri la sua compagna di casa, Carla. Completa i dialoghi secondo il modello.

ESEMPIO: (telefonare) in cucina / lavare i piatti →
LAURA: Dov'eri quando ho telefonato?
CARLA: Ero in cucina.
LAURA: Ah sì? E che cosa facevi?
CARLA: Lavavo i piatti.

1. (andare al cinema) in biblioteca / leggere una rivista

   LAURA: ________________
   CARLA: ________________
   LAURA: ________________
   CARLA: ________________

2. (ritornare a casa) al supermercato / fare la spesa

   LAURA: ________________
   CARLA: ________________
   LAURA: ________________
   CARLA: ________________

3. (passare a trovarti) in palestra / giocare a pallone

   LAURA: ________________
   CARLA: ________________
   LAURA: ________________
   CARLA: ________________

❖ **E. Una giornata diversa.** Pierina ha deciso di fare qualcosa di diverso oggi. Leggi la sua routine tipica e di' cosa ha fatto di diverso.

ESEMPIO: Si sveglia di cattivo umore (*in a bad mood*). → Oggi si è svegliata di buon umore.

1. Si alza dopo mezzogiorno. ________________
2. Si veste mentre fa da mangiare. ________________
3. Si mette i jeans e una brutta maglietta. ________________
4. Lei e le amiche si incontrano al solito (*usual*) bar. ________________

5. Lei e il suo ragazzo si fanno regali noiosi (*boring*). ______________________________

____

6. Lei e Laura si telefonano. ____

____

F. Traduzioni. Traduci in italiano. Scrivi su un tuo foglio.

1. s1: How are you feeling today? A little better?
   s2: No, Doctor, I feel worse!
2. s1: Angela, I was looking just for you! Come to my house at 5:00. I have a surprise for you two.
   s2: Dario is working tonight. I have to come without him.
3. s1: Did you know that Stefania is older than her husband?
   s2: Really? She looks much younger than him!
4. s1: It was the worst game of the year! You have to train (**allenarsi**) more.
   s2: It's true. It wasn't my best game.
5. s1: Do you speak Italian as well as your grandfather?
   s2: No, but I speak it better than my brother.
6. s1: My younger sister Patrizia is getting married at the end of the month.
   s2: Isn't her boyfriend, Piero, the oldest son of Mr. Baresi?

LETTURA

La sanità in Italia

Alice parla della sua esperienza col sistema sanitario italiano. Leggi il testo e poi rispondi alle domande.

Che dire del sistema di assistenza sanitaria in Italia? C'è chi dice che è lento, costoso e inefficiente, e c'è chi, come me, dice che funziona abbastanza bene, perché ha avuto un buon rapporto con ospedali e medici. Per me, che mi sono rotta un braccio mentre sciavo l'anno scorso sulle Dolomiti, è andato tutto bene.

Non appena[a] mi hanno portato all'ospedale (al Pronto Soccorso) con l'ambulanza, i dottori hanno fatto subito le radiografie[b] e hanno anche ordinato un check-up completo, per cominciare subito una terapia. Odio[c] prendere le medicine, ma ne ho dovute prendere molte, specialmente gli antidolorifici[d], perché oltre al male al braccio avevo sempre mal di testa. Il dottore ha poi prescritto una terapia riabilitativa, con massaggio incluso.

Il sistema sanitario ha coperto quasi tutte le spese e sono contenta perché altrimenti il conto sarebbe stato[e] proibitivo. È vero che il sistema è costoso (una parte del mio stipendio va verso il sistema nazionale) e non sempre efficiente, ma avere la copertura[f] medica è un vero vantaggio, specialmente quando i giorni all'ospedale sono molti, sono molte le medicine e la malattia è cronica.

Sono stata col gesso[g] al braccio per più di tre mesi e sono andata dal dottore regolarmente ogni due settimane, e certe volte anche di più, quando invece di sentirmi meglio mi sentivo peggio. Meno male che[h] alla fine non ho pagato molto per tutte le mie disavventure[i]!

[a]Non... *As soon as*
[b]*X-rays*
[c]*I hate*
[d]*painkillers*
[e]sarebbe... *would have been*
[f]*coverage*
[g]*cast*
[h]Meno... *At least*
[i]*mishaps*

1. Che posizione ha Alice nei confronti del sistema sanitario? È a favore o contro?

____

2. Cosa è successo a Alice l'anno scorso?

____

3. Che rapporto ha avuto coi dottori?

____

❖ 4. E tu, che rapporto hai con il tuo dottore o con la tua dottoressa?

____

❖ 5. Hai un'assicurazione privata? È molto costosa?

____

❖ 6. Cosa pensi di un'assicurazione universale? È solo un'utopia? È troppo costosa per la nazione?

____

UN PO' DI SCRITTURA

❖ **A. Parlando di sport.** Sei appassionato/a (*fond*) di uno sport in particolare? Ti interessi di uno sport? È importante per te praticare un'attività fisica? Parla del tuo rapporto con lo sport. Scrivi una pagina. Scrivi su un tuo foglio.

ESEMPIO: Io sono appassionata di canottaggio; è uno sport faticoso e rilassante allo stesso tempo. Anche se non ho mai partecipato a questo sport, lo seguo molto alla televisione...

❖ **B. La salute incomincia nel piatto!** Cosa dobbiamo fare per seguire la giusta alimentazione, per restare in forma, per godere la vita (*enjoy life*) in modo sano ed equilibrato? È sufficiente mangiare bene e fare sport? Scrivi una pagina. Scrivi su un tuo foglio.

ESEMPIO: Secondo me, per seguire una giusta alimentazione dobbiamo mangiare meno carne. Per restare in forma, è molto importante rilassarsi, non lavorare troppo, meditare e fare esercizi di yoga...

(continua nella prossima pagina)

A. Scopriamo le parti del nostro corpo! Guarda questo corpo umano e cerca di imparare i nomi delle sue parti.

Adesso copri la figura con un foglio e rispondi a questa domanda: quali sono le parti del corpo più usate dai ciclisti (dalle cicliste)? Indicale con una crocetta (X).

_____ la bocca	_____ le ginocchia
_____ le braccia	_____ le orecchie
_____ il collo	_____ i piedi
_____ le dita	_____ le spalle
_____ le gambe	_____ il torace

Name ____________________ Date __________ Class ____________________

B. Mangiare sano! Leggi questa pubblicità della pasta Barilla e indica se le affermazioni che seguono sono vere o false.

Fonte: United States Department of Agriculture.

LA PASTA E' ALLA BASE DI UNA SANA ALIMENTAZIONE.

Di recente, il governo americano ha reso ufficiali attraverso "La Piramide del Mangiar Sano" i principi per una sana ed equilibrata alimentazione. La Piramide rappresenta in modo facile ed intuitivo la varietà e il ruolo che grassi, proteine, carboidrati e gli altri principi nutritivi devono avere in una alimentazione quotidiana equilibrata e completa. Questi stessi principi, indicati dall'Istituto Nazionale della Nutrizione nelle "Linee guida per una sana alimentazione italiana", sono alla base della tradizione alimentare dell'Italia dove la pasta ha un ruolo primario. Un motivo in più per portare in tavola un piatto di pasta. Non solo buono, ma anche molto sano.

vero falso 1. La pasta fa ingrassare (*makes you put on weight*) e bisogna mangiarne il meno possible.

vero falso 2. Gli alimenti di origine animale sono necessari per l'apporto quotidiano (*daily intake*) di vitamine.

vero falso 3. I sali minerali derivano principalmente dai carboidrati.

vero falso 4. Il governo americano ha dichiarato che la pasta è nociva (*harmful*) alla salute.

Name ______________________

Date ______________________

Class ______________________

BUON VIAGGIO!

VOCABOLARIO PRELIMINARE

A. Vacanze, che mal di testa! Leggi il dialogo e rispondi alle domande.

MARIO: Allora, che hai intenzione di fare per le vacanze?

DANIELE: Mah, a dire il vero cerchiamo qualcosa da affittare in Sicilia, sul mare, ma per quest'agosto sembra difficile.

MARIO: Ma hai ancora tre mesi, sono sicuro che un appartamento o una casa li trovi... Che avevi fatto l'anno scorso?

DANIELE: Abbiamo passato le ferie a Cefalù, ma in albergo, e tra camera matrimoniale, camera singola e pensione completa abbiamo speso tantissimo! Conveniva affittare davvero una casa e avere più spazio.

MARIO: E come vai in Sicilia?

DANIELE: Come l'anno scorso, voliamo da Milano a Palermo e poi noleggiamo una macchina per le tappe interne. Stiamo soprattutto sulla costa e ci divertiamo al mare.

1. Dove ha intenzione di andare Daniele quest'estate?

____

2. Che mese è adesso?

____

3. Dove ha passato le vacanze l'anno scorso?

____

4. Cosa fa Daniele quando è in Sicilia?

____

B. Io vado all'estero! Dove vanno queste persone? Usa espressioni con il verbo **andare.**

ESEMPIO: I signori Moretti *vanno in vacanza*.

1. Paola e Andrea ______________________________
____
2. La famiglia Sbraccia ______________________________
____
3. I ragazzi ______________________________
____
4. Io e Gabriele ______________________________
____

C. Viva le vacanze! Completa le frasi con le forme adatte delle seguenti espressioni: affittare, una cartolina, con l'aria condizionata, con televisore, con tutte le comodità, economico, fare una crociera, l'itinerario, lasciare un deposito, Natale, noleggiare, la tappa.

ESEMPIO: A Franco e Daniele piace molto il mare; quest'anno hanno deciso di *fare una crociera*.

1. Donata è un tipo molto indipendente; non le piacciono gli ______________________________ fissi.
2. Se vai in Umbria ti conviene (*you should*) ______________________________ una macchina.
3. La signora Peccianti è giornalista. Prenota sempre camere ______________________________ perché non può perdere il telegiornale (*news*).
4. Andiamo in moto da Los Angeles a New York. Dobbiamo dividere il viaggio in varie ______________________________.
5. Piera e Daniele sono studenti. Cercano un alloggio (*lodging*) ______________________________.
6. Ho due mesi di vacanza; penso di ______________________________ una casa al mare.
7. Il signor Caretti non sopporta (*tolerate*) il caldo. Vuole sempre camere ______________________________.
8. Adele, sapevi che la signora Luciani era in vacanza? Ho appena ricevuto ______________________________.

9. Il dottor Bruscagli e il dottor Tellini sono professori universitari. Possono permettersi (*afford*) un albergo ______________________.

10. La signora Dei mi ha detto che ha già ______________________ per la casa che affitta per le vacanze di ______________________.

PROVERBI E MODI DI DIRE

Chi tardi arriva, male alloggia.
Those who arrive late get the worst accomodations (lit., lodge poorly).

Smuovere mare e monti.
To move heaven and earth (lit., the sea and the mountains).

❖ **D. Domande personali.** Rispondi alle seguenti domande.

1. Cosa hai intenzione di fare per le vacanze (quest'inverno / quest'estate)?

____

____

2. Stai di solito negli Stati Uniti quando vai in vacanza o vai all'estero? Dove?

____

3. Vai da solo / da sola o con la famiglia? O con amici?

____

4. Che tipo di albergo preferisci?

____

5. Cosa fai per divertirti quando sei in vacanza?

____

____

GRAMMATICA

A. Futuro semplice

A. Partire è un po' morire. Quali sono i programmi di Jeff per le vacanze? Leggi il monologo e poi rispondi alle domande.

Alla fine di giugno sarò in volo per l'Italia con i miei genitori e mia sorella. Saliremo in aereo a New York, faremo tappa a Londra e poi voleremo fino a Roma. Staremo una settimana insieme a Roma, poi i miei genitori torneranno a Londra e mia sorella continuerà il suo viaggio da sola: noleggerà una macchina e andrà in Sicilia. Nella prima tappa, visiterà Pompei ed Ercolano e starà qualche giorno a Capri. Io, invece, da Roma andrò a Siena, dove studierò italiano e farò corsi in inglese di letteratura, per cinque settimane. Quando tornerò a casa alla fine di agosto probabilmente parlerò un italiano migliore. Mi dispiacerà lasciare l'Italia, che amo molto. Capisco bene il proverbio che dice: «partire è un po' morire», anche per me sarà così...

1. Quali sono le tappe della vacanza di Jeff?

   ____

2. Quali sono le tappe della vacanza di sua sorella?

   ____

3. Che cosa farà Jeff a Siena?

   ____

4. Come si sentirà Jeff quando ritorna a casa alla fine di agosto?

   ____

B. Domani! Di' cosa tu ed i tuoi amici non avete ancora fatto, ma avete intenzione di fare.

ESEMPIO: Non ti hanno scritto, ma *ti scriveranno*.

1. Non si sono sposati, ma ______________________
2. Non è venuto a casa mia, ma ______________________
3. Non l'avete detto, ma ______________________
4. Non hai comprato la moto, ma ______________________
5. Non hanno visto il film, ma ______________________
6. Non siete andate a Parigi, ma ______________________
7. Non ho capito la lezione, ma ______________________

C. L'anno che verrà... Scrivi per tutti i buoni propositi dell'anno nuovo.

ESEMPIO: io / imparare una lingua straniera. → Quest'anno imparerò una lingua straniera.

1. io / scrivere agli amici italiani ogni mese.

   ____

2. tu / finire di scrivere il romanzo.

   ____

3. Paolo e Gabriele / giocare a tennis ogni settimana.

   ____

4. io e mia sorella / non guardare la TV ogni sera.

   ____

5. voi / laurearsi

   ____

6. Priscilla / non mangiare tanti dolci.

   ____

❖ **D. È già fortuna se...** Segui il modello del fumetto per completare le frasi che seguono. A quali altre situazioni ti fa pensare il fumetto?

—Non possiamo andare in vacanza: è già una fortuna se potremo restare in città!

1. Non posso ______________________: è già una fortuna se ______________________
____
2. Gli studenti non possono ______________________: è già una fortuna se ____________
____
3. L'insegnante non può ______________________: è già una fortuna se ____________
____
4. Gli amici ed io non possiamo ______________________: è già una fortuna se __________
____

❖ **E. Non più!** Elenca le cose che fai ora da studente ma che non farai più dopo la laurea. Segui l'esempio.

ESEMPIO: Ora passo i weekend in biblioteca. →
Dopo la laurea, non passerò più i weekend in biblioteca.

ORA	DOPO LA LAUREA
1. Ora mangio alla mensa dell'università.	______________________
2. Ora mi alzo presto per studiare.	______________________
3. ______________________	______________________
4. ______________________	______________________
5. ______________________	______________________

B. Usi speciali del futuro

A. Forse. Hai appena conosciuto una giovane donna a Roma, sull'autobus per il Vaticano. Il suo accento e la guida che tiene in mano ti dicono che è staniera. Ti chiedi da dove verrà e cosa farà qui. Completa le frasi che esprimono i tuoi pensieri con il futuro di probabilità.

_______________[1] (essere) francese. No, forse _______________[2] (venire) dalla Spagna, perché parla un po' come Carmencita. _______________[3] (avere) più o meno venticinque anni, _______________[4] (viaggiare) per motivi di lavoro o forse _______________[5] (seguire) un corso di lingua italiana. Sicuramente _______________[6] (volere) vedere le città italiane più famose. Oggi, probabilmente _______________[7] (andare) in Piazza San Pietro o _______________[8] (visitare) i Musei Vaticani. Stasera, _______________[9] (salire [*to go up*]) a Trinità dei Monti e _______________[10] (guardare) tutta Roma dal Pincio.

B. Se, quando, appena. Carlo cerca di rassicurare i suoi genitori sul fatto che si comporterà bene mentre loro saranno via per due settimane. Scrivi quello che dice Carlo. Segui l'esempio.

ESEMPIO: telefonare alla polizia / se / sentire un rumore →
Telefonerò alla polizia se sentirò un rumore.

1. chiamare la zia Pina / se / avere bisogno di soldi

____

2. andare dal dottore / se / stare male

____

3. fare il letto / appena / alzarmi la mattina

____

4. non prendere la macchina di papà / quando / uscire la sera

____

5. non organizzare feste / quando / voi non esserci

____

6. bere il latte / quando / fare colazione

____

7. dare da mangiare ai gatti / quando / tornare a casa

____

8. lavare i piatti / appena / finire di mangiare

____

Name ______________________ Date ____________ Class ______________________

❖ **C. Un grosso colpo.** Segui il modello del fumetto per completare le frasi che seguno. Cosa sarà un colpo (*shock*) per le seguenti persone?

—Sarà un grosso colpo per mia moglie quando le dirò che non potete rimanere a pranzo...

1. l'insegnante

   ____

2. il mio compagno / la mia compagna di camera

   ____

3. i miei genitori

   ____

4. gli studenti

   ____

C. Il **si** impersonale

—Quando non si hanno i soldi per comprare la benzina, la macchina è meglio venderla!

A. Come si preparano? Completa le battute (*exchanges*) con la forma corretta dei verbi tra parentesi. Usa il **si** impersonale.

1. s1: Come ______________ (preparare) gli spaghetti alla carbonara?

   s2: ______________ (fare) soffriggere (*to brown*) la pancetta e ______________ (aggiungere) a questa delle uova sbattute e del formaggio. ______________ (mettere) questa salsa sugli spaghetti cotti al dente.

2. s1: Cosa ______________ (fare) in montagna?

   s2: ______________ (Dormire) fino a tardi e ______________ (divertirsi) a giocare a carte o a fare passeggiate.

3. s1: Ci sono tanti film da vedere! Come ______________ (fare) a decidere?

   s2: Bo', ______________ (potere) semplicemente andare al cinema più vicino.

4. s1: A che ora ______________ (partire) domani mattina?

   s2: ______________ (Partire) molto presto e non ______________ (fermarsi) da nessuna parte (*anywhere*), così ______________ (arrivare) al mare in serata (*by evening*).

B. Una visita a Milano. Barbara ti racconta del suo viaggio a Milano con suo fratello. Cambia le sue frasi al passato, secondo l'esempio.

ESEMPIO: Si vedono delle mostre interessanti. → Si sono viste delle mostre interessanti.

1. Si arriva all'aeroporto Malpensa.

   ____

2. Si trova un albergo nel centro storico.

   ____

3. Si mangia fuori ogni sera.

   ____

4. Ci si ferma sui navigli (*canals*).

   ____

5. Si fanno tante foto.

   ____

6. Si visita il museo di Brera.

   ____

7. Si va a vedere la casa di Manzoni.

   ____

8. Ci si diverte un mondo (*tons*)!

   ____

❖ **C. Tutto da scoprire.** Osvaldo è arrivato da poco in paese. Rispondi liberamente alle sue domande.

ESEMPIO: Dove si danno i film migliori in questa città? →
I film migliori si danno al cinema Astoria.

1. Dove si fanno le pizze migliori?

   ____

2. Dove si va per noleggiare una macchina?

   ____

3. Dove si vendono le riviste e i giornali stranieri?

   ____

4. Dove si mangia il miglior gelato?

   ____

5. Dove si comprano vestiti a buon mercato (*at a good price*)?

____

6. Dove si trovano i musei più interessanti?

____

7. Dove si ascolta la musica rock più originale?

____

8. Dove ci si diverte di più in questa città?

____

❖ **D. Se non si hanno i soldi...** Completa le seguenti frasi. Usa la costruzione impersonale e il tempo adeguato del verbo.

ESEMPIO: Se non si hanno i soldi... → ci si può divertire in modo semplice!

1. Ci si diverte di più quando ______________________________
2. Quando non si sa cosa fare ______________________________
3. Quando si è camminato molto ______________________________
4. Ci si lamentava ogni volta che ______________________________

PROVERBI E MODI DI DIRE

Morto un papa, se ne fa un altro.
Life goes on. (Lit., When one pope dies, they find another.)

Quando si è in ballo, bisogna ballare.
In for a penny, in for a pound. (Lit., When you're at the ball, you have to dance.)

D. La formazione dei nomi femminili

Chi sono? Guarda i disegni e scrivi chi sono.

ESEMPIO:

un operaio comunista e un'operaia comunista

1. ______________________________
2. ______________________________
3. ______________________________
4. ______________________________
5. ______________________________
6. ______________________________

PROVERBI E MODI DI DIRE

Tra moglie e marito non mettere il dito.
Don't interfere with a husband and wife. (Lit., Don't put a finger between a wife and a husband.)

LETTURA

Le vacanze negli Stati Uniti

Enrico racconta la sua vacanza negli Stati Uniti. Leggi la descrizione e rispondi alle domande.

Anche l'anno prossimo, se avrò abbastanza soldi, tornerò in vacanza negli Stati Uniti, così potrò perfezionare il mio inglese. La prossima volta, però, sarò meglio preparato psicologicamente per questa esperienza che mi ha conquistato.[a] Ho passato due mesi con una famiglia di Brooklyn, New York, e per la prima volta ho conosciuto la «grande mela» come turista italiano e come abitante.

New York City per il turista italiano è una componente essenziale. New York, Los Angeles e San Francisco, forse Miami e il Grand Canyon sono infatti le tappe dei tipici viaggi turistici italiani. Anche Chicago adesso sta diventando famosa grazie a due trasmissioni televisive: «ER» e «Chicago Hope».

[a]mi... *won me over*

L'America che ho visto non è stata solo un'America da cartolina. Ho parlato con la gente, ho vissuto le «distance», sono andato al supermercato alle due di notte (cosa impossibile in Italia dopo le otto di sera), sono stato in enormi alberghi di lusso, e ho fatto esperienza del cinema americano nei cinema giganti. Insomma, ho voluto vedere cosa è vivere in una città americana, le cose che offre. Mi sono svegliato la mattina per bere succo di arancia e mangiare bagels (che in Italia praticamente non esistono) e ho provato ristoranti di ogni tipo.

A New York il traffico è terribile, ma forse non è meno terribile a Roma o Milano o Napoli. Nelle grandi città americane è quasi impossibile muoversi a piedi.[b] Le distanze sono grandi ed è necessario prendere la macchina o la metropolitana. Diventa impossibile ogni forma di spontaneità nei contatti umani. È davvero necessario «prendere un appuntamento» con gli amici per vederli! Ma la verità è che New York è incredibile. I suoi monumenti sono giganti e inquietanti.[c] Davvero capisco l'ossessione di Woody Allen per questa magnifica città nervosa, dinamica, ossessiva, ottimista. Una città che offre tutto ai suoi abitanti, è veramente la città che non dorme mai.

[b]muoversi... *to go places on foot*

[c]*disquieting*

1. Che cosa conosce il turista italiano dell'America?

____

____

2. Quali sono gli elementi che colpiscono (*strike*) maggiormente l'immaginazione di un italiano? Secondo te, perché?

____

____

____

____

3. Perché le distanze americane sono un problema per il turista italiano?

____

____

4. Come viene descritta New York da Enrico? Con più qualità negative o positive?

____

____

UN PO' DI SCRITTURA

❖ **A. Una vacanza disastrosa!** Descrivi una vacanza disastrosa! Può essere una tua vacanza, una vacanza di amici o una vacanza inventata. Scrivi una pagina. Scrivi su un tuo foglio.

ESEMPIO: L'inverno scorso Laura e Renato hanno deciso di passare le vacanze invernali in Tunisia. Quando sono arrivati a Tunisi faceva un freddo cane (*bitterly cold*) e pioveva, così hanno deciso di noleggiare una macchina e di andare nel sud, verso il deserto...

❖ **B. Una vacanza ideale.** Immagina di avere molto tempo, molti soldi e di poter andare in vacanza dove e con chi vuoi. Descrivi con ricchezza di particolari e usa il futuro (quando necessario). Scrivi una pagina. Scrivi su un tuo foglio.

ESEMPIO: Tra due settimane partirò per il Perù con Leonardo DiCaprio. Ci incontreremo a Los Angeles e poi prenderemo l'aereo per Lima dove...

ATTUALITÀ

Andiamo in vacanza! L'estate è vicina e chi non l'ha ancora fatto deve cominciare a fare progetti per le vacanze. Dai un'occhiata (*Take a look*) alla pubblicità dell'agenzia Comet e rispondi alle domande.

Parole utili: su misura (*tailor made*), tale (*such*), approfondito (*investigative*), ausilio (*assistance*), preconfezionato (*ready-made*), assiduo (*steady*)

1. In quali città italiane sono gli uffici dell'agenzia Comet?

2. In quale parte del mondo organizza viaggi l'agenzia?

3. Per chi sono i viaggi organizzati da quest'agenzia? Sono solamente per un tipo particolare di viaggiatore?

4. Che tipo di esperienza ha l'agenzia Comet nelle isole della Polinesia? Perché?

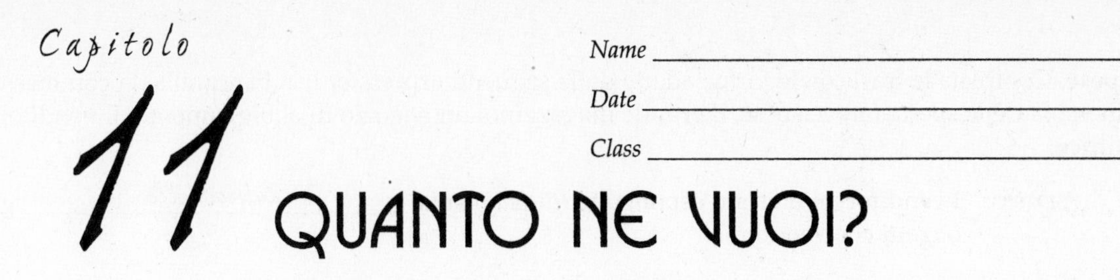

Name ____________________

Date ____________________

Class ____________________

QUANTO NE VUOI?

VOCABOLARIO PRELIMINARE

A. Negozi e negozianti. Chi vende il pane e dove lavora? Seguendo l'esempio, di' cosa vendono e dove lavorano le persone rappresentate.

ESEMPIO: Il fruttivendolo vende frutta e verdura e lavora al mercato.

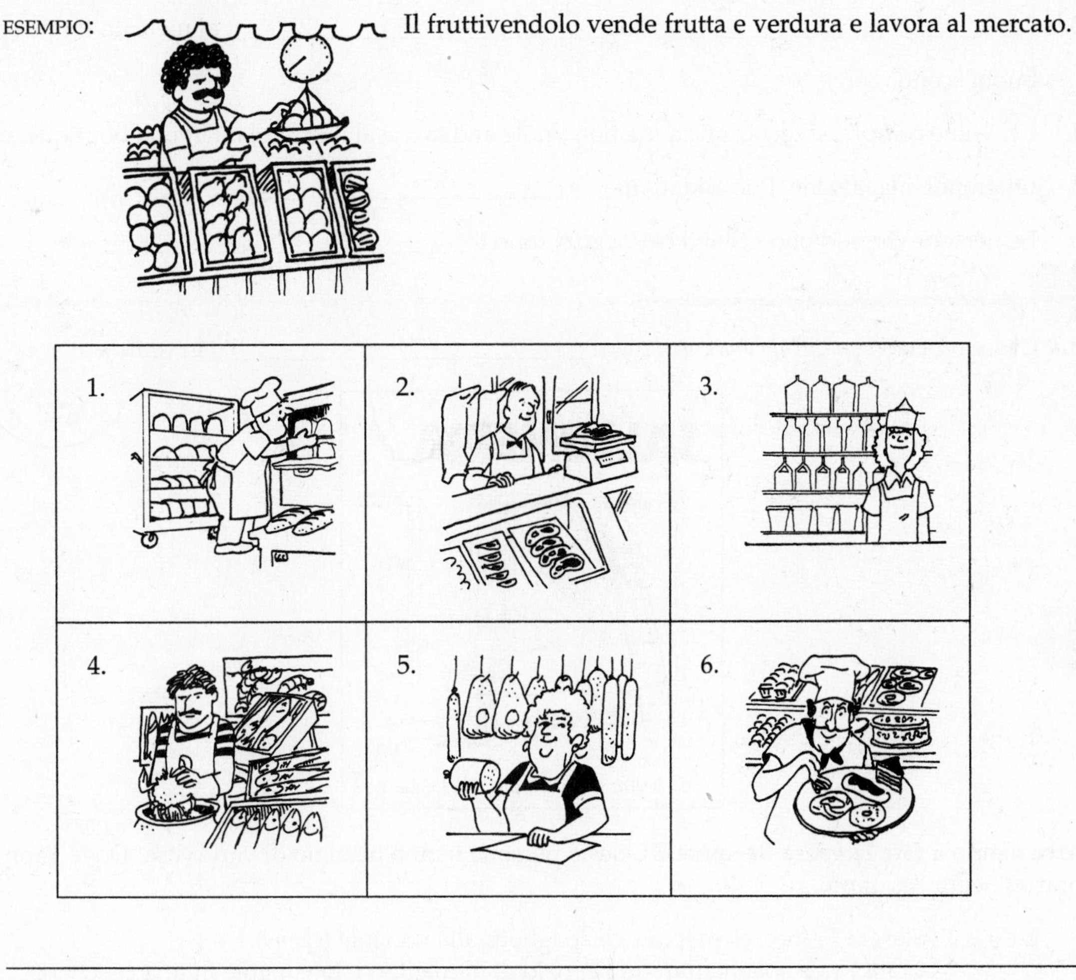

1. ____________________
2. ____________________
3. ____________________
4. ____________________
5. ____________________
6. ____________________

B. Spese. Completa le frasi con le forme adatte delle seguenti espressioni: la bancarella, la commessa, il commesso, fare la spesa, fare le spese, il grande magazzino, un negozio di abbigliamento, il venditore, la venditrice.

ESEMPIO: I venditori al mercato espongono (*display*) sulle ___bancarelle___ gli oggetti che vendono.

1. Il ______________________ è un negozio che vende vestiti, oggetti per la casa, elettrodomestici (*home appliances*), ecc.
2. In Italia molte persone ______________________ tutti i giorni: dal fruttivendolo, dal panettiere, o nel negozio di alimentari vicino a casa loro.
3. I ______________________ e le ______________________ al mercato fanno spesso buoni sconti.
4. Lei vuole comprarsi una camicia ma non vuole andare né al mercato, né in una boutique, né in un grande magazzino. Può andare in ______________________.
5. Le persone che servono i clienti nei negozi sono i ______________________ e le ______________________.
6. Ci sono persone a cui (*whom*) non piace ______________________ in centro.

—C'è una «elle» in più... la lasciamo?

❖ **C. Dove vanno a fare la spesa (le spese)?** Queste persone hanno bisogno di varie cose. Dove vanno a comprarle? Segui l'esempio.

ESEMPIO: Stasera Francesca prepara gli spaghetti alle vongole (*clams*). →
Compra gli spaghetti in un negozio di alimentari e le vongole in una pescheria.

1. Lucia ha intenzione di fare una gita domani. Vuole preparare dei panini con prosciutto, salame e formaggio. Vuole anche portare una bottiglia d'acqua e una di vino.

____

____

2. Il signor Lazzarini ha invitato degli amici a cena. Vuole servire un arrosto di maiale, patate al forno, un'insalata, delle paste e una bottiglia di spumante (*sparkling wine*).

____

____

3. Il bambino della signora Ghidini sta male. Ha bisogno di molte spremute d'arancia e può mangiare solo yogurt e pollo.

____

____

4. La settimana prossima Fiorella ricomincia l'università. Ha bisogno di una giacca nuova, di un paio di jeans e di un paio di stivali. Non vuole spendere troppo.

____

____

5. Domani è il compleanno di Giovanna. Sua madre vuole comprarle un cappotto all'ultima moda (*in the latest style*) molto elegante.

____

____

❖ **D. Domande personali.** Rispondi alle seguenti domande.

1. Dove vai quando vai a fare la spesa? _______________

____

2. Descrivi il negozio o il supermercato che ti piace di più. Perché ci vai? _______________

____

3. Vai spesso a fare le spese? Cosa compri di solito? _______________

____

4. Vai mai in libreria? Che tipi di libri ti piace comprare? _______________

____

5. Usi i contanti, la carta di credito o gli assegni quando fai la spesa o le spese? _______________

____

GRAMMATICA

A. Usi di **ne**

A. Ne parli? Chiedi ad un amico se parla spesso dei seguenti argomenti. Rispondi di sì o di no e usa **ne** nella tua risposta.

ESEMPIO: religione →
s1: Parli spesso della religione?
s2: Sì, ne parlo spesso. (No, non ne parlo spesso.)

1. filosofia

s1: _______________

s2: _______________

2. moda (*fashion*)

s1: ______________________________

s2: ______________________________

3. letteratura

s1: ______________________________

s2: ______________________________

4. sport

s1: ______________________________

s2: ______________________________

5. la violenza nella società moderna

s1: ______________________________

s2: ______________________________

—E bambini, ne ha?

B. No, ne voglio... Sei molto particolare e vuoi sempre qualcosa di diverso da quello che ti viene offerto. Rispondi di no alle seguenti domande. Usa **ne** e le informazioni date tra parentesi per spiegare esattamente cosa vuoi.

ESEMPIO: Non vuoi una casa in città? (in campagna) → No, ne voglio una in campagna.

1. Non vuoi un gelato al limone? (al cioccolato)

____

2. Non vuoi molti dischi di musica classica? (di musica country)

____

3. Non vuoi due etti di prosciutto cotto? (mezzo chilo)

____

4. Non vuoi una camicetta di cotone (*cotton*)? (di seta [*silk*])

____

5. Non vuoi comprare un negozio di abbigliamento? (di alimentari)

____

6. Non vuoi studiare solo una lingua? (molte)

____

PROVERBI E MODI DI DIRE

Chi cento ne fa, una ne aspetti.
What goes around comes around. (Lit., Those who commit a hundred misdeeds must expect one in return.)

C. Perché mi piace! Le seguenti persone hanno delle ragioni molto semplici per fare quello che fanno. Segui l'esempio e rispondi alle domande.

ESEMPIO: Perché compri sempre molte cravatte? → Perché mi piace comprarne molte.

1. Perché mangi sempre molto pane a tavola?
   ____
2. Perché vedete sempre molti film classici il sabato sera?
   ____
3. Perché fa sempre molte foto Gianna?
   ____
4. Perché danno sempre molti esami ogni semestre?
   ____
5. Perché fa sempre tanti sconti il tuo commesso?
   ____
6. Perché porti sempre molti anelli (*rings*)?
   ____

B. Usi di **ci**

❖ **A. Domande personali.** Rispondi alle seguenti domande secondo la tua esperienza. Usa **ci** nella tua risposta.

ESEMPIO: Mangi spesso alla mensa universitaria? →
Sì, ci mangio spesso. (*o* No, non ci mangio mai.)

1. Vai tutti i giorni in biblioteca?
   ____
2. Vai spesso a fare compere ai grandi magazzini?
   ____
3. Sei mai andato/a a fare la spesa al mercato?
   ____
4. Credi all'astrologia?
   ____
5. Pensi spesso ai problemi politici e sociali?
   ____

❖ **B. Ci o ne?** Vuoi affittare una stanza in un appartamento a Roma. La tua futura padrona di casa ti fa delle domande. Rispondi alle sue domande con frasi complete. Usa **ci** o **ne,** secondo la necessità.

1. Hai animali domestici?

   ____

2. A che ora vai a letto di solito?

   ____

3. Ricevi molte telefonate di sera tardi?

   ____

4. Torni sempre a casa per pranzare?

   ____

5. Hai intenzione di invitare molti amici?

   ____

6. Vai all'università tutti i giorni?

   ____

7. Da quanto tempo abiti in questa città?

   ____

C. Pronomi doppi

A. Ha provato tutto? Leggi il dialogo e completa le domande.

COMMESSA: Allora, che gliene sembra della giacca e dei pantaloni? Ha provato tutto? Come va?
SIGNORE: La giacca è troppo larga, glielo avevo detto, ho bisogno di una misura più piccola, mentre per i pantaloni non c'è male. Li prendo.
COMMESSA: Vuole provare un'altra giacca? Posso prendergliene un'altra di un'altra misura, se vuole.
SIGNORE: No, grazie, mi bastano i pantaloni.
COMMESSA: Va bene. Glieli metto in una borsa, un momento...
SIGNORE: Grazie.

1. «Che gliene sembra» si riferisce a...
   a. la giacca e i pantaloni. b. la giacca. c. i pantaloni.
2. «Posso prendergliene un'altra» si riferisce a...
   a. posso prendere un'altra giacca, in generale, per farla provare a Lei.
   b. posso prendere un'altra giacca di un'altra misura.
   c. posso andare a prendere un'altra giacca di un altro colore.
3. «Glieli metto in una borsa» si riferisce a...
   a. i pantaloni. b. la giacca e i pantaloni. c. la giacca.

B. Sì, te la compro! Sei molto disponibile e fai tutto quello che ti chiedono gli altri. Rispondi di sì alle loro richieste. Usa i pronomi doppi adeguati.

ESEMPIO: Mi dai la tua macchina? → Sì, te la do.

1. Mi offri una sigaretta?

____

2. Mi fai lo sconto?

____

3. Mi paghi i corsi?

____

4. Mi presti la tua carta di credito per questo acquisto?

____

5. Ci prendi i vestiti in lavanderia (*laundromat*)?

____

6. Mi compri queste scarpe?

____

7. Regali ad Alberto un libro di cucina?

____

8. Spieghi la lezione di ieri a Elisabetta ed Enrico?

____

C. Quanti? Nino è curioso di tutto quello che fai. Rispondi alle sue domande. Usa le informazioni date tra parentesi.

ESEMPIO: Quante fotografie hai fatto a Caterina? (3) → Gliene ho fatte tre.

1. Quante rose hai dato alla mamma? (6)

____

2. Quante cartoline hai scritto a Enrico? (molte)

____

3. Quanti dollari hai regalato a Doriana? (5)

____

4. Quanti dischi hai portato a Carmela? (2)

____

5. Quante riviste hai prestato al professore? (1)

____

6. Quanti libri hai venduto alla signora? (pochi)

____

D. Chi te l'ha regalata? Carlo è molto elegante. Parla con un suo amico che gli fa i complimenti sui suoi vestiti e gli chiede chi glieli ha regalati. Carlo risponde sempre che glieli ha regalati la sua ragazza. Scrivi il loro dialogo.

ESEMPIO: cravatta →
s1: Che bella cravatta, Carlo! Chi te l'ha regalata?
s2: Me l'ha regalata la mia ragazza.

1. orologio
   s1: ______________________________
   s2: ______________________________
2. guanti
   s1: ______________________________
   s2: ______________________________
3. sciarpa (*scarf*)
   s1: ______________________________
   s2: ______________________________
4. stivali
   s1: ______________________________
   s2: ______________________________

D. Imperativo (**tu, noi, voi**)

A. Non fare così! Teresa chiede i tuoi consigli su tutto. Dille cosa fare e cosa non fare, secondo i suggerimenti.

ESEMPIO: Che cosa devo servire: tè o caffè? → Non servire tè: servi caffè!

1. Che cosa devo comprare: carne o pesce?
   ____
2. Che cosa devo studiare: il francese o lo spagnolo?
   ____
3. Dove devo vivere: in campagna o in città?
   ____
4. Che cosa devo mettermi: la gonna o i jeans?
   ____
5. Che cosa devo pulire: il bagno o la cucina?
   ____
6. Dove devo andare: dal macellaio o dal salumiere?
   ____

7. Che cosa devo dire al signor Branca: «Ciao!» o «Buon giorno!»?

____

8. Che cosa devo fare: le crêpe o una torta?

____

B. Entra! Fai il pediatra e devi dire ai tuoi pazienti cosa fare durante la visita. Scrivi le frasi alla seconda persona dell'imperativo (**tu**).

1. aprire la bocca ____
2. mostrare la lingua ____
3. guardare in alto ____
4. stare fermo (*still*) ____
5. prendere la medicina prima dei pasti ______________________________

____

6. bere tanta acqua ____

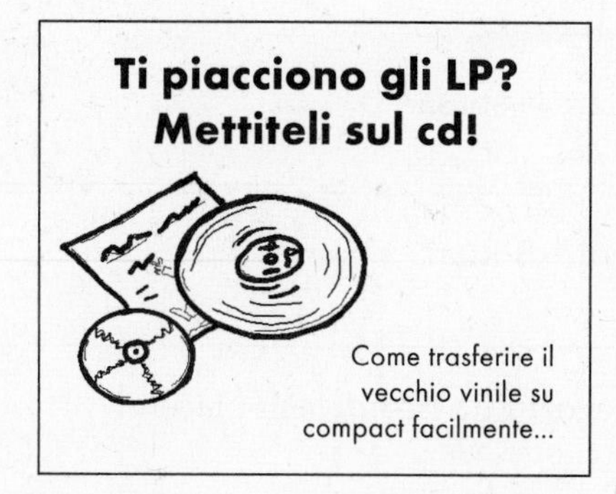

C. State fermi! I nostri genitori ci hanno detto tante cose quando eravamo piccoli. Segui l'esempio e scrivi frasi positive o negative all'imperativo, secondo i suggerimenti.

ESEMPIO: Quando noi non volevamo dormire, i nostri genitori ci dicevano... → Dormite!

1. Quando mangiavamo con la bocca aperta, i nostri genitori ci dicevano...

____

2. Quando non volevamo fare i compiti, i nostri genitori ci dicevano...

____

3. Quando non eravamo buoni, i nostri genitori ci dicevano...

____

4. Quando non avevamo pazienza, i nostri genitori ci dicevano...

____

5. Quando volevamo tornare a casa tardi, i nostri genitori ci dicevano...

____

6. Quando non volevamo alzarci per andare a scuola, i nostri genitori ci dicevano...

____

LETTURA

Fare la spesa

Rita, una dottoressa di 28 anni, ricorda com'era diverso fare la spesa quando era bambina. Leggi il brano e rispondi alle domande.

Adesso, con i supermercati, fare la spesa è diventata un'avventura meno eccitante di quando io ero bambina. Si andava con mamma e papà di negozio in negozio, si incontravano nuove persone, si parlava dei prodotti diversi e si tornava verso la macchina carichi di pacchi.[a] Si andava prima all'alimentari (il mio negozio favorito), per il pane, i panini, il prosciutto, i formaggi, la pasta e i biscotti per la colazione... Poi c'era il lattaio, per il latte fresco, le uova, spesso la panna, e poi il macellaio (per il vitello, pollo, la bistecca) e il fruttivendolo. Ricordo ancora gli odori di questi negozi, ma anche le chiacchiere e l'attenzione personale per ogni cliente. Ricordo anche i comandi di mamma e papà quando io volevo «aiutare»: «Prendi *un* pacco di biscotti, non due!» «Non toccare la frutta, non mangiare le noccioline[b]!» Ma anche i supermercati hanno il loro fascino: contenitori giganteschi di ogni tipo di biscotti o dolci possibili, pieni di oggetti curiosi, colorati...

[a]carichi... *loaded with bags*

[b]*peanuts*

Domande:

1. Che effetto aveva su Rita fare la spesa?

   ____

2. Quale negozio era il preferito di Rita?

   ____

3. Quali caratteristiche dei negozi Rita ricorda con piacere?

   ____

4. Cosa pensa dei supermercati?

   ____

❖ 5. E tu, che ricordi hai di quando andavi a fare la spesa da bambino?

   ____

   ____

   ____

UN PO' DI SCRITTURA

❖ **A. Vestirsi.** Ci tieni a (*Do you care about*) vestirti con capi firmati (*designer clothing*)? È importante per te vestire all'ultima moda? Secondo te, l'abbigliamento di una persona è indicativo della sua personalità? C'è un proverbio che dice, «L'abito non fa il monaco» (*The cowl does not make the monk*). Sei d'accordo? Scrivi una pagina in cui rispondi a queste domande. Scrivi su un tuo foglio.

ESEMPIO: Non ci tengo affatto a vestirmi con capi firmati; vestirsi all'ultima moda per me non vuol dire niente...

Name ______________________ Date ____________ Class ______________________

B. Compere! Immagina di aver vinto una vacanza di una settimana in Italia. Vuoi dedicare tutto il tuo tempo a fare compere. Da dove cominci? Dove vai? Cosa compri? Cosa cerchi? Cosa vuoi assolutamente trovare? Scrivi una pagina. Scrivi su un tuo foglio.

ESEMPIO: La mia passione è la storia dell'arte italiana, quindi per prima cosa comincio a cercare fiere (*fairs*), mercatini dell'usato (*second-hand merchandise*) e librerie per trovare libri d'arte a buon prezzo...

ATTUALITÀ

Tutto in vendita (*sale*)! Leggi il seguente annuncio e rispondi alle domande. Scrivi frasi complete.

[a]cessione... *going out of business* / [b]*designer labels*

1. Perché Creso ha annunciato una vendita totale?

   ____

2. La vendita include anche l'abbigliamento per bambino?

   ____

3. Sono in vendita anche capi firmati?

   ____

4. È in vendita la collezione primavera-estate?

   ____

5. Quando incomincia la vendita e dove?

   ____

6. Ci sono mezzi di trasporto pubblici per arrivare al negozio di via Vitruvio?

   ____

Name ______________________

Date ______________________

Class ______________________

12 ARREDARE LA CASA

VOCABOLARIO PRELIMINARE

A. La casa e l'affitto. Leggi il dialogo tra Carmen e Pina e rispondi alle domande.

CARMEN: Allora, hai trovato casa?

PINA: Sì, l'ho trovata, ma adesso devo trovare un secondo lavoro per pagare l'affitto! È praticamente una soffitta! È monolocale non ammobiliato in un palazzo senza ascensore e con poche finestre. Almeno è vicino a dove lavoro...

CARMEN: Anche un mio amico ha fatto fatica trovare un appartamento. Lui poi non è molto contento: l'appartamento va bene, dice, perché è anche ammobiliato, ma ha poca luce. Il palazzo ha altri palazzi accanto, davanti e dietro. E così è un po' triste perché anche se ha moltissime finestre, non vede mai il sole...

PINA: Beh, meglio due stanze buie ma ben sistemate che una soffitta senza mobili!

1. Qual è il problema di Pina?

____

____

2. Com'è l'appartamento dell'amico di Carmen?

____

____

3. Com'è l'appartamento di Pina?

____

____

4. Come risponde Pina alle osservazioni di Carmen?

____

____

B. Abitazioni. Guarda il disegno e scrivi il nome di ogni locale nello spazio corrispondente.

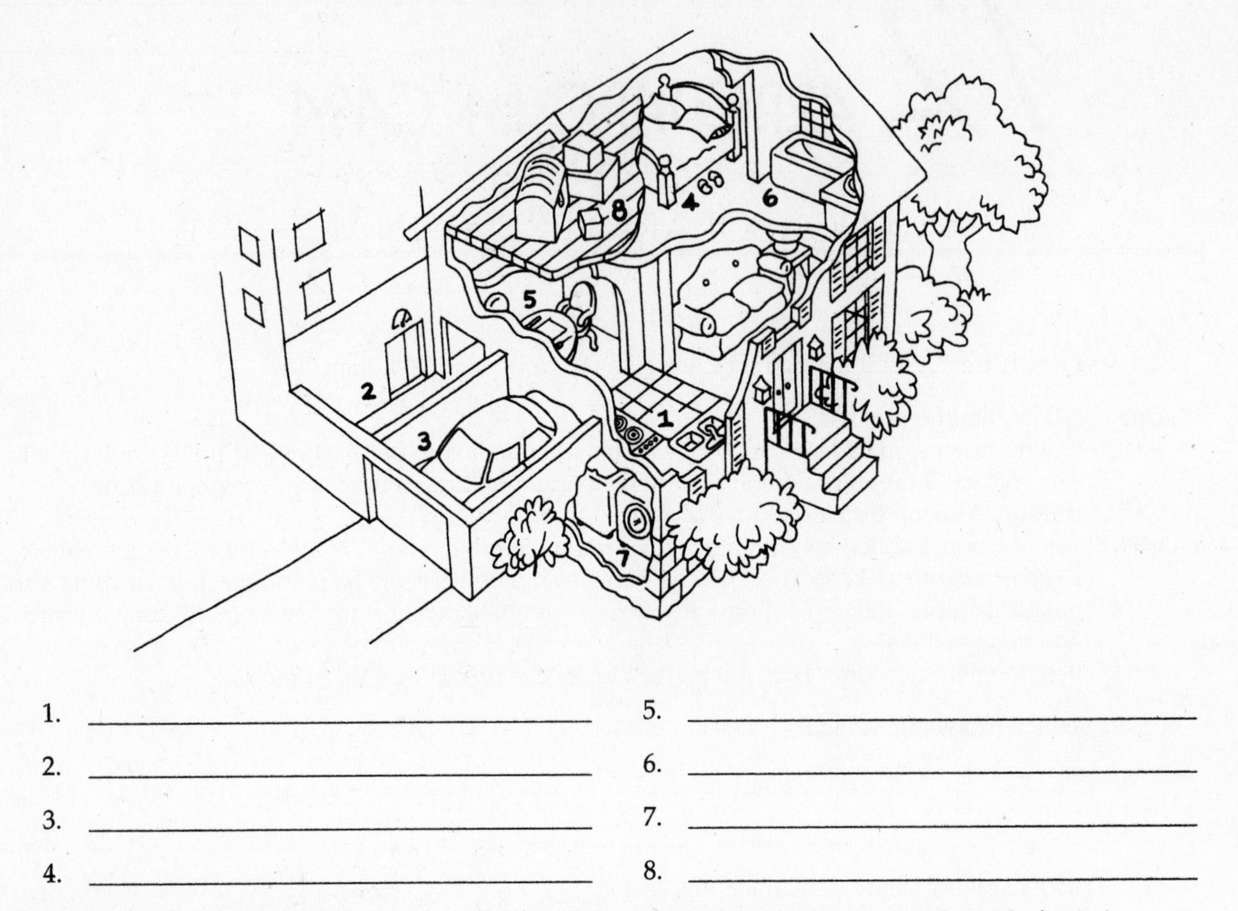

1. ______________________ 5. ______________________
2. ______________________ 6. ______________________
3. ______________________ 7. ______________________
4. ______________________ 8. ______________________

C. Da Simonetta. Simonetta ha una grande casa, sempre piena di amici e parenti. Leggi le frasi e completale con il nome delle stanze in cui le varie persone si trovano.

Espressioni utili: il bagno, il balcone, la camera da letto, la camera per gli ospiti, la cucina, il garage, il salotto, lo studio.

ESEMPIO: Simonetta prepara la cena *in cucina*.

1. Nanni è un amico di famiglia. È arrivato ieri sera da Firenze. In questo momento dorme ______________________.
2. Marcella ripara la sua macchina ______________________.
3. Franco, il marito di Simonetta, non si sente bene e si riposa (*he's resting*) ______________________.
4. La madre di Simonetta prepara la lezione per domani e corregge (*corrects*) i compiti dei suoi studenti ______________________.
5. La nonna legge una rivista e il nonno fuma la pipa ______________________.
6. Lorenzo si prepara ad uscire. In questo momento si fa la barba ______________________.
7. A Mariella piace il sole. Si sta abbronzando (*She's getting a tan*) ______________________.

D. Cambiare casa. Completa il paragrafo con la forma adatta delle seguenti parole: l'attico, l'ascensore, l'inquilino, il monolocale, la padrona di casa, il riscaldamento, la vista.

Alessandra è stanca del suo piccolissimo ______________________[1] all'ultimo piano senza ______________________.[2] D'inverno ha freddo perché il ______________________[3] non è molto efficiente. Non le piace l'______________________[4] che abita allo stesso piano e ha litigato con la ______________________[5] perché voleva aumentare l'affitto. Sta cercando un ______________________[6] con ______________________[7] sui tetti (*roofs*) di Roma e... qualche amica per dividere le spese!

GRAMMATICA

A. Aggettivi indefiniti

A. E l'ascensore? Paolo e Gabriella cercano casa, senza successo. C'è qualcosa che non va in tutte le case che hanno visto. Riscrivi le loro lamentele (*complaints*). Cambia **qualche** in **alcuni/e.**

ESEMPIO: Qualche palazzo non aveva l'ascensore. → Alcuni palazzi non avevano l'ascensore.

1. Qualche mansarda costava 500 milioni.

   ____

2. Qualche appartamento non aveva balconi.

   ____

3. Qualche stanza era troppo piccola.

   ____

4. C'era qualche topo in cantina.

   ____

5. Qualche inquilino faceva troppo rumore.

   ____

6. Qualche villetta era senza garage e senza soffitta.

   ____

B. Non tutti. Domenico è un tipo entusiasta e a volte esagera. Correggi i suoi commenti riguardo alla festa che avete fatto. Cambia **tutti** in **alcuni/e.**

ESEMPIO: Tutti i ragazzi cantavano. → Alcuni ragazzi cantavano.

1. Tutte le ragazze erano belle.

 ____

2. Tutti gli ospiti si sono divertiti.

 ____

3. Tutti i vini costavano molto.

 ____

4. Tutti i nostri amici sono venuti.

 ____

5. Tutte le stanze erano affollate.

 ____

6. Tutte le persone hanno ballato sul tavolo.

 ____

C. Un appartamento in centro o una casa in campagna? Completa il dialogo con le espressioni mancanti (*missing*). Alcune espressioni possono essere usate più di una volta.

Espressioni: alcune, alcuni, ogni, qualunque, tutte, tutti i giorni

GIGI: Ciao, Claudio, come stai? È da ____________________[1] giorni che non ti vedo. Ho sentito che hai cambiato casa. Dove abiti adesso?

CLAUDIO: Prima vivevo in un appartamento in centro, ma c'era troppo traffico e troppo rumore. ____________________[2] notte non potevo dormire e ____________________[3] era la stessa storia: difficilissimo trovare parcheggio per la macchina...

GIGI: E allora che hai fatto?

CLAUDIO: Ho deciso di andare a vivere in campagna. Ho consultato ____________________[4] le possibili immobiliari, e non per una zona ____________________,[5] ma per una con molte case con giardino e orto. Ho trovato alla fine una bella casa tutta di pietra, con un orto enorme pieno di alberi da frutta. ____________________[6] stanza è dipinta con colore diverso. È grande e ____________________[7] le finestre al secondo piano danno su un balcone...

GIGI: Sono contento per te! Sai che ti dico? ____________________[8] persone nascono fortunate!

PROVERBI E MODI DI DIRE

Tutto è bene quel che finisce bene.
All's well that ends well.

❖ **D. Ogni volta che...** Segui il modello del fumetto e scrivi quattro frasi in cui dici cosa succede ogni volta che fai certe cose.

—Ogni volta che lo vedo, questo vestito mi piace sempre...

ESEMPI: Ogni volta che mangio alla mensa, sto male.
Ogni volta che vedo il professore d'italiano, gli parlo.
Ogni volta che mi lavo, uso l'acqua calda.

1. ______________________________
2. ______________________________
3. ______________________________
4. ______________________________

B. Pronomi indefiniti

Qualcuno. Riscrivi le seguenti frasi. Sostituisci le parole in corsivo con i pronomi indefiniti.

ESEMPIO: *Qualche persona* vuole accompagnarmi (*to come with me*)? →
Qualcuno vuole accompagnarmi?

1. *Alcune persone* parlavano, *alcune persone* ascoltavano.

____

2. *Qualche persona* può aiutarci.

____

3. *Ogni persona* ha il diritto di protestare.

____

4. È una persona impossibile! Si lamenta di *ogni cosa* e di *ogni persona*!

____

C. Negativi

A. Né questo né quello. Silvia è molto curiosa di sapere di Paolo e Francesca. Rispondi negativamente alle sue domande.

ESEMPIO: Frequentano ancora l'università? → No, non frequentano più l'università.

1. Ti telefonano qualche volta?

____

2. Sono già partiti per Siena?

____

3. Conoscono qualcuno in Italia?

____

4. Hanno un cane o un gatto?

____

5. Ti hanno portato qualcosa dalla Francia?

____

—Sei sicuro che non ci vede nessuno?

B. Pessimisti ed ottimisti. Dario vede tutto nero, mentre Mario è ottimista. Riscrivi le frasi di Dario dal punto di vista di Mario.

ESEMPIO: Nessuno è felice. → Tutti sono felici!

1. Le persone non si aiutano mai.

____

2. Non fanno più dei bei film.

____

3. Non c'è rispetto (*respect*) né per i vecchi né per i giovani.

____

4. Non succede niente di interessante nel mondo (*world*).

____

5. Nessuno mi ama.

____

PROVERBI E MODI DI DIRE

Nessuna nuova, buona nuova.
No news is good news.

Con niente non si fa niente.
You can't make something from nothing.

❖ C. **Delle domande per te.** Rispondi alle seguenti domande. Scrivi frasi complete.

1. Cosa hai in mente (*mind*) di fare quest'estate?

   ____

2. Hai già trovato un compagno / una compagna di camera per l'anno prossimo?

   ____

3. Tu e il tuo compagno / la tua compagna di camera litigate qualche volta?

   ____

4. Qualcuno ti aiuta nelle faccende (*chores*) di casa?

   ____

D. Le forme **Lei** e **Loro** dell'imperativo

A. Mi dica! Una rinomata (*renowned*) professoressa italiana è in visita alla tua università. Incoraggiala (*encourage her*) a fare le seguenti cose.

ESEMPIO: accomodarsi (*to make oneself comfortable*) → Professoressa, si accomodi!

1. parlarcene ____
2. prendere un caffè ____
3. aspettare un momento ____
4. finire con calma ____
5. riposarsi un po' ____
6. venire in giardino ____

Ora ripeti gli stessi incoraggiamenti a lei e un suo collega.

ESEMPIO: Professori, si accomodino!

1. ______________________________
2. ______________________________
3. ______________________________
4. ______________________________
5. ______________________________
6. ______________________________

SORRIDA[a], PURE! NON SI PREOCCUPI, SIGNORA! STAMATTINA HA USATO DENTI-WHITE

[a]*Smile*

B. Sempre in ufficio. Ripeti le istruzioni della dottoressa Ongetta alla sua segretaria. Sostituisci le espressioni in corsivo con i pronomi adeguati.

ESEMPIO: Signorina, telefoni *all'avvocato!* → Signorina, gli telefoni!

1. Signorina, mi porti *l'agenda*!

____

2. Signorina, scriva *quelle lettere* subito!

____

3. Signorina, le spedisca *il pacco* oggi!

____

4. Signorina, non parli *dei prezzi* con nessuno!

____

5. Signorina, mi prenoti *l'albergo*!

____

6. Signorina, vada *alla posta* stamattina!

____

PROVA-QUIZ

A. A che piano? Lucia non riesce a decidersi sul piano al quale vuole abitare perché ogni piano ha i suoi vantaggi e svantaggi (*advantages and disadvantages*). Completa il dialogo con una delle seguenti espressioni: ogni, ottavo, primo, qualcosa, qualunque, terzo, tutti.

SIMONETTA: Allora, hai deciso? Lo sai che per ____________[1] piano ci può essere un problema.

LUCIA: Infatti! Il ____________[2] piano è troppo vicino alla strada. Non c'è molta luce ed è troppo rumoroso... ma l'____________[3] piano è pericoloso. Pensa se si rompe l'ascensore!

SIMONETTA: Allora il ____________[4] piano! Non è troppo in alto e non è troppo in basso.

LUCIA: Sì, ma puoi sentire ____________[5] gli inquilini del piano di sopra e quelli del piano di sotto. No, dopotutto (*in the end*) preferisco la mansarda.

SIMONETTA: Per me non c'è problema: ____________[6] piano va bene. L'importante è trovare ____________![7]

B. Mini-dialoghi. Completa i dialoghetti con le espressioni adeguate.

Possibilità: ci, comprarmi, incartarmela, me ne, ne, parlagliene

1. GIOVANNA: Non ho ancora parlato a Paolo del nostro progetto.
   SILVANA: Ma cosa aspetti? ____________ stasera!
2. COMMESSO: Questa camicia, è per un regalo?
   CLIENTE: Sì, può ____________?
3. LINA: Sei già andata al mercato oggi?
   FRANCA: No, ____________ vado più tardi; vuoi venire con me?
4. NINA: Se vai alla bancarella del formaggio, puoi ____________ del provolone?
   GIANNI: Di quanto ____________ hai bisogno?
5. ANNA: Guarda che bei pantaloni in vetrina!
   DONATO: Belli veramente! ____________ compro un paio.

C. Tutti, ognuno. Riscrivi le seguenti frasi. Cambia **tutto** ad **ogni, ogni cosa,** o **ognuno.**

ESEMPIO: Tutti hanno trovato una stanza. → Ognuno ha trovato una stanza.

1. Guardiamo la TV tutte le sere.
   ____
2. Mi hanno raccontato tutto.
   ____
3. Tutti gli inquilini hanno pagato l'affitto.
   ____

4. Tutti hanno visto l'appartamento.

____

5. Vado all'università tutti i giorni, anche il sabato.

____

6. Hanno perso tutto durante (*during*) la guerra.

____

7. Perché ti fermi davanti a tutte le vetrine (*shop windows*)?

____

D. Parlane! Incoraggia Marisa a fare le seguenti cose. Segui l'esempio.

ESEMPIO: Non mangi frutta? → Mangiane!

1. Non compri libri? _______________________
2. Non scrivi lettere? _______________________
3. Non leggi riviste? _______________________
4. Non bevi latte? _______________________

E. Dategliele subito! I tuoi amici devono ancora fare molte cose. Dagli una mossa (*Get them started*). Segui l'esempio.

ESEMPIO: Non avete dato le chiavi a Giuseppe? → Dategliele subito!

1. Non avete riportato i libri al professore? _______________________
2. Non avete dato il numero a Gilda? _______________________
3. Non avete spiegato la lezione agli studenti? _______________________
4. Non avete parlato della spesa a Carlo? _______________________

F. Un seminario. Il professore Di Franco è appena tornato da un seminario di un antropologo famoso. Utilizza i suoi appunti, dati qui sotto, per scrivere una breve relazione su ciò che si è fatto.

ESEMPIO: discutere sulle origini dell'uomo → Si è discusso sulle origini dell'uomo.

1. fare confronti costruttivi

____

2. distruggere (*to destroy, p.p.* **distrutto**) dei miti

____

3. criticare l'atteggiamento (*attitude*) di alcuni

____

4. lamentarsi dei pregiudizi di molti

____

5. studiare le usanze (*customs*) di alcuni popoli

____

6. rintracciare (*to trace*) le radici (*roots*) di una famiglia di immigrati

____

G. Traduzioni. Traduci in italiano.

1. s1: English pronunciation is difficult. I'll never learn it!
   s2: But Miss Duranti, you already speak English very well.
2. Nobody likes a person who brings bad news.
3. Ask me no questions and I'll tell you no lies.
4. Everybody loves somebody sometime.

LETTURA

❖ L'appartamento ideale

Lanfranco è veramente felice: ha trovato un appartamento ideale per lui. Leggi la descrizione del suo appartamento e rispondi alle domande.

Penso proprio di avere trovato il mio appartamento ideale. È in centro città, al sesto piano di un palazzo modernissimo. È un appartamento piuttosto piccolo e stretto, ma con un sacco di finestre, almeno due per ogni stanza. Quando si entra, c'è subito un corridoio che divide l'appartamento in due parti. Sulla sinistra c'è la cucina, piccola piccola, e davanti alla porta della cucina due belle finestre. C'è sempre molta luce in cucina. Accanto alla cucina c'è la sala da pranzo, con altre due finestre, sulla destra della porta. Accanto alla sala da pranzo c'è un bagno piccolo, con una sola finestra. Davanti al bagno, sulla destra, c'è uno studio minuscolo. Poi c'è la camera da letto, accanto a questa camera c'è anche un ripostiglio,[a] che è davanti alla cucina. Una casa veramente confortevole!

[a]*closet*

1. Com'è la tua casa o il tuo appartamento? Puoi descriverla/lo?

____

____

2. Che tipo di mobili hai nell'appartamento o nella casa?

____

____

3. Hai la lavastovoglie (*dishwasher*) e la lavatrice (*washing machine*) nel tuo appartamento o nella tua casa?

____

____

4. Dove tieni i tuoi libri, i tuoi Cd e il computer? In stanze differenti? Quali?

____

____

UN PO' DI SCRITTURA

❖ **A. Il problema della casa.** Nella tua città c'è il problema della casa? Ci sono molti senzatetto (*homeless people*)? Tu, personalmente, hai mai avuto difficoltà a trovare una stanza, un appartamento o una casa ad un prezzo accessibile? Descrivi la situazione e proponi possibili soluzioni. Scrivi su un tuo foglio.

ESEMPIO: Nella mia città (una piccola città di provincia), il problema della casa non è molto grave, ma a Berkeley, dove sto studiando, la situazione è un po' diversa...

❖ **B. Una casa perfetta.** Hai la possibilità di costruire una casa adatta ai tuoi bisogni e alle tue esigenze estetiche. Come la costruisci? Dove? Descrivi con tutti i particolari. Scrivi su un tuo foglio.

ESEMPIO: Per me, la casa perfetta è una casa di campagna, costruita sulle colline (*hills*) della Toscana. Non deve essere una casa nuova, può anche essere un rudere ristrutturato (*rebuilt wreck*) ma deve essere molto grande...

ATTUALITÀ

A. Il valore della casa. Guarda attentamente questa pagina del settimanale *L'Espresso*, poi rispondi alle domande.

MERCATO IMMOBILIARE/RAPPORTO GABETTI-"L'ESPRESSO"

Aiuto, qui crolla la casa

Via Veneto, Roma: 33 per cento in meno. Via Montenapoleone, Milano: il 23 in meno. In un anno, il valore degli appartamenti è precipitato. Lo rivela uno studio esclusivo. Città per città

1. Di che cosa parla questo articolo?

   ____

   ____

2. A quali città italiane si riferisce questo studio?

   ____

   ____

3. Il valore degli appartamenti è precipitato (*fallen*) solo a Milano?

   ____

   ____

4. Qual è la zona di Milano più costosa?

   ____

   ____

5. In quale zone di Milano i prezzi in percentuale sono crollati (*fallen*) di più?

   ____

   ____

❖ **B. Una casa da costruire** (*build*)! Scrivi un dialogo tra un architetto* e un (una) cliente molto esigente (*demanding*)! Il cliente descrive le sue necessità, l'architetto deve trovare le soluzioni. Scrivi una pagina.

ESEMPIO:
CLIENTE: Mi piace avere molti ospiti ma non voglio vederli sempre.
ARCHITETTO: Allora dobbiamo costruire una casa per gli ospiti nel giardino, lontano della casa principale, con molti alberi nel mezzo (*in the middle*).
CLIENTE: Mi piace dipingere con molta luce.
ARCHITETTO: Allora...

---

*The word **architetto** refers to both male and female architects.

Capitolo

Name ______________________

Date ______________________

Class ______________________

13 È FINITA LA BENZINA!

VOCABOLARIO PRELIMINARE

A. Il traffico e l'ambiente. Abbina le espressioni della colonna A con le parole e le frasi della colonna B.

A	B
1. _____ l'inquinamento	a. l'indicazione, l'avviso
2. _____ i rifiuti	b. gli pneumatici
3. _____ l'autostrada	c. se lo superiamo prendiamo la multa
4. _____ la benzina verde	d. se ci parcheggiamo prendiamo la multa
5. _____ il divieto di sosta	e. troppo spesso li scarichiamo invece di riciclarli
6. _____ il limite di velocità	f. è un problema ecologico serio
7. _____ il segnale	g. la benzina senza piombo (*lead*)
8. _____ le gomme	h. gli automobilisti possono guidare più velocemente su questa strada

❖ **B. Cosa non va?** Trova la parola che, secondo te, ha poco in comune con le altre. Poi scrivi una frase usando questa parola in un contesto logico.

ESEMPIO: il distributore di benzina, (il riciclaggio), i mezzi di trasporto →
Il riciclaggio della plastica, della carta e del vetro è molto importante per la protezione dell'ambiente.

1. l'effetto serra, la fascia di ozono, la targa

____

2. inquinare, depurare, il limite di velocità

____

3. i rifiuti, la patente, scaricare

____

4. la protezione dell'ambiente, ecologico, guidare

____

C. Guidare, parcheggiare. Guarda il disegno e scrivi cosa fanno le persone rappresentate. I numeri nel disegno corrispondono ai numeri delle frasi.

1. L'automobilista ______________________________.
2. Dario e Daniele ______________________________.
3. Renata ______________________________.
4. Claudia e Patrizia ______________________________.

5. Pina ______________________ a Giorgio.
6. Il signor Ronconi ______________________.
7. Il meccanico ______________________.
8. Graziano e Lara ______________________ senza benzina!

—Non hai rispettato il cartello!

GRAMMATICA

A. Condizionale presente

A. Cosa faresti per non guidare? Un tuo amico ti chiede cosa saresti disposto (*willing*) a fare per evitare di guidare. Scrivi le sue domande e le tue risposte personali.

ESEMPIO: uscire sempre a piedi →
s1: Usciresti sempre a piedi?
s2: Sì, uscirei sempre a piedi. (No, non uscirei sempre a piedi.)

1. vendere la tua macchina
   s1: ______________________
   s2: ______________________
2. fare l'autostop tutte le mattine
   s1: ______________________
   s2: ______________________
3. chiedere un passaggio a un amico
   s1: ______________________
   s2: ______________________
4. prendere l'autobus tutti i giorni
   s1: ______________________
   s2: ______________________

5. andare a lavorare a piedi

   s1: ___

   s2: ___

6. comprare un motorino o una bicicletta

   s1: ___

   s2: ___

7. viaggiare solo in treno

   s1: ___

   s2: ___

❖ **B. Non mi stancherei mai di** (*I would never get tired of*)... Segui il modello del fumetto e scrivi quattro frasi sulle cose che tu o altre persone non vi stanchereste mai di fare.

—Giuro[a] che non mi stancherei mai di starti vicino!

[a] *I swear*

1. io

   ___

   ___

2. il mio compagno / la mia compagna di camera

   ___

   ___

3. i miei genitori

   ___

   ___

4. l'insegnante d'italiano

   ___

   ___

B. **Dovere, potere** e **volere** al condizionale

A. Dovresti aiutarmi... Qualche volta non va bene dire le cose in modo troppo deciso. Riscrivi le seguenti frasi al condizionale.

ESEMPIO: Puoi darmi un passaggio? → Potresti darmi un passaggio?

1. Dobbiamo allacciare le cinture di sicurezza.

   ____

2. Voglio fare il pieno.

   ____

3. Potete parcheggiare qui?

   ____

4. Scusi, può controllare l'olio?

   ____

5. Dovete pagare prima di fare benzina.

   ____

6. Vogliamo guidare il meno possibile.

   ____

B. Potrebbe? In una situazione particolare, cosa diresti? Segui l'esempio del fumetto e fai, per ognuna delle seguenti situazioni, una domanda con **potere** al condizionale.

—Sono scappato di[a] casa: potrebbe indicarmi una meta[b]?

[a]Sono... *I ran away from*
[b]*destination*

1. Non riesci a trovare il Centro per la protezione dell'ambiente. Fermi un vigile e domandi:

   ____

2. Vuoi comprare un orologio nuovo. Ce n'è uno che ti piace nella vetrina di una gioielleria (*jeweler's shop*). Entri nel negozio e dici:

   ____

3. Sei seduto/a al tavolino di un caffè. Non c'è zucchero sul tavolo. Chiami il cameriere e dici:

   ____

❖ **C. Brevi pensieri.** Rispondi alle seguenti domande secondo le tue esperienze personali.

1. Che cosa dovresti fare per contribuire a proteggere l'ambiente?

   ____

2. Che cosa potresti fare per avere più tempo da dedicare alle questioni sociali?

   ____

3. Che cosa vorresti fare quest'anno che non hai potuto fare l'anno scorso?

   ____

❖ **D. Dovresti...** Dici mai ai tuoi amici cosa dovrebbero o non dovrebbero fare? Segui l'esempio del fumetto e di' ad un buon amico tre cose che dovrebbe o non dovrebbe fare.

—Non dovresti giocare a poker se non sai controllare le tue emozioni...

1. ____

2. ____

3. ____

C. Condizionale passato

A. Io pensavo... Rimani sorpreso delle scelte di alcune persone. Di' che pensavi che avrebbero fatto altre cose, secondo i suggerimenti.

ESEMPIO: Studierà recitazione. (musica) → Io invece pensavo che avrebbe studiato musica.

1. Suonerà il flauto. (la batteria)
   ____
2. Studierete all'Università di Bologna. (all'Università di Roma)
   ____
3. Si metteranno un vestito lungo. (i jeans)
   ____
4. Diventerai cantautrice. (cantante d'opera)
   ____
5. Passerà due settimane a Parigi. (a Roma)
   ____
6. Andrai all'opera. (a teatro)
   ____

❖ **B. Ripensamenti** (*Second thoughts*). Roberta è una persona impulsiva e rimpiange (*regrets*) sempre le sue decisioni. Completa le sue frasi. Segui l'esempio.

ESEMPIO: Ho imparato a suonare il piano; *avrei preferito imparare a suonare la chitarra*.

1. Ho studiato arte drammatica; ______________________________
   ____
2. Sono andata al Festival di Spoleto; ______________________________
   ____
3. Ho messo in scena una tragedia; ______________________________
   ____
4. Ho preso l'aereo; ______________________________
   ____
5. Sono ritornata a casa a mezzanotte; ______________________________
   ____
6. Sono partita alle quattro di mattina; ______________________________
   ____

❖ **C. Che cosa avresti fatto tu?** Cosa hanno fatto le seguenti persone? Cosa avresti fatto tu al posto loro (*in their shoes*)?

1. Era la settimana degli esami. Giuseppina era a casa e studiava. Le ha telefonato una sua amica per invitarla ad andare con lei a un concerto di musica rock. Cosa ha fatto Giuseppina? Cosa avresti fatto tu? Avresti accettato o saresti restato/a a casa a studiare?

   ____

   ____

2. Osvaldo aveva trovato un lavoro per l'estate: avrebbe fatto il cameriere in un ristorante chic. Ha saputo che suo cugino Leo aveva intenzione di fare il giro d'Europa in motocicletta e che cercava un compagno. Cosa ha fatto Osvaldo? Cosa avresti fatto tu?

   ____

   ____

3. Antonella è al ristorante coi suoi genitori. Ha mangiato molto e ora vuole solo un po' di frutta. Il cameriere porta in tavola una torta di cioccolato offerta dalla casa. Cosa ha fatto Antonella? Cosa avresti fatto tu?

   ____

   ____

[a]*size*

❖ **D. Ho detto che...** Cosa hai detto che avresti fatto e cosa hai fatto invece? Completa le frasi.

ESEMPIO: Ho detto che ___*avrei scritto*___ e invece non ho scritto.

1. Ho detto che ____

   e invece non ho telefonato.

2. Ho detto che ____

   e invece mi sono sposato/a.

3. Ho detto che ____

   e invece ____

4. Ho detto che ____

   e invece ____

D. Pronomi possessivi

A. Il nostro è quello. Rispondi alle seguenti domande con le forme adeguate del pronome **quello.**

ESEMPIO: Ecco il nostro tavolino! Dov'è il vostro? → Il nostro è quello.

1. Ecco la nostra macchina! Dov'è la vostra?

   ____

2. Ecco le nostre chiavi! Dove sono le vostre?

   ____

3. Ecco i nostri posti! Dove sono i vostri?

   ____

4. Ecco il nostro regalo! Dov'è il vostro?

   ____

5. Ecco nostro figlio! Dov'è il vostro?

   ____

B. La tua com'è? Sei stato/a appena presentato/a a Stefano e gli racconti della tua vita. Chiedigli anche com'è la sua vita.

ESEMPIO: La mia casa è piccola. → La tua com'è?

1. La mia famiglia è numerosa. ______________________________
2. Il mio lavoro è interessante. ______________________________
3. Le mie amiche sono simpatiche. ______________________________
4. Mio fratello è allegro. ______________________________
5. Mia sorella è molto attiva. ______________________________
6. I miei compagni di camera sono pigri. ______________________________

PROVERBI E MODI DI DIRE

A ciascuno il suo.
To each his own.

C. **Bandiere** (*flags*). Leggi le istruzioni di questo enigma (*logic game*) e prova a scoprire la risposta.

Parole utili: quadrata (*square*), lo stemma (*coat of arms*), la striscia (*stripe*), intruso (*intruder*)

LE SEI BANDIERE

Tra le sei bandiere che vedi qui sopra ci sono quelle dei cinque soldati più una «intrusa». Sapresti individuare quest'ultima?

LETTURA

La patente in Italia

In Italia, per prendere la patente di guida bisogna avere diciotto anni. Di solito si va a «scuola-guida» dove si fanno lezioni di teoria e si inizia subito a guidare con una macchina speciale che ha i comandi anche dalla parte dell'istruttore. Così chi non sa guidare non causa incidenti, perché il controllo è comunque[a] mantenuto[b] dall'istruttore.

Quando si inizia a guidare viene dato al guidatore un foglio chiamato «foglio rosa», un permesso provvisorio[c] di guida. Con quel permesso è possibile fare pratica con la propria macchina. Freno,[d] frizione,[e] acceleratore, cambio[f]: è tutto quello che c'è da imparare ma non è facilissimo. In Italia le macchine automatiche praticamente non esistono e guidare nel traffico intenso delle città italiane è una sfida.[g]

[a]*in any case*
[b]*maintained*
[c]permesso... *temporary permit* / [d]*Brake* / [e]*clutch* / [f]*gearshift*
[g]*challenge*

Per avere la patente è necessario passare un esame di guida. C'è prima lo scritto (riconoscere i segnali stradali e rispondere a domande sul traffico, sulle regole della strada e sul motore) e poi la prova pratica (guidare per circa venti minuti). Quando si guida per l'esame, mettere la cintura, fermarsi agli stop, stare attenti ai segnali e parcheggiare in parallelo sono elementi importanti. Passare l'esame non è tanto difficile, ma è anche facile commettere[h] errori che non vengono perdonati.[i] Guidare nelle grandi città italiane è comunque molto simile a guidare nelle metropoli americane: guida aggressiva, un po' caotica, e grandi file[j] a tutte le ore del giorno...

[h] *to make*
[i] non... *are inexcusable*
[j] *traffic jams*

1. Quando si prende la patente in Italia?

   ____

2. Cosa è necessario fare per prendere la patente?

   ____

3. Cos'è il «foglio rosa»?

   ____

❖ 4. Hai la patente? Secondo quello che dice il testo, ci sono differenze tra il sistema in questo paese e quello italiano?

   ____

❖ 5. Quali sono le regole più importanti di rispettare nella guida in questo paese?

   ____

UN PO' DI SCRITTURA

❖ **A. Pensiamo all'ambiente!** Quali sono i problemi ecologici più importanti di oggi? Secondo te, esagerano quelli che dicono che la terra (*earth*) è in serio pericolo? Scrivi una pagina su questo argomento. Scrivi su un tuo foglio.

ESEMPIO: Secondo me, i problemi ecologici più importanti sono l'inquinamento dell'acqua e la distruzione delle foreste vergini...

❖ **B. Il traffico.** Immagina di essere il sindaco (*mayor*) di una grande città. Cosa faresti per risolvere il problema del traffico cittadino? Da dove cominceresti? Di chi chiederesti l'aiuto? Scrivi una pagina. Scrivi su un tuo foglio.

ESEMPIO: Per risolvere il problema del traffico cittadino, comincerei ad andare a lavorare in bicicletta. Cercherei di riservare il centro ai pedoni (*pedestrians*) e ai ciclisti...

A. Interamente riciclabile! Leggi questo breve articolo e cerca di capirne il senso generale. Poi rispondi alle seguenti domande.

ECOLOGIA

Arriva il televisore riciclabile

È totalmente ecologico ed è fatto apposta per piacere ai ragazzi. Si chiama «Jim Nature» ed è l'ultima Tv creata dalla Saba. È un televisore con schermo 14 pollici a colori e ha due caratteristiche che lo rendono unico: l'estetica accattivante «anni 50», tanto di moda in questo periodo, e l'uso di materiali (come il legno, la colla priva di formalina e la vernice ad acqua) interamente riciclabili, per la gioia di chi non vuole avere sulla coscienza un rifiuto inquinante. Il prezzo è tutto sommato ragionevole: il Saba «Jim Nature» viene venduto a 700 mila lire circa.

«Jim Nature», il nuovissimo televisore «verde» della Saba.

1. Qual è la compagnia che ha creato *Jim Nature*?

____

2. Qual è la caratteristica più importante di questo nuovo televisore?

____

3. Costa molto?

___

❖ 4. Conosci altri prodotti interamente riciclabili?

___

❖ **B. Cerchiamo di capire!** Adesso cerca di capire il significato delle espressioni in corsivo. I primi esempi sono presi dal testo, gli altri due ti aiuteranno a capire il significato dell'espressione. Scrivi poi una tua frase usando la stessa espressione.

1. (Questo televisore) è fatto *apposta* per piacere ai ragazzi.
   Scusami! Non l'ho fatto *apposta*!
   Ho comprato questo regalo *apposta* per te.

   ___

2. (Questo televisore è fatto) per la gioia di chi non vuole *avere sulla coscienza* un rifiuto inquinante.
   Non puoi venire con me! È troppo pericoloso! Non voglio *averti sulla coscienza*!
   Se non passo questo esame, *avrai* sempre *sulla coscienza* il fatto di non avermi aiutato!

   ___

3. Il prezzo è *tutto sommato* ragionevole.
   Devo ammettere che, *tutto sommato,* hai ragione.
   Tutto sommato, non è una grande perdita (*loss*).

   ___

Capitolo

Name ______________________

Date ______________________

Class ______________________

14 UNO SPETTACOLO DA NON PERDERE!

VOCABOLARIO PRELIMINARE

A. Vero o falso? Se è falso, correggi!

ESEMPIO: Il (La) musicista scrive poesie. → Falso; il (la) musicista scrive musica.

1. Il (La) regista mette in (*sets to*) musica opere.

   ____

2. Il cantautore (La cantautrice) dirige un'orchestra.

   ____

3. Il compositore (La compositrice) scrive commedie.

   ____

4. Il baritono e il basso sono voci femminili.

   ____

5. *Musica leggera* è un sinonimo di *musica classica.*

   ____

6. La soprano e il tenore cantano nel melodramma.

   ____

7. La prima è l'ultima rappresentazione teatrale della stagione.

   ____

8. Quando il pubblico è soddisfatto fischia.

   ____

B. La parola giusta. Completa le frasi con le forme adatte delle seguenti espressioni: l'autrice, il balletto, la canzone, dilettante, mettere in scena, la tragedia.

1. Il regista Giorgio Strehler ha ______________ molte rappresentazioni teatrali.
2. Sono una cantante ______________; non sono una cantante di professione.
3. Stasera andiamo a vedere l'*Edipo Re,* una ______________ greca.
4. Valentina ama ______________. Adesso studia danza perché vuole diventare ballerina.
5. Chi è ______________ di questa commedia.
6. Le ______________ di Andrea Bocelli sono molto popolari negli Stati Uniti.

C. Fuori posto. Trova l'espressione che sembra fuori posto e spiega perché.

ESEMPIO: la tragedia, il baritono, la commedia →
Il baritono è l'espressione fuori luogo perché non è una rappresentazione teatrale.

1. il palcoscenico, l'orchestra, recitare

____

2. allestire uno spettacolo, fischiare, applaudire

____

3. l'aria, lirico, il cantautore

____

GRAMMATICA

A. Pronomi relativi

A. Che o cui? Completa le frasi con **che** o **cui.**

1. Chi è il regista _____ ha allestito questo spettacolo?
2. Il ragazzo con _____ esce Gianna è attore.
3. Non ho capito la ragione per _____ hanno fischiato.
4. Non sono d'accordo con quello _____ mi hai detto del concerto di Luciano Pavarotti.
5. Vi è piaciuta la commedia _____ avete visto ieri sera?
6. La signora a _____ ti ho presentato è una cantante bravissima.
7. Qual è l'opera da _____ viene l'aria «La donna è mobile»?
8. L'attrice _____ preferisco è Valeria Golino.

B. Qual è? Ad Antonio piace sapere tutto quello che fanno o pensano i suoi amici. Scrivi le domande che Antonio fa quando sente le seguenti informazioni. Comincia ogni domanda con **Qual è...**

ESEMPIO: Ha parlato con un regista. → Qual è il regista con cui ha parlato?

1. Ero innamorato di una studentessa del mio corso.

   ____

2. Pensiamo a una canzone.

   ____

3. Lavoreranno per una musicista.

   ____

4. Ho sentito parlare di uno scittore.

   ____

5. Abbiamo bisogno di un libro.

   ____

6. Dovrebbe rispondere a una lettera.

   ____

7. Uscirò con una compositrice.

   ____

PROVERBI E MODI DI DIRE

Cane che abbaia non morde.
A dog that barks doesn't bite.

C. A cui, di cui... Completa i dialoghetti con **cui,** con o senza la preposizione.

1. S1: È questo il libretto ____________ ha bisogno?

   S2: Sì, grazie. Non dimenticherò mai l'estate ____________ ho visto quest'opera per la prima volta.

2. S1: Gianna, chi è il ragazzo ____________ dai lezioni di piano?

   S2: Quello ____________ frequento il corso di recitazione.

3. S1: Dai, Sergio, dimmi la ragione ____________ sei tanto distratto!

   S2: Pensavo a quella musicista ____________ ho parlato ieri sera...

❖ **D. Quello che mi piace di Lei...** Segui l'esempio del fumetto e di' alle persone elencate che qualità o abitudine ti piace o non ti piace. Comincia ogni frase con **Quello che (non) mi piace...**

—Quello che non mi piace di te, è che sei troppo legato[a] al passato.

[a]*tied*

1. un amico / un'amica

____

2. il presidente degli Stati Uniti

____

3. il tuo / la tua cantante preferito/a

____

B. Chi

> ## PROVERBI E MODI DI DIRE
> Ride bene chi ride ultimo.
> *He who laughs last laughs best.*

A. Chi sta attento, capisce! Sostituisci le parole in corsivo con **chi.** Fa' tutti gli altri cambiamenti necessari.

ESEMPIO: *Quelli che* mangiano troppo ingrassano → Chi mangia troppo ingrassa.

1. *Quelli che* hanno studiato hanno fatto bene l'esame.

____

2. *La persona che* ha applaudito non ha capito niente.

____

3. I bambini non dovrebbero parlare con *le persone che* non conoscono.

____

4. Ad Elisabetta non piacciono *quelli che* cercano di attirare sempre l'attenzione.

____

5. *Quelli che* vanno nei ristoranti giapponesi amano mangiare il pesce crudo (*raw*).

   ____

6. *La persona che* suona il violino di professione è un/una violinista.

   ____

—Lo vedi cosa succede a chi continua a rosicchiarsi le unghie[a]?

[a]rosicchiarsi... *chew their nails*

B. Di chi parli? Completa con **chi,** con o senza una preposizione.

1. La professoressa ha dato un buon voto ____________ ha fatto bene il compito di matematica.
2. ____________ prende i libri dalla biblioteca, deve riportarceli.
3. Hai paura ____________ non rispetta i limiti di velocità?
4. ____________ hai telefonato?
5. A Marcello non piace uscire ____________ beve troppo.
6. ____________ dorme poco è molto nervoso.
7. La signora darà 100.000 lire ____________ troverà il suo cane Fido.
8. ____________ è il tenore italiano più famoso?

C. Chi prima arriva, meglio s'accomoda! Sapresti dire i seguenti proverbi in inglese?

1. Chi cerca, trova.

   ____

2. Chi sa, fa, e chi non sa, insegna.

   ____

3. Chi tardi arriva, male alloggia (**alloggiare** = *to lodge*).

   ____

4. Chi dorme, non piglia (prende) pesci.

   ____

C. Costruzioni con l'infinito

A. In ufficio. Completa le seguenti frasi con l'espressione corretta.

1. Preferisce _____ qualcuno con più esperienza.
   a. di assumere b. assumere
2. È vietato (*prohibited*) _____ in ufficio.
   a. fumare b. fumando
3. _____ un concorso non è facile.
   a. Vincendo b. Vincere
4. Bisogna _____ all'annuncio immediatamente.
   a. rispondere b. a rispondere

B. La preposizione corretta. Completa le battute con le preposizioni adeguate, quando necessario. (Se non ci vuole la preposizione, scrivi /.)

1. s1: Quando pensi _____ smettere _____ lavorare?
   s2: Ho intenzione _____ continuare _____ lavorare fino alla fine del mese; poi comincerò _____ stare a casa.
2. s1: Abbiamo paura _____ non ottenere tutto quello che abbiamo chiesto. Speriamo _____ ricevere almeno l'aumento.
   s2: Non dovete accettare _____ lavorare alle loro condizioni!
3. s1: Fermati _____ mangiare a casa mia stasera! Posso passare _____ prenderti al lavoro.
   s2: Stasera non posso; devo passare _____ salutare un mio vecchio collega.
4. s1: Non sono riuscita _____ finire _____ scrivere l'articolo.
   s2: Vuoi _____ fare sempre troppe cose! Devi _____ abituarti _____ lavorare di meno.

❖ **C. Un po' di fantasia.** Completa le frasi secondo le tue esperienze personali.

ESEMPIO: Invece di... → Invece di cercare lavoro ho deciso di specializzarmi.

1. Dopo aver...
   ____
2. Dopo essermi...
   ____
3. Per imparare...
   ____
4. Prima di...
   ____
5. Non sono mai riuscito/a a...
   ____

D. Nomi e aggettivi in -a

A. Risposte facili. Guarda i disegni e rispondi alle domande.

ESEMPIO: È ottimista Marco? → No, è pessimista.

1. Chi sono?

____

2. Sono delle artiste?

____

3. Chi è?

____

4. È pessimista Flavia?

____

5.  Chi è?

____

B. Femminili e maschili. Cambia al maschile le seguenti espressioni.

ESEMPIO: quella poetessa pessimista → quel poeta pessimista

1. una ragazza ottimista ______________________________
2. le professoresse comuniste ______________________________
3. la famosa pianista ______________________________
4. delle presentatrici entusiaste ______________________________
5. le artiste interessanti ______________________________
6. le peggiori turiste ______________________________

C. Plurali e singolari. Riscrivi al singolare le seguenti espressioni plurali.

ESEMPIO: i migliori panorami → il migliore panorama

1. gli ultimi problemi ______________________________
2. i papi stranieri ______________________________
3. nei programmi comunisti ______________________________
4. ai poeti originali ______________________________
5. le registe italiane ______________________________
6. i partiti socialisti ______________________________

LETTURA

L'educazione musicale in Italia

Leggi il testo e poi rispondi alle domande.

L'Italia è considerata il paese del bel canto. E non perché c'è Andrea Bocelli che oggi è molto famoso, ma perché in Italia la musica ha una tradizione vecchia di secoli. Certo l'Italia ha sempre avuto cantanti lirici famosi come oggi Bocelli, Cecilia Bartoli e Luciano Pavarotti, e prima Enrico Caruso, Renata Tebaldi o Renata Scotto. Ma sono stati soprattutto i grandi compositori come Rossini, Bellini, Donizetti, Verdi, Puccini, Mascagni, fino al Giancarlo Menotti di oggi, fondatore del Festival dei Due Mondi, a fare dell'Italia la patria della musica.

Ogni estate, in tutta Italia, ci sono tantissime manifestazioni musicali conosciute in tutto il mondo, come il Maggio Musicale Fiorentino, Umbria Jazz (dove vanno a suonare tutti i grandi jazzisti, e Perugia diventa il centro del mondo jazz per un mese), o l'Arena di Verona con la sua stagione operistica, dove possono essere viste grandi opere come *Aida* e *Turandot.* E naturalmente, conosciuta in tutto il mondo è La Scala di Milano, il teatro dell'opera forse più importante del mondo.

Gli italiani, però, studiano poco la musica, e questo è davvero un paradosso per un paese che ama la musica così tanto. Gli italiani hanno lezione obbligatoria di musica solo quando hanno tra gli undici e i tredici anni, nella scuola media, poi la musica scompare[a] dal curriculum. Se si vuole studiare la musica, è necessario andare al Conservatorio, una vera scuola musicale. All'università la musica non si studia quasi mai. La musica si studia solo nei pochi DAMS (Dipartimenti di Arte, Musica e Spettacolo) che ci sono in Italia, il più famoso dei quali è quello di Bologna. Fa parte dei piani di studio delle facoltà di lettere, ma solo come storia della musica, non come pratica.

[a]*disappears*

1. Quali sono i maggiori compositori italiani d'opera?

____

____

2. Quali sono le manifestazioni musicali più importanti in Italia durante l'estate?

____

____

3. Qual è il paradosso della situazione musicale in Italia?

____

____

4. Dove viene studiata la musica in Italia?

____

____

UN PO' DI SCRITTURA

❖ **A. Una vita d'artista.** C'è una carriera nel campo teatrale o in quello musicale che avresti voluto intraprendere (*pursue*)? Se sì, quale? Spiega il perché. Scrivi su un tuo foglio.

ESEMPIO: Io avrei voluto fare la direttrice d'orchestra. Da piccola ho visto Leonard Bernstein alla televisione e da allora...

❖ **B. Maschere.** «Tutto il mondo è un palcoscenico e l'uomo è un attore che cambia continuamente maschera». Sei d'accordo con quest'affermazione? Come la interpreti? Scrivi su un tuo foglio.

ESEMPIO: Secondo me, quest'affermazione significa che nella vita tutti dobbiamo recitare varie parti...

A. Roma punta su Verdi. Dai un'occhiata al programma della stagione operistica in Italia e impara i nomi dei maggiori teatri d'opera!

Roma punta su Verdi e Napoli su Rossini

Oltre alla Scala, riaprono i maggiori teatri d'opera con una serie di proposte davvero valide e di gran qualità. Vediamole.

● **Bologna.** *Il «Comunale» ha in scena, fino al 15 dicembre, diretto da Riccardo Chailly, il* Trittico *di Puccini formato dai tre atti unici* Il tabarro, Suor Angelica *(questa, con un brano non più eseguito dal 1922, recuperato da Alfredo Mandelli e dallo stesso Chailly) e* Gianni Schicchi; *regia di Luìs Pascual (tel. 051/529999).*

● **Napoli.** *Il «San Carlo» rappresenta il* Mosè in Egitto *di Rossini (versione originaria del* Moïse *francese e del* Mosè *italiano) dal 10 al 22 dicembre; dirige Salvatore Accardo ancora una volta lasciando il violino, che lo rese celebre, per il podio in teatro; con le voci «rossiniane» Devìa e Blake; regia di De Ahna (tel. 081/417144).*

● **Torino.** *Il «Regio», dal 9 al 23 dicembre, dà* Il caso Makropoulos *di Janacek dal dramma di Capek con Raina Kabaivanska nella parte di una donna vissuta 300 anni (la stessa edizione si darà a Bologna in marzo). Tel. 011/8815209-383210.*

● **Catania.** *Il «Bellini», dal 3 al 14 dicembre, accoppia* La medium *di Menotti al* Castello di Barbablù *di Bartok (tel. 095/7150921).*

● **Trieste.** *Il «Verdi» in Sala Tripcovich riapre con la celebre fiaba* Haensel & Gretel *di Umperdinck con Fiamma Izzo dal 10 al 22 dicembre (tel. 040/631948-62931).*

● **Roma.** Aida *di Verdi, all'«Opera», nella famosa messinscena Zeffirelli - Lilla De Nobili (tel. 06/461755).*

● **Genova.** *Il «Carlo Felice» inaugura con il* Don Giovanni *di Mozart, messinscena di Strehler, dal 9 al 21 dicembre (tel. 010/589329).*

1. _____ Trieste
2. _____ Genova
3. _____ Catania
4. _____ Roma
5. _____ Torino
6. _____ Napoli
7. _____ Bologna
8. _____ Milano

a. il Teatro alla Scala
b. il Regio
c. il Comunale
d. il San Carlo
e. il Bellini
f. il Carlo Felice
g. il Verdi
h. l'Opera

❖ **B. Parole in musica.** Scrivi una breve canzone in italiano. Oppure, se preferisci, traduci in italiano una strofa (*verse*) della tua canzone preferita.

Capitolo

15 CHI FU DANTE?

Name ______________________

Date ______________________

Class ______________________

VOCABOLARIO PRELIMINARE

A. Un'interrogazione su Dante... Leggi il dialogo e poi rispondi alle domande.

PROF.SSA STEFANIN: Allora, vediamo chi chiamo oggi per l'interrogazione orale su Dante. Marco Bosca. Sei preparato, Marco? Vediamo, cominciamo da una citazione famosa: «Un giorno leggiavamo per diletto[a] di Lancialotto[b] come amor lo strinse[c] soli eravamo e senza alcun sospetto»...

MARCO: Sono versi che fanno parte del racconto di Francesca, nel canto quinto dell' *Inferno.* Francesca racconta a Dante le circostanze del suo peccato[d] con Paolo, il fratello del marito. È dà la colpa[e] al tipo di lettura che facevano insieme: «Galeotto fu il libro e chi lo scrisse»...

PROF.SSA STEFANIN: Puoi essere più preciso?

MARCO: Dà la colpa della sua morte (il marito la uccise insieme al cognato) alla lettura della storia di Lancialotto e del suo bacio a Ginevra, moglie di Re Artù, che loro hanno imitato.

PROF.SSA STEFANIN: Francesca non ha responsabilità, allora?

MARCO: Secondo me, Dante crede alla responsabilità di un certo tipo di letteratura, ma vuole anche dirci che dobbiamo usare la nostra intelligenza, e la fede[f], per non commettere[g] peccato. Francesca accusa il libro per diminuire[h] la sua responsabilità personale.

PROF.SSA STEFANIN: Bravo Marco, sei un lettore sensibile!

[a] *pleasure* / [b] *Lancelot* / [c] *grasped*

[d] *sin*

[e] *blame*

[f] *faith* / [g] *to commit*

[h] *to reduce*

1. Da dove viene la citazione?

____

____

2. Che cosa hanno imitato Paolo e Francesca?

____

____

3. Come interpreta Marco la posizione di Dante sul peccato di Francesca?

____

____

4. Secondo Francesca, chi è responsabile della sua morte?

____

____

B. Chi sono? Che cosa fanno? Guarda il disegno e di' qual è la professione delle seguenti persone e che cosa fanno.

ESEMPIO:

Gabriella è *un'archeologa; Fa uno scavo archeologico*.

1. Paolo è ______________________________
____
2. Claudia è ______________________________
____
3. Giuliano è ______________________________
____
4. Lina è ______________________________
____

❖ **C. Il linguaggio della letteratura.** Scrivi cinque frasi che includono le seguenti paroli.

1. la citazione: ______________________________
2. la relazione: ______________________________
3. il riassunto: ______________________________
4. il brano: ______________________________
5. il/la protagonista: ______________________________

D. Preferenze. Valerio e Giovanna discutono delle loro preferenze letterarie. Completa il dialogo con la forma adatta delle seguenti parole: il capolavoro, la poesia, il poeta, il racconto, il romanzo, lo scrittore, la scrittrice.

VALERIO: Io preferisco leggere ____________________[1] di venti o trenta pagine, non di più! I ____________________[2] sono troppo lunghi per il mio carattere, non ho pazienza.

GIOVANNA: E le ____________________[3]? Di solito sono brevi e intense. Sono la mia lettura preferita!

VALERIO: No, anche la rima non fa per me. La prosa è il mio genere.

GIOVANNA: C'è uno ____________________[4] o una ____________________[5] che leggi più spesso?

VALERIO: Be', in questo momento sto leggendo Tabucchi e mi piace molto; poi rileggo spesso Calvino... I suoi racconti sono affascinanti. E tu, invece?

GIOVANNA: Il mio ____________________[6] preferito è Leopardi. Certo, non è un poeta contemporaneo, ma le sue poesie sono uniche. Sono dei ____________________[7]!

PROVERBI E MODI DI DIRE

Fermo come una statua.
Still as a statue.

Ogni medaglia ha il suo rovescio.
Every cloud has a silver lining. (Lit., Every medal has its reverse side.)

E. Il linguaggio dell'arte. Guarda il giochetto e cerca di trovare le seguenti parole: affrescare, archeologia, architettura, dipinto, mosaico, opera, paesaggio, pittura, quadro, restauro, rovine, ruderi.

C	A	R	O	A	D	I	P	I	N	T	O	H
R	L	L	O	I	G	G	A	S	E	A	P	P
E	N	T	E	G	R	U	D	E	R	O	N	I
S	O	M	M	O	S	A	I	C	O	E	R	T
T	E	A	R	L	A	R	C	H	E	N	G	T
A	R	E	P	O	I	R	E	D	U	R	O	U
U	S	T	R	E	L	L	E	N	I	V	O	R
R	A	R	C	H	I	T	E	T	T	U	R	A
O	S	T	R	C	C	A	N	I	N	O	B	E
O	S	F	(E	R	A	C	S	E	R	F	F	A)
I	N	Q	U	A	D	R	O	T	R	I	A	N

GRAMMATICA

A. Passato remoto

A. Parliamo d'arte. Riscrivi le seguenti frasi prima con il passato prossimo e poi con il passato remoto.

ESEMPIO: Michelangelo scolpisce la Pietà →
Michelangelo ha scolpito la Pietà.
Michelangelo scolpì la Pietà.

1. Michelangelo affresca la Cappella Sistina.

___

___

2. Botticelli dipinge la *Primavera.*

___

___

3. Gli studenti di storia dell'arte ammirano i disegni di Leonardo.

___

___

4. Giovanni fotografa i mosaici di Ravenna.

___

___

5. La guida mostra le rovine del Foro Romano ai turisti.

___

___

6. I greci costruiscono molti templi in Sicilia.

___

___

B. Dante Alighieri. Completa il seguente testo su Dante. Scegli le espressioni giuste fra quelle date.

Espressioni: andò, apparteneva (*belonged to*), aveva visto, capolavoro, morì, nacque, opera, poeta, si sposò, tornò

Il ___[1] Dante Alighieri ___[2] a Firenze nel 1265. La sua famiglia ___[3] alla piccola nobiltà fiorentina. Nel 1295 ___[4] con Gemma Donati ma nel 1274 ___[5] per la prima volta Beatrice, la sua musa, la sua ispirazione spirituale. Per motivi politici Dante ___[6] in esilio nel 1301 e non ___[7] mai più a Firenze. La sua prima ___[8] letteraria importante è *La vita nuova* e il suo ___[9] è il poema *La Divina Commedia.* ___[10] a Ravenna nel 1321.

C. Gli zii d'America. Il nonno racconta una storia ai suoi nipotini. Riscrivi la storia. Cambia i verbi dal passato remoto al passato prossimo.

Un giorno lo zio Antonio ________________________[1] (prese) la nave da Genova e ________________________[2] (partì) per gli Stati Uniti. Il viaggio ________________________[3] (durò [*lasted*]) molte settimane e quando finalmente lo zio Antonio ________________________[4] (arrivò) a New York ________________________[5] (ebbe) paura di trovarsi in una città così grande dove non conosceva nessuno. ________________________[6] (Cercò) lavoro per molto tempo, poi finalmente lo ________________________[7] (trovò) in una piccola fabbrica (*factory*) di scarpe. Dopo un anno, ________________________[8] (conobbe) Elisabetta, una ragazza del suo paese (*village*). Dopo un po' di tempo lo zio Antonio ________________________[9] (chiese) ad Elisabetta se si voleva sposare con lui. Lei ________________________[10] (rispose) di sì e così dopo due mesi ________________________[11] (si sposarono). Non ________________________[12] (fecero) una grande festa perché erano soli e i loro parenti ed amici erano tutti in Italia. Gli zii ________________________[13] (ebbero) cinque figli. ________________________[14] (Vissero) sempre negli Stati Uniti e non ________________________[15] (ritornarono mai) in Italia.

D. Avvenimenti del passato. Completa le frasi con i verbi al passato remoto.

1. I miei antenati (venire) ________________________ dall'Irlanda nel 1830.
2. L'anno scorso, gli studenti del corso di cinema italiano (vedere) ________________________ tutti i film di Federico Fellini.
3. Quando Cristoforo Colombo, nel 1492, (mettere) ________________________ piede nell'isola di San Salvador, (credere) ________________________ di aver raggiunto le Indie Orientali.
4. Michelangelo (vivere) ________________________ per molti anni della sua vita a Roma, dove (dipingere) ________________________ gli affreschi della Cappella Sistina, nel Vaticano.
5. Io e Cosetta (andare ad abitare) ________________________ a Napoli nel 1998. Due anni dopo, (tornare) ________________________ qui a Bologna.
6. Roma (diventare) ________________________ la capitale d'Italia nel 1870.
7. Amerigo Vespucci (1454–1512) (esplorare) ________________________ le coste del «Nuovo Mondo» e (dare) ________________________ il suo nome al nuovo continente.

E. Una favola: Cappuccetto Rosso. Completa la favola con il passato remoto o l'imperfetto.

_________________________[1] (Esserci) una volta una bambina che _________________________[2] (chiamarsi) Cappuccetto Rosso. Un giorno Cappuccetto Rosso _________________________[3] (dovere) andare dalla nonna a portarle un cestino di cibo, perché la nonna _________________________[4] (essere) ammalata. Cappuccetto Rosso _________________________[5] (uscire) di casa ed _________________________[6] (entrare) nel bosco. Cappuccetto Rosso _________________________[7] (vedere) dei fiori e _________________________[8] (decidere) di raccoglierne (*to pick*) alcuni per la nonna. Improvvisamente _________________________[9] (incontrare) un grosso lupo che le _________________________[10] (chiedere) dove _________________________[11] (andare). «Dalla nonna» _________________________[12] (rispondere) Cappuccetto. Il lupo la _________________________[13] (salutare) e _________________________[14] (andare) via. Il lupo _________________________[15] (correre) a casa della nonna, la _________________________[16] (mangiare) e _________________________[17] (mettersi) a letto al suo posto. Quando Cappuccetto Rosso _________________________[18] (arrivare) dalla nonna, la _________________________[19] (trovare) a letto. Ma la nonna _________________________[20] (sembrare) un po' strana. «Nonna, che orecchie lunghe che hai» _________________________[21] (dire) la bambina. «È per sentirti meglio» _________________________[22] (rispondere) la nonna. «Nonna, che bocca grande che hai, che denti grandi che hai...» «È per mangiarti meglio!» E il lupo _________________________[23] (saltare) dal letto e _________________________[24] (mangiare) la bambina.

F. Piccoli dialoghi. Completa i dialoghi o con il passato prossimo e l'imperfetto o con il passato remoto e l'imperfetto.

1. s1: Quando _________________________ (trasferirsi) in America i tuoi nonni?
   s2: Quando mio padre _________________________ (avere) due anni. Ma poi mio nonno _________________________ (dovere) tornare in Italia, due anni dopo.
2. s1: Luigi, come mai _________________________ (leggere) tutti quei libri?
   s2: Be', _________________________ (volere) fare bella figura (*a good impression*) con il nuovo professore.
3. s1: _________________________ (Uscire) in fretta stamattina Marco e Nino. Perché?
   s2: _________________________ (Avere) un esame di storia e non _________________________ (potere) arrivare tardi all'università.

B. Numeri ordinali

A. Personaggi storici. Scrivi in lettere il numero ordinale.

1. Luigi IX, re di Francia ______________________
2. Leone XIII, papa nel XIX secolo ______________________
3. Enrico IV, imperatore di Germania nel Medioevo ______________________
4. Bonifacio VIII, papa nel Medioevo ______________________
5. Vittorio Emanuele III, penultimo re d'Italia ______________________
6. Elisabetta II d'Inghilterra ______________________

B. In quale secolo? Scrivi a quale secolo appartengono questi anni.

1. L'anno 2000 ______________________
2. Il 1492 ______________________
3. Il 1776 ______________________
4. Il 1865 ______________________
5. Il 1620 ______________________

C. **Volerci** vs **metterci**

A. Cosa ci vuole? Completa con la forma corretta di **volerci.**

1. Per fare un tavolo, ______________________ il legno.
2. Nel secolo passato ______________________ tre giorni per andare da Firenze a Milano.
3. ______________________ sei uova per fare questo dolce.
4. L'anno prossimo ______________________ più professori di italiano per questa università.
5. ______________________ coraggio per fare questo esame domani.

❖ **B. Volerci o metterci?** Completa le seguenti frasi con **volerci** o **metterci,** secondo la costruzione della frase. Presta particolare attenzione al soggetto della frase.

ESEMPI: Io ci metto cinque minuti per arrivare all'università.
Per Gianni ci vuole molta volontà per studiare la chimica.

1. Mio padre dice sempre che ______________________
2. Secondo mia madre ______________________
3. I miei fratelli (Le mie sorelle) ______________________
4. Per mia nonna ______________________
5. I miei amici ______________________

PROVA-QUIZ

A. Io, al tuo posto... Marisa ti racconta dei suoi programmi di vacanza in Brasile sulle spiaggie di Rio de Janeiro. Tu, invece, hai in mente una vacanza sempre in Brasile, ma meno convenzionale. Rispondi alle affermazioni di Marisa usando le informazioni date tra parentesi. Comincia con **Io al tuo posto...**

ESEMPIO: Andrò solo nelle grandi città. (in Amazzonia) →
Io, al tuo posto, andrei in Amazzonia.

1. Dormirò tutti i giorni fino a mezzogiorno. (alzarmi presto)

   ____

   ____

2. Viaggerò solo in aereo. (in treno)

   ____

   ____

3. Visiterò i posti più popolari. (i piccoli paesi)

   ____

   ____

4. Mangerò nei grandi ristoranti. (nelle trattorie locali)

   ____

   ____

5. Farò il giro dei quartieri più chic. (dei quartieri popolari, *working class*)

   ____

   ____

6. Ballerò in discoteca tutte le sere. (andare a visitare i centri sociali)

   ____

   ____

B. La ragione per cui... Completa il seguente paragrafo con i pronomi relativi appropriati.

Ci sono varie ragioni per _____________[1] gli americani studiano l'italiano: ci sono studenti _____________[2] sono d'origine italiana, altri _____________[3] s'interessano alla musica e all'arte, altri ancora _____________[4] sono stati in Italia e vogliono tornarci. Io domando sempre ai miei studenti, il primo giorno di lezione, perché studiano i'italiano. La risposta più originale _____________[5] ho avuto finora (*so far*) è la seguente: «Studio l'italiano perché ho un compagno di camera _____________[6] è italiano. Lui parla nel sonno (*sleep*) e io voglio capire quello _____________[7] dice!»

C. Scrittori e opere del medioevo. Riscrivi il seguente testo usando il passato remoto, l'imperfetto o il trapassato prossimo, come necessario.

ESEMPIO: I tre grandi del Medioevo italiano furono Dante...

I tre grandi del Medioevo italiano sono Dante, Petrarca e Boccaccio. Dante nasce e vive a Firenze. Partecipa attivamente alla vita politica della città. Si occupa di questioni filosofiche, teologiche e linguistiche. Scrive, quando ha circa trentatré anni, la sua opera più famosa, *La Divina Commedia.*

L'opera più nota di Petrarca è invece *Il Canzoniere.* Il poeta dedica la sua opera alla donna amata, Laura, che ha incontrato ad Avignone nel 1327. Nel corso della sua vita Petrarca prepara nove versioni del *Canzoniere.*

Boccaccio scrive il suo capolavoro, *Il Decameron,* subito dopo la peste[a] di Firenze del 1348. Come anticipa il titolo greco (che significa «Dieci giornate»), l'azione rappresentata si svolge[b] in dieci giorni. In questo periodo di tempo, mentre infuria[c] la peste a Firenze, sette donne e tre uomini si riuniscono in una villa di campagna e raccontano le novelle che leggiamo nel *Decameron.*

[a] *plague*
[b] si... *takes place*
[c] *rages*

D. Traduzioni. Traduci in italiano. Scrivi su un tuo foglio.

1. A date we'll never forget is July 21, 1969, the day when (on which) man set foot (*to set foot* = **mettere piedi**) on the moon (**luna**) for the first time.
2. As soon as they went out, it began to rain. They tried to get a cab (**tassì,** *m.*) but there were too many people who were trying to do the same thing. They ended up (**finire per** + *inf.*) walking.
3. s1: Fabio, tell me the reason why you're so worried (**preoccupato**).
   s2: Nothing, really—only that I didn't do all I could do.
4. s1: Gina, could you give me a hand?
   s2: Sure, but you should really learn to change the tires by yourself.

LETTURA

Dall' *Inferno* di Dante: Canto V, l'episodio di Paolo e Francesca

Dante parla con Francesca, morta (uccisa, anzi) per amore. Un amore peccaminoso (*sinful*). Nel suo dialogo con Dante, Francesca racconta la sua versione di come lei e Paolo, suo cognato, si innamorarono.

Noi leggiavamo un giorno per diletto[a]
di Lancialotto come amor lo strinse[b];
soli eravamo e sanza alcun sospetto.
Per più fiate[c] li occhi ci sospinse[d]
quella lettura, e scolorocci[e] il viso;
ma solo un punto fu quel che ci vinse.
Quando leggemmo il disiato riso[f]
esser baciato da cotanto[g] amante,
questi, che mai da me non fia[h] diviso,
la bocca mi baciò tutto tremante.

[a] per passatempo, per piacere
[b] (da **stringere**)
[c] volte / [d] ci spinse in avanti
[e] ci scolorì, ci fece perdere colore
[f] il desiderato sorriso
[g] tanto grande
[h] sarà

1. Cosa facevano Paolo e Francesca prima di commettere il loro peccato d'amore?

   ____

2. Perché, secondo Francesca, commettono questo peccato?

   ____

3. Fai una lista dei verbi al passato remoto, e poi riscrivi il brano usando verbi al passato prossimo. Scrivi su un tuo foglio.

UN PO' DI SCRITTURA

❖ **A. Una lettura amata.** C'è un racconto o un romanzo che ami particolarmente? Perché? Racconta prima la trama (*plot*) (usando il passato remoto e l'imperfetto), poi cerca di dire in poche parole perché ti piace tanto. Scrivi una pagina. Scrivi su un tuo foglio.

ESEMPIO: Il mio romanzo preferito è *Sostiene Pereira* di Antonio Tabucchi. Il protagonista è un vecchio giornalista portoghese che viveva di ricordi e di rimpianti (*regrets*) finché (*until*) un giorno qualcosa di diverso accadde (*happened*) nella sua vita...

❖ **B. Esperienze diverse.** Conosci uno scrittore (una scrittrice) o un (un') artista la cui vita ti sembra diversa, strana o comunque interessante? Raccontala usando i tempi del passato. Scrivi una pagina. Scrivi su un tuo foglio.

ESEMPIO: La vita di Dacia Maraini mi sembra ricca di esperienze diverse che hanno sicuramente influito sulla (*influenced*) sua carriera di scrittrice. Nata in Italia, dovette lasciare il paese ancora piccolissima perché fu imprigionata con i genitori antifascisti in un campo di concentramento giapponese...

ATTUALITÀ

Sull'arte. Leggi le notizie qui riportate, poi rispondi alle domande.

Parole utili: il periodico (*periodical*), affermare (*to affirm*), risalente (*dating back*)

• Il periodico americano «Art and Antiques» afferma nel suo numero di gennaio '87 che una ricerca condotta negli Usa con l'ausilio di un computer stabilisce che il famoso quadro di Leonardo da Vinci «Monna Lisa» non sarebbe altro che la copia al femminile del volto dello stesso Leonardo.

1. Di quale artista italiano parla l'articolo pubblicato nel periodico americano *Art and Antiques*?

   ____

2. Chi sarebbe veramente Monna Lisa secondo i ricercatori americani?

   ____

3. Come sono arrivati a questa conclusione?

   ____

   ____

4. Dove lavora la ragazza nella foto?

   ____

   ____

UN'ANTICA ARTE
Ravenna. Una ragazza al lavoro nella Cooperativa Mosaicisti. «A Ravenna il mosaico viene ancora eseguito secondo la tecnica e la metodologia aulica bizantina», afferma Bruno Bandini, direttore della Pinacoteca Comunale di Ravenna.

5. Che cosa fa?

____

6. Che tecnica usa per fare i mosaici?

____

7. Chi è Bruno Bandini?

____

Capitolo 16 PER CHI VOTI?

Name ______________________

Date ______________________

Class ______________________

VOCABOLARIO PRELIMINARE

A. Un'Europa unita, con una sola moneta. Leggi il dialogo e rispondi alle domande.

MARISA: Cosa pensi di quest'Europa unita, con una sola moneta?
ADRIANA: Un po' mi dispiace che la lira scompaia ma penso che sia un bene per l'economia europea. Così sarà possibile essere più forti contro il dollaro...
MARISA: Non credo che quest'unità porti moltissimi vantaggi.
ADRIANA: Marisa! Sono sorpresa! Che dici? Un libero mercato, molte leggi uguali per gli stati dell'Unione, una legislazione sociale più avanzata..Credo che sia un vantaggio sicuro!
MARISA: E tu, per chi voti per il nuovo parlamento europeo?
ADRIANA: Sai, io sono di sinistra, voto per un partito progressista...
MARISA: E io sono di centro, ma devo ancora decidere chi votare!
ADRIANA: Spero che sia una decisione veloce, la tua! Le elezioni sono domani!

1. Che giorno è domani?

   ____

   ____

2. Cosa pensa Marisa dell'unificazione economica dell'Europa?

   ____

   ____

3. Per quale tipo di partito vuole votare Adriana?

   ____

   ____

B. Definizioni. Abbina le parole della colonna A con le parole e le definizioni della colonna B.

A	B
1. _____ eleggere	a. le leggi, lo statuto
2. _____ la riduzione	b. lo stipendio, la paga
3. _____ la costituzione	c. il membro del governo
4. _____ la disoccupazione	d. nominare, votare
5. _____ il ministro	e. la mancanza (*lack*) di lavoro
6. _____ il salario	f. la diminuzione, la limitazione

C. La Repubblica. Completa le frasi con le parole adatte.

1. Il ____________________ è il capo dello stato italiano.
2. Il ____________________ è il capo del governo.
3. Al governo partecipano i rappresentanti dei maggiori ____________________ italiani.
4. La ____________________ e il ____________________ formano il Parlamento.
5. Le ____________________ e il ____________________ sono gli strumenti della democrazia.

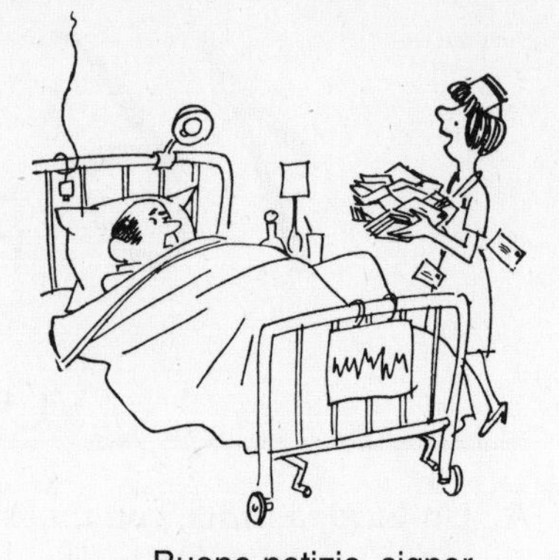

—...Buone notizie, signor ministro: il 60% della popolazione si augura una sua guarigione,[a] il 40% invece è decisamente contrario...

[a]si... *hopes that you recover*

D. Il costo della vita. Giulia e Guido sono preoccupati del continuo aumento del costo della vita. Completa il dialogo con la forma adatta delle seguenti parole: aumentare, aumento, diminuire, lo stipendio, le tasse.

GIULIA: Il costo della vita è in continuo ____________________![1]

GUIDO: Sì, è sempre peggio! I prezzi ____________________,[2] le ____________________[3] non ____________________ ....[4]

GIULIA: Tra poco ci ridurranno (*they'll reduce*) anche gli ____________________![5]

GUIDO: Io faccio sciopero!

E. Cittadini e rappresentanti. Rispondi alle seguenti domande.

1. Come si chiamano i membri della Camera?

   ____

2. Come si chiamano i membri del Senato?

   ____

3. Chi sono i disoccupati?

   ____

4. Dove lavorano gli operai?

   ____

5. Dove lavorano gli impiegati?

   ____

6. Chi fa gli scioperi? Perché?

   ____

❖ **F. Domande personali.** Rispondi alle seguenti domande secondo la tua esperienza personale.

1. Chi sono i rappresentanti al Senato del tuo Stato? Conosci i loro programmi?

   ______

2. Vai a votare alle elezioni nazionali e federali? Perché sì, perché no?

   ______

3. Cosa pensi del leader di questo paese?

   ______

4. Quali sono i maggiori partiti in questo paese?

   ______

5. Secondo te, è importante interessarsi di politica?

   ______

—Oh, sì, lo so benissimo che cosa succede ai piccoli bugiardi: crescono e si danno[a] alla politica!

[a]si... *they devote themselves*

GRAMMATICA

A. Congiuntivo presente

A. Un padre troppo protettivo. Il padre di Marina è molto severo (*strict*) e protettivo. Scrivi le sue risposte alle richieste di sua figlia.

ESEMPIO: Posso uscire con Claudio? → No, non voglio che tu esca con Claudio.

1. Posso prendere la macchina stasera?

   ______

2. Posso andare in discoteca con gli amici?

   ______

3. Possiamo fare una passeggiata dopo cena, io e Claudio?

   ______

4. Posso mettermi la minigonna?

____

5. Posso tornare dopo mezzanotte il sabato sera?

____

6. Posso frequentare un corso di nuoto?

____

B. Io non credo! Enrico ha poca fede nelle dichiarazioni di politica del governo. Segui l'esempio e scrivi le opinioni di Enrico.

ESEMPIO: il governo / aumentare gli stipendi →
Io non credo che il governo aumenti davvero gli stipendi.

1. il governo / diminuire le tasse

____

2. il governo / aiutare gli immigrati

____

3. i ministri / risolvere il problema del deficit finanziario

____

4. i ministri / migliorare l'assistenza medica

____

5. il governo / fare qualcosa per l'Aids

____

6. il parlamento / approvare leggi per cambiare il sistema universitario

____

C. Bisogna! Il signor Francesco è avanti con gli anni (*on in years*) ma molto vivace. Ti preoccupi per la sua salute. Incoraggialo a fare ciò che dovrebbe fare. Comincia ogni frase con **Ma bisogna che Lei...**

ESEMPIO: Non voglio andare dal dottore. → Ma bisogna che Lei vada dal dottore!

1. Non voglio guidare piano (*slowly*).

____

2. Non voglio smettere di fumare.

____

3. Non voglio bere meno vino.

____

4. Non voglio riposarmi.

____

D. Spero che... Sei preoccupato/preoccupata per la visita dei tuoi cognati presuntuosi (*opinionated*). Ne parli con tua madre. Rispondi alle sue domande con **Non so, ma spero che...** e le informazioni suggerite.

ESEMPIO: A che ora arriveranno? (tardi) → Non so, ma spero che arrivino tardi.

1. Quando partiranno? (domenica sera)

   ____

2. Dove dormiranno? (nella stanza degli ospiti)

   ____

3. A che ora si alzeranno? (presto)

   ____

4. Di che cosa discuteremo? (di arte e di cultura, non di politica)

   ____

B. Verbi ed espressioni che richiedono il congiuntivo

A. È bene? Esprimi la tua opinione riguardo ai seguenti fatti. Reagisci ad ogni affermazione cominciando con **È bene che..** o **Non è bene che...**

ESEMPIO: Il governo aumenta le tasse. →
È bene che (Non è bene che) il governo aumenti le tasse.

1. Il governo è principalmente un sistema di due partiti.

   ____

2. Negli Stati Uniti non c'è assistenza medica per tutti i cittadini.

   ____

3. Le Nazioni Unite aiutano i paesi più poveri.

   ____

4. I lavoratori esigono stipendi migliori.

   ____

5. Le femministe organizzano una manifestazione per la parità dei diritti.

   ____

B. Indicativo o congiuntivo? Completa i dialoghetti con la forma adeguata del indicativo o del congiuntivo.

1. S1: Peccato che tu oggi non ____________ (stare) bene, perché volevo andare a fare una passeggiata.

   S2: Ho un brutto raffreddore ed è bene che io non ____________ (uscire) e che ____________ (bere) molto succo d'arancia.

2. s1: Penso che stasera _______________ (arrivare) Valeria dall'Inghilterra. Vorresti andare a prenderla all'aeroporto?

   s2: No, non posso. È meglio che io _______________ (leggere) un po' e che poi _______________ (andare) a letto presto.

—Credi che stia bene un vaso del paleolitico insieme ad un tavolo del paleozoico?

3. s1: Bambini, è ora che _______________ (alzarsi) e _______________ (prepararsi) per andare a scuola.

   s2: Mamma, è proprio necessario che noi _______________ (andare) a scuola?

❖ **C. Opinioni personali.** Completa le frasi secondo le tue opinioni personali.

ESEMPIO: È importante che il governo... →
È importante che il governo faccia di più per le persone povere.

1. Ho l'impressione che il presidente _______________
2. È ora che i nostri senatori _______________
3. Sembra che gli operai in questo paese _______________
4. È strano che il papa _______________
5. Spero che alle prossime elezioni _______________
6. Ho paura che nel nostro paese _______________

❖ **D. Peccato!** Quali situazioni o avvenimenti ti fanno dire «Che peccato!» Scrivi tre frasi cominciando con **Peccato che...**

ESEMPIO: Peccato che siano pochi i progressisti al governo!

1. _______________
2. _______________
3. _______________

C. Congiuntivo passato

A. Ieri. Completa le seguenti frasi con il congiuntivo passato del verbo.

ESEMPIO: Voi non avete scioperato. Speriamo che almeno Giovanni *abbia scioperato*!

1. Io non ho finito. È possibile che gli altri _______________!
2. Hai votato! Sono contenta che tu _______________!
3. Non si sono divertiti? Peccato che non si _______________!
4. Vi siete trasferiti a Milano? È strano che vi _______________ così lontano!
5. Non avete chiesto l'aumento? Mi dispiace che non _______________ l'aumento!
6. Ho capito tutto! È incredibile che io _______________ tutto!

B. Può darsi. Roberto non ha molte certezze. Scrivi le sue risposte alle seguenti domande. Comincia con **Può darsi che...** segui l'esempio.

ESEMPIO: Sai quando arriva l'aereo? → Può darsi che sia già arrivato.

1. Sai quando vanno a dormire?

   ____

2. Sai quando fanno colazione?

   ____

3. Sai quando pagano?

   ____

4. Sai quando escono?

   ____

5. Sai quando parte il treno?

   ____

   ____

6. Sai quando danno i risultati delle elezioni?

   ____

   ____

—Sembra che abbia perso tutta la sua capacità di ricupero...

C. Piccoli dialoghi. Completa i dialoghetti con la forma adeguata del congiuntivo presente o passato.

1. S1: Sono contenta che Renata e Gianni ______________ (incontrare) mio fratello ieri sera.

   S2: Ne sono contenta anch'io. Ho l'impressione che quei due non ______________ (avere) molti amici qui a Roma.

2. S1: Credi che il signor Albi ______________ (annoiarsi) alle feste?

   S2: Direi di no. Pare che lui ______________ (divertirsi) tanto alla festa dei Mauri la settimana scorsa.

3. S1: Carlo, dove sono i ragazzi? Ho paura che ______________ (succedere) qualcosa.

   S2: Non ti preoccupare, Franca. Immagino che quel distratto di nostro figlio ______________ (dimenticare) di fare benzina.

4. S1: Spero che non ci ______________ (essere) lo sciopero dei treni domani.

   S2: Ho appena sentito il giornale radio e pare che gli operai ______________ (ottenere) l'aumento che chiedevano.

LETTURA

La politica in Italia

Leggi cosa pensa Stefania, una segretaria di 35 anni, della politica italiana. Poi rispondi alle domande.

Per votare in Italia, alla Camera dei Deputati, bisogna avere 18 anni, mentre per il Senato sono necessari 21 anni. Io ho votato la prima volta, nel lontano 1983 e mi sembra un secolo fa. A leggere i nomi dei partiti adesso e a paragonarli con quelli che esistevano vent'anni fa, mi trovo infatti disorientata.

Anche se i partiti sono cambiati, lo spirito italiano riguardo alla politica credo sia rimasto immutato. Gli italiani sono abbastanza scettici.[a] Non credono ai partiti, ma vanno a votare in massa lo stesso perché vogliono fare sentire la loro voce. La politica poi è un po' come lo sport del calcio: è un argomento che appassiona la gente. Gli italiani litigano quando parlano di politica, sono sarcastici, eppure[b] la seguono giorno dopo giorno.

L'italiano medio conosce bene i nomi dei ministri, segue l'itinerario delle leggi, ed ascolta con attenzione chi promette di far pagare meno tasse. Le tasse! Sono queste l'argomento più spinoso.[c] In Italia esistono tasse per ogni cosa possibile e immaginabile e il fisco (*Italian IRS*) ovviamente, è odiato anche perché molto denaro[d] non viene speso bene. Ma forse questo non è solo un male italiano.

Secondo me, un problema è invece che ci sono troppi partiti. Negli Stati Uniti è l'opposto, ce ne sono troppo pochi, mentre in Italia chi non è d'accordo con le politiche correnti forma un partito e prova ad andare al parlamento.

Negli ultimi dieci anni è cambiato molto nella politica italiana, e molto cambierà ancora. Adesso che l'Italia è parte integrante della Comunità Europea, per molte cose dovrà adeguarsi alla legislazione europea. E questo, secondo me, avrà un effetto positivo, perché la politica italiana sarà legata a quella degli altri paesi in Europa e sarà più responsabile.

[a] *skeptical*
[b] *yet*
[c] *thorny*
[d] *money*

1. Che spirito hanno gli italiani nei confronti della politica secondo Stefania?

___

___

2. Che cosa pensano gli italiani delle tasse?

___

___

3. Cosa dice Stefania del numero dei partiti in Italia e negli Stati Uniti? È un bene o un male secondo lei che ci siano tanti partiti?

___

___

4. Cosa pensa Stefania dell'Italia nell'Unione Europea?

___

___

UN PO' DI SCRITTURA

❖ **A. Discussioni politiche.** Ricordi una discussione politica con amici o parenti? Di che cosa avete parlato? Riporta la discussione alternando la prosa con il dialogo e usando il congiuntivo quando necessario. Scrivi una pagina e mezzo. Scrivi su un tuo foglio.

ESEMPIO: Due settimane fa ho avuto una discussione piuttosto accesa (*heated*) con Roberta. L'argomento in discussione era la politica governativa sulla scuola. Roberta diceva: «Io penso che sia giusto che il governo aiuti le scuole private!» E io dicevo: «Ma perché dobbiamo avere scuole pubbliche e scuole private? L'istruzione deve essere uguale per tutti. Io penso che ricchi e poveri debbano avere le stesse possibilità di accesso alla migliore istruzione possibile e che il governo... »

❖ **B. Uno stato ideale.** Come dovrebbe funzionare, secondo te, uno stato che faccia davvero gli interessi di tutti i cittadini? Immagina questo stato ideale e descrivilo con tutti i particolari. Scrivi una pagina e mezzo. Scrivi su un tuo foglio.

ESEMPIO: Secondo me lo stato dovrebbe garantire alcune cose essenziali a tutti i cittadini. Innanzitutto (*First of all*) la possibilità di lavorare e di vivere dignitosamente (*with dignity*), con assistenza medica, istruzione...

ATTUALITÀ

A. La fine di un'epoca. L'articolo in pagina 212 è dedicato al crollo (*collapse*), nel 1992–93, di uno dei maggiori partiti italiani, il partito dei cattolici, la Dc (Democrazia cristiana, detto anche il partito bianco, in contrapposizione al vecchio partito comunista, PCI, detto anche il partito rosso). Prima leggi le domande, poi leggi i titoli e i brani riportati. Rispondi con frasi complete.

1. Che cosa può significare il titolo?

   ____

2. Perché la Dc, secondo il giornalista, «ha le maggiori responsabilità della catastrofe»?

   ____

3. Perché nel 1945 «le macerie (*rubble*) invadevano i marciapiedi (*sidewalks*)»?

   ____

4. Perché nel 1945 «i fascisti si nascondevano sotto i letti»?

   ____

5. Questi tre partiti sono ancora importanti?

   ____

6. Che cosa pensano gli italiani della vecchia classe dirigente (*ruling*)?

   ____

Requiem in bianco

Ha le maggiori responsabilità della catastrofe, per la sua vocazione alle transazioni, al malgoverno. Non poteva bastare un segretario integerrimo come Martinazzoli. Il trasformismo le ha tolto credibilità. E i cattolici devono ricominciare...

di ENZO BIAGI

Si conclude un'epoca che ha segnato mezzo secolo di vita italiana. Una storia cominciata nel 1945: c'erano ancora i governatori alleati, gli sciuscià (chi ricorda questo nome?) pulivano le scarpe ai soldati dell'US Army e del re d'Inghilterra, le «signorine» facevano compagnia anche ai disertori nella pineta di Tombolo, le macerie invadevano i marciapiedi, i fascisti di Salò si nascondevano sotto i letti, occorrevano le tessere coi punti per mangiare e per vestirsi...

C'erano tre grandi partiti; due sono praticamente finiti, il Pc ha cambiato faccia e programma. È caduto un muro e sotto i detriti sono scomparsi i socialisti, i comunisti e i democristiani, e la polvere rende quasi irrespirabile l'aria. Il dollaro è oggi la moneta che conta. I tribunali si stanno occupando di una classe dirigente che i cittadini considerano traditrice. Sono mille le cause avviate: che numero fatale. O sbarcano a Marsala o sbancano il Paese.

AMICI AMERICANI. *Aldo Moro e Amintore Fanfani in visita a Washington.*

❖ **B. Politica italiana, politica americana.** Quali sono le principali differenze tra il sistema politico italiano e quello di questo paese? La storia di questo paese nell'ultimo secolo è simile o diversa da quella italiana? Perché? Sei soddisfatto/a del sistema politico di questo paese? Che cosa vorresti cambiare o migliorare?

Scrivi una pagina pensando a questi temi: partiti, economia, sistema assistenziale (*welfare*), politica interna, politica estera, eccètera. Poi confronta le tue conclusioni con il resto della classe. Scrivi su un tuo foglio.

ESEMPIO: Secondo me, il sistema politico italiano e quello degli Stati Uniti sono molto diversi. Per esempio, noi abbiamo solo due partiti...

Capitolo

Name ______________________

Date ______________________

Class ______________________

17 IL MONDO DEL LAVORO

VOCABOLARIO PRELIMINARE

A. Trovare un lavoro... Leggi il dialogo e rispondi alle domande.

EMANUELE: Forse è vero che l'inflazione e la disoccupazione sono in diminuzione, e che la crisi economica è una cosa del passato, ma intanto[a] sono disoccupato. E come lo trovo un lavoro? Ho fatto tutto, domande, concorsi, ho risposto ad annunci...

GABRIELLA: Bisogna aver pazienza e persistere. Poi dipende dal tipo di curriculum che mandi, dalle mansioni che cerchi e anche dalla zona. Noi siamo più fortunati che al Sud, dove la disoccupazione è grande.

EMANUELE: Mah, saremo anche più fortunati, ma io il lavoro non ce l'ho. Forse dovrei trasferirmi a Milano, o andare a Torino, lì forse c'è meno crisi. O no?

GABRIELLA: A dire il vero non lo so. Con il tuo curriculum puoi avere molte possibilità, dipende anche dalla tua flessibilità. E ricorda che puoi sempre chiedere aiuto al sindacato, e io lo so bene. Lavoro per il sindacato, io!

[a] *in the meantime*

1. Cosa ha fatto Emanuele per trovare un lavoro? ______________________

____

2. Qual è l'opinione di Gabriella? ______________________

____

3. Cosa pensa di fare Emanuele? ______________________

____

4. Quale aiuto propone Gabriella? ______________________

____

B. Un colloquio di lavoro. Emanuele scrive a Gabriella. Usa il **Vocabolario preliminare** dal tuo testo per completare la sua lettera.

Cara Gabriella, finalmente ho ______________[1] con una grande ______________[2] di Milano. Avevo fatto ______________[3] un mese fa, spedito il mio ______________[4] e riempito tutti i ______________[5] ma poi non avevo sentito più nulla. Adesso hanno ______________[6] per martedì prossimo. Spero che mi ______________,[7] sono qualificato per il ______________[8] e spero che ______________[9] economica sia adeguata al ______________[10] di Milano.

C. La parola giusta. Abbina le parole della colonna A e le definizioni della colonna B.

A		B	
1.	_____ un sindacato	a.	offrire un lavoro
2.	_____ un dirigente	b.	una persona con cui si lavora
3.	_____ assumere	c.	rinunciare al proprio lavoro
4.	_____ licenziarsi	d.	un incontro tra due (o più) persone
5.	_____ un colloquio	e.	un compito di lavoro
6.	_____ un'azienda	f.	un'organizzazione dei lavoratori
7.	_____ una mansione	g.	una ditta
8.	_____ un collega	h.	un direttore, un capo

PROVERBI E MODI DI DIRE

A rubar poco si va in galera, a rubar tanto si fa carriera.
By stealing a little one goes to jail, by stealing a lot one moves up in the world.

❖ **D. A caccia di lavoro** (*Job hunting*). Pensa un po' al tuo ultimo lavoro. Perché cercavi lavoro? Com'è andato il colloquio? Quali erano le tue mansioni? Scrivi una pagina usando almeno cinque delle seguenti espressioni. Scrivi su un tuo foglio. (Se non hai lavorato recentemente, scrivi di un tuo lavoro ideale.)

Espressioni utili: cercare lavoro, fare domanda, fissare un colloquio, l'offerta, partecipare a un concorso, il requisito, la richiesta, riempire un modulo, rispondere ad un annuncio

ESEMPIO: L'anno scorso ho lavorato come bagnina (*lifeguard*) alla piscina comunale. Cercavo lavoro perché avevo bisogno di soldi per andare in Europa...

GRAMMATICA

A. Congiunzioni che richiedono il congiuntivo

A. Il verbo giusto. Completa le seguenti frasi con la forma adeguata dell'indicativo o del congiuntivo dei verbi tra parentesi.

ESEMPIO: Vi telefoneremo appena ____*potremo*____.

1. Chiudo la finestra perché la nonna ____________________ (avere) freddo.
2. Chiudo la finestra perché non ____________________ (entrare) l'aria fredda.
3. Vieni qui prima che io ____________________ (arrabbiarsi)!
4. Telefonami appena ____________________ (potere).

5. Benché non ________________ (esserci) il sole, fa abbastanza caldo.
6. Non mi parlare di linguistica perché non ne ________________ (capire) niente!
7. Io lavo i piatti mentre Renata ________________ (studiare).
8. Uscite di casa senza che i bambini vi ________________ (vedere).
9. Stiamo a casa perché ________________ (piovere).
10. Usciremo purché non ________________ (piovere).

B. In azienda. Stefano non è contento del suo lavoro. Scrivi le sue risposte alle seguenti domande. Usa **a meno che... non** e le informazioni date tra parentesi. Segui l'esempio.

ESEMPIO: Pensi di andare dal direttore? (loro / darci migliori condizioni di lavoro) →
Andrò dal direttore a meno che non ci diano migliori condizioni di lavoro.

1. Pensi di licenziarti? (loro / darmi un aumento)

____

2. Pensi di organizzare una dimostrazione? (il sindacato / dire di no)

____

3. Pensi di partecipare al concorso dei Telefoni di Stato? (esserci pochi posti)

____

4. Pensi di rispondere a degli annunci? (trovare lavoro prima)

____

5. Pensi di trasferirti a Milano? (trovare lavoro a Torino)

____

6. Pensi di partecipare allo sciopero? (succedere qualcosa)

____

C. Il mondo del lavoro. Completa le frasi con le congiunzioni appropriate.

1. Un dirigente agli operai: «parlerò col rappresentante del sindacato ____________ capiate meglio la mia posizione.»
2. Parteciperemo al concorso insieme ____________ tu non preferisca cercare un lavoro diverso.
3. Ti aiuto a riempire il modulo ____________ tu prometta di fare davvero domanda.
4. ____________ loro mi licenzino, mi licenzio io!
5. ____________ abbia già avuto due colloqui, è ancora disoccupato.
6. Posso aumentare gli stipendi ____________ voi lavoriate di sabato.
7. Te lo ripetono ____________ tu lo ricordi: il sindacato può aiutarti a trovare un lavoro!
8. Ho una buona professione: mi hanno dato un aumento ____________ io lo chiedessi!

❖ **D. Cerco un lavoro...** Completa le seguenti frasi secondo le tue abitudini. (Se la frase non corrisponde alle tue abitudini, inventa la risposta.)

ESEMPIO: Cerco un lavoro part-time per... →
Cerco un lavoro part-time per pagarmi le lezioni di musica.

1. Mi licenzio a meno che...
____
2. Continuo a frequentare l'università sebbene...
____
3. Faccio il (la) dirigente benché...
____
4. Parto senza che...
____
5. Faccio domanda prima di...
____
6. Telefono subito prima che...
____
7. Accetto quest'offerta di lavoro purché...
____
8. Non esco con un ragazzo (una ragazza) senza...
____

—Carlo è il cacciatore più leale[a] che abbia mai visto!

[a]*honorable*

B. Altri usi del congiuntivo

A. Comunque... Completa le frasi con **chiunque, comunque, dovunque,** o **qualunque.**

ESEMPIO: ___Chiunque___ mi telefoni, rispondete che non sono in casa.

1. Io non la lascerò _______________ cosa succeda.
2. Verremo a trovarvi in _______________ paese vi trasferiate.
3. _______________ voglia, può far domanda.
4. _______________ tu lavorerai, avrai successo.
5. _______________ vadano le cose, Le scriverò.
6. Vi seguiranno _______________ voi andiate.

B. Esagerazioni. A Giorgio piace esagerare sempre. Scrivi le sue risposte alle seguenti domande. Segui l'esempio.

ESEMPIO: È difficile questa lingua? → Sì, è la più difficile che io conosca.

1. È alto il costo della vita a Venezia?

   ____
2. È buono questo lavoro che hai?

   ____
3. Sono simpatiche queste colleghe di lavoro?

   ____
4. È caro questo tipo di assistenza medica?

   ____
5. Sono esigenti questi requisiti?

   ____
6. Sono ragionevoli (*reasonable*) quelle richieste sindacali?

   ____

C. Non c'è proprio nessuno! Ti sei rotto il braccio e stai sempre a casa perché non puoi guidare la macchina. Ti chiama la tua mamma, che abita distante, e ti fa tante domande. Rispondile in modo negativo. Segui l'esempio.

ESEMPIO: Ti fa da mangiare qualcuno? → No, non c'è nessuno che mi faccia da mangiare.

1. Qualcuno ti porta al cinema?

   ____
2. Passa a trovarti qualcuno?

   ____
3. Qualcuno guarda la TV con te?

   ____
4. Qualcuno esce con te stasera?

   ____
5. Viene a farti compagnia qualcuno?

   ____

D. Piccoli dialoghi. Completa i dialoghetti con la forma adeguata dell'indicativo o del congiuntivo dei verbi tra parentesi.

1. s1: Ragazzi, non c'è nessuno qui che ________________ (sapere) leggere il russo?

   s2: Qui no, ma c'è qualcuno che ________________ (parlare) russo nell'ufficio di mio marito. Gli telefono?

2. s1: Ho bisogno di un dizionario che ________________ (dare) le forme dei verbi irregolari.

   s2: Vediamo... c'è questo che ________________ (avere) delle tabelle in fondo (*in the back*). Lo vuole vedere?

3. s1: Mia moglio conosce una signora che ________________ (avere) intenzione di vendere la propria macchina, un'Alfa Romeo del '99.

   s2: Grazie, Mauro, ma io cerco una macchina che ________________ (essere) un po' meno costosa.

4. s1: Per arrivare a Milano prima delle nove, posso prendere il treno che ________________ (partire) alle tre?

   s2: No, signore, deve prendere un treno che non ________________ (fermarsi) a tutte le stazioni!

C. Congiuntivo o infinito?

❖ **A. L'aspettativa per donne e uomini.** Leggi il dialogo tra Fiorella e Valentina e rispondi alle domande.

FIORELLA: Ciao, Valentina! Come vanno le cose con il lavoro e la maternità?

VALENTINA: Oh, non sai! Pensavo di chiedere sei mesi di aspettativa per stare con Davide e invece ne ho chiesti solo tre.

FIORELLA: Come mai? Mandi il bambino all'asilo-nido, o tua madre fa la babysitter?

VALENTINA: A dire il vero no, Roberto ha deciso di stare con Davide per tre mesi. Penso abbia ragione a dire che vuole passare più tempo col bambino, e per fortuna la legge lo permette.

FIORELLA: Quando torni a lavorare, allora?

VALENTINA: Ho l'aspettativa per altri due mesi, ma sarò comunque impegnata a tempo pieno. Crescere un figlio è il vero lavoro, adesso!

1. Esiste l'aspettativa per maternità in questo paese?

   ____

2. Cosa dice la legge in questo paese sui padri e le madri che lavorano? Che diritti hanno?

   ____

   ____

   ____

   ____

   ____

E Lei, signore,

farebbe il mammo[a]?

[a]*Mr. Mom*

B. È importante! Crea delle frasi nuove con le espressioni date tra parentesi.

ESEMPIO: Voto domani. (È importante / Ho intenzione / Voglio) →
È importante che io voti domani.
Ho intenzione di votare domani.
Voglio votare domani.

1. Si sono fatti sentire. (Sono contento / Pare / Credo)

____

____

2. Il governo applica le riforme. (È ora / Voglio / È importante)

____

____

3. Hai ripreso il lavoro. (È meglio / Sei felice / Lui spera)

____

____

4. Chiedete un grosso aumento. (È opportuno / Desiderate / Avete bisogno)

____

____

❖ **C. Obiettivi.** Di' cosa dovrebbe essere fatto in generale per ottenere i seguenti risultati, e poi di' cosa tu personalmente dovresti fare. Segui l'esempio.

ESEMPIO: per imparare bene l'italiano →
Per imparare bene l'italiano bisogna studiare ogni giorno.
Per imparare bene l'italiano bisogna che io vada al laboratorio.

1. per avere buona salute

____

____

2. per trovare un lavoro

____

____

3. per essere simpatico/a a tutti

____

____

4. per riuscire nella vita

____

____

LETTURA

Il mio primo lavoro

Silvia, una professoressa italiana di lingue, ci parla delle difficoltà del primo lavoro. Leggi il brano e rispondi alle domande.

Trovare lavoro in Italia, diciamocelo subito, non è una cosa facilissima, specialmente appena usciti dall'Università, con la laurea in mano. Dipende dal mercato, da cosa si ha in mente, dalla voglia di andare ad abitare lontano dalla famiglia e fare tanti sacrifici. Principalmente, dipende dal tipo di laurea che si ha e dai compromessi a cui siamo disposti. Per me, per esempio, è stata un po' dura: sono «emigrata» dalla Toscana in Val d'Aosta, dal momento che lì c'erano posti per l'insegnamento dell'inglese al liceo e alle scuole medie. Per insegnare in quella regione bisogna conoscere il francese, che io per fortuna conosco bene. Però trasferirmi dalla mia città a Courmayer non è stato facile. Anche avere il posto di insegnamento è stato lungo: ho fatto tanti concorsi, ho mandato tante domande, ho scritto tanti curriculi e ho ricevuto anche tanti rifiuti.[a] Ma non ho rinunciato, ho perseverato. Poi ho provato come sia difficile l'adattamento ad un nuovo ambiente anche con un lavoro. A Courmayer non avevo amici, solo colleghi di lavoro. E le mie mansioni nel lavoro non corrispondevano veramente al mio sogno (insegnare a studenti della scuola media è duro), per non parlare[b] dello stipendio, che non mi permetteva una vita molto agiata.[c] Non ho una visione negativa del lavoro di insegnante, comunque. Tra tante difficoltà, ci sono molte soddisfazioni: la possibilità di vedere «crescere» intellettualmente gli studenti, la possibilità di fare delle escursioni guidate, vedere posti nuovi, e imparare le lingue sempre meglio. Certo sarebbe bello vivere in Toscana, più vicino alla mia famiglia, ma nel complesso[d] sono contenta del mio lavoro e non lo cambierei.

[a] *rejections*
[b] per... *not to mention*
[c] *comfortable*
[d] nel... *all in all*

1. Secondo Silvia, perché è difficile trovare lavoro in Italia?

   ____

   ____

   ____

2. Cosa ha dovuto fare Silvia per trovare un posto di insegnamento?

   ____

   ____

   ____

3. Perché le piace il lavoro di insegnante?

   ____

   ____

   ____

UN PO' DI SCRITTURA

❖ **A. Accettare o rifiutare?** Scrivi una lettera al direttore (alla direttrice) della ditta a cui hai fatto domanda, accettando o rifiutando un'offerta di lavoro. Spiega il perché della tua decisione. Scrivi una pagina e mezzo. Scrivi su un tuo foglio.

ESEMPIO: Gentile Signora Scalfi,
sono molto felice di comunicarLe che ho deciso di accettare la Sua offerta di lavoro, benché le mie mansioni non siano state ancora ben definite...

❖ **B. Il mondo del lavoro.** Scegli un aspetto del mondo del lavoro in questo paese (disoccupazione, sindacati, ore lavorative, condizioni di lavoro, prospettive di lavoro per il futuro) e parlane, facendo riferimento ad altri paesi e a qualche esperienza personale. Scrivi una pagina e mezzo. Scrivi su un tuo foglio.

ESEMPIO: Io finora ho fatto solo qualche lavoro part-time, ma mia sorella lavora a Minneapolis per una ditta le cui condizioni di lavoro sono veramente buone. La ditta ha un asilo per i bambini dei dipendenti...

ATTUALITÀ

Cercate un lavoro? Le offerte d'impiego (lavoro) in pagina 94 sono state messe insieme dalla redazione della rivista *Epoca* dopo aver fatto «un rapido giro tra le aziende più in forma sul mercato». Leggi gli annunci di lavoro e trova un posto per le seguenti persone.

ESEMPIO: Daniele, 30 anni, laureato in economia e commercio, 110 e lode (*the highest score at the university*) →
Mi sembra che Daniele abbia tutti i requisiti necessari per lavorare come consulente... Daniele dovrebbe fare domanda...

1. Maria, 28 anni, laureata in ingegneria, residente a Milano

____

____

____

2. Caterina, 25 anni, diplomata in ragioneria (*accounting*), residente a Torino, disponibile a (*willing to*) trasferirsi

____

____

____

3. Debora, 21 anni, brava in tutti gli sport, energica, suona la chitarra, cerca un lavoro per l'estate in Calabria

____

____

____

4. Federico, 38 anni, laureato in scienze politiche, residente in provincia di Brindisi

____

____

____

UN SERVIZIO ESCLUSIVO DI EPOCA

Lavoro

Devi trovarlo? Vuoi cambiarlo? Ecco 6.000 posti in tutta Italia

346 posti pubblici

10 laureati in ingegneria o economia e commercio cerca Bain, Cuneo e Associati (società per la consulenza di strategia) voto 110 e lode, età tra i 28 e i 32 anni, per ruoli di dirigenza. Possibilità di partnership.
Telefonare a Bain, Cuneo e Associati: 02-58.28.81 (dott.ssa Nicoletta Nefri).

100 posti di lavoro. Sgs Thomson Semiconducteurs cerca 50 addetti tecnici che posseggano il titolo di studio di perito elettronico e 50 laureati in ingegneria elettronica.
Inviare un dettagliato curriculum a: Sgs-Thomson Microelectronics. Direzione Generale del Personale, Via Camillo Olivetti, 2 - 20041 Agrate Brianza, Milano, Casella postale 3651.

16 Regione **Piemonte** (Usl 72): 16 posti di infermiere professionale. Per i requisiti e le modalità della domanda fare riferimento all'ufficio del bollettino ufficiale, Piazza Castello, 165 - Torino - tel. 011/4323453.
Ultimo termine per inviare la domanda 10/3/00.

5 La Regione **Campania** bandisce 5 posti di autista di ambulanza, dei quali tre riservati al personale interno della Usl n.46. Per i requisiti richiesti e le modalità della domanda fare riferimento al Bollettino ufficiale della Regione n.5 del 24/1/2000 (tel. 081/7961111).
Ultimo termine per la domanda 27/3/2000.

6 La provincia di **Brindisi** bandisce un concorso per 2 posti da bibliotecario e 4 per aiuto bibliotecari a tempo determinato (un anno). Requisiti per i 2 posti da bibliotecario: età compresa tra i 18 e i 40 anni; laurea in lettere o storia o filosofia o giurisprudenza o scienze politiche o sociologia o magistero o lingue straniere o psicologia. Requisiti per i 4 posti da aiuto bibliotecario: diploma di maturità. Per ulteriori informazioni fare riferimento alla G.U. IV serie speciale n.9 dell'1/2/2000. Inviare la domanda a: Amministrazione provinciale, Via De Leo, 3 - 72100 Brindisi - tel 0831/221111.

1.670 assunzioni in aziende private

30 persone dai 20 ai 50 anni Mirino Marketing Srl ricerca per l'apertura e la direzione di nuovi uffici nell'area nord Italia.
Telefonare allo 02-98282221.

10 giovani, diplomati e laureati tra i 24 e i 28 anni, Gruppo Pam cerca. Anche senza precedenti esperienze per svolgere il ruolo di allievi direttori in supermercati di media grandezza. Preferibile la residenza a Roma, Milano, Torino o nel Triveneto, altrimenti la disponibilità al trasferimento. La selezione avverrà nella seconda metà di marzo, il contratto è a tempo indeterminato e la formazione dura dai 15 ai 18 mesi.
Il curriculum va inviato a Supermercati Pam, Direzione del personale, via delle Industrie, 8 - 30038 - Spinea (Venezia).

8 Regione **Lombardia**: 8 posti di cui uno di assistente medico di cardiologia, uno di assistente medico di psichiatria, uno di assistente medico di urologia, uno di assistente medico di organizzazione dei sistemi sanitari di base, uno di fisico coadiutore, tre di tecnico di neurofisiopatologia presso la Usl n.11. Per i requisiti fare riferimento al bollettino ufficiale della Regione n.1 del 5/1/2000. Per informazioni ufficio del bollettino ufficiale della Regione, via F. Filzi, 22 - Milano - 02/67654600.
Ultimo termine per la domanda 4/3/2000.

operatori turistici. Villaggi Vacanze Spa cerca per la prossima stagione estiva 200 giovani, e meno giovani, per i propri villaggi turistici in Calabria, Sardegna, Sicilia e Trentino Alto Adige. Il contratto stagionale (maggio-settembre). Le selezioni partono ora e la richiesta è molto ampia: direttori, vicedirettori, cuochi, maitre, chef de rang, barman, parrucchieri, massaggiatori, estetiste, bagnini, capi animazione, capi sport, istruttori (sub, velisti, canoisti, arcieri e tennisti), musicisti, disc-jockey, tecnici del suono e delle luci.
Inviare un dettagliato curriculum a: Villaggi Vacanze Spa, Via Paolo da Cannobio, 33 - 20122 Milano.

Comune di **Seregno**: 5 posti di vigile urbano. Requisiti: tra i 18 e i 40 anni, diploma di maturità. Per ulteriori informazioni fare riferimento alla G.U. IV serie speciale n.12 del 11/2/2000.
Ultimo termine per la domanda 12/3/2000.

Name ______________________

Date ______________________

Class ______________________

VOCABOLARIO PRELIMINARE

A. Contro il razzismo. Leggi il dialogo e rispondi alle domande.

ANTONIO: Sei proprio impegnato tu! Ho saputo che tu e Carla siete andati alla manifestazione contro il razzismo di ieri...

FABRIZIO: Sì, questo razzismo non è solo contro gli extracomunitari, è un razzismo contro tutti gli immigrati, del Nord contro il Sud, dei ricchi contro i poveri, dell'intolleranza e del materialismo...

ANTONIO: Capisco, Antonio! Non farmi una lezione di educazione civica! Qui in Italia non c'è un reale pericolo...

FABRIZIO: Non sono d'accordo, basta leggere i giornali. C'è sempre molta diffidenza verso gli immigrati. Sono emarginati. Finiscono per stare in miseria, o diventano senzatetto, o anche sono spinti alla criminalità. Dobbiamo mostrare la nostra solidarietà.

ANTONIO: Per questo hai portato i tuoi figli?

FABRIZIO: Certo. E anche i loro amici nordafricani. I giovani sono la nostra speranza. Il razzismo non è genetico, è una cosa che impariamo quando ascoltiamo chi ci dice che dobbiamo avere paura di chi è diverso. Quello che dico sempre ai miei figli è, invece, che la diversità è un valore positivo, che possiamo imparare tanto dalle altre culture...

1. A che tipo di manifestazione ha partecipato Fabrizio?

____

____

2. Chi è andato con Fabrizio?

____

____

3. Cosa pensa dei giovani Fabrizio?

____

____

4. Cosa pensa Antonio? Perché lui e Fabrizio non sono d'accordo?

____

____

B. La parola giusta. Abbina le parole della colonna A e le definizioni della colonna B.

A	B
1. _____ convivere	a. rimuovere
2. _____ essere a favore di	b. avere fiducia (*faith*) in
3. _____ eliminare	c. esprimere un giudizio
4. _____ apprezzare	d. vivere insieme
5. _____ fidarsi di	e. obiettare
6. _____ essere contro	f. stimare (*to esteem*)
7. _____ assicurare	g. favorire
8. _____ giudicare	h. rendere certo

—Ho dei problemi con i miei genitori: si ribellano reclamando[a] i loro diritti.

[a]*claiming*

C. Temi e problemi. Riscrivi le frasi sostituendo le parti indicate con un'espressione simile.

ESEMPIO: Il problema *della cocaina, dell'eroina e di altri stupefacenti* nelle scuole preoccupa molti genitori. →
Il problema *della droga* nelle scuole preoccupa molti genitori.

1. I giornalisti scrivono molti articoli *sui problemi di chi beve molti alcolici.*

   ____

2. Molti giovani oggi sono *coinvolti* (*engaged*) in varie questioni sociali.

   ____

3. La pubblicità alimenta (*encourages*) *il desiderio di comprare e di avere le cose di cui non abbiamo veramente bisogno.*

   ____

4. *Avere amici* è più importante che *avere molti soldi.*

   ____

5. *Il modo di vivere non pacifico* nelle grandi città è un altro grosso problema che la società d'oggi deve risolvere.

   ____

Proverbi e modi di dire

Moglie e buoi dei paesi tuoi.
(Take) a wife and oxen from your own parts.

Il mondo è bello perché è vario.
The world is beautiful because it's varied. (Vive la différence!)

D. La società d'oggi. Completa le frasi con la forma adatta delle seguenti parole. Usa le preposizioni articolate quando necessario.

Espressioni: la droga, l'ingiustizia, la giustizia, il materialismo, la povertà, il razzismo, l'uguaglianza

ESEMPIO: ___*Il materialismo*___ e il consumismo sono due grossi problemi della società capitalista.

1. Il ______________________ è una delle ragioni per cui i nuovi immigrati hanno difficoltà a trovare lavoro.
2. Purtroppo, molti giovani oggi cercano di risolvere i loro problemi con l'aiuto (di) ______________________.
3. I parenti della vittima hanno richiesto (*demanded*) che ______________________ sia fatta.
4. In una società ideale non ci dovrebbe essere né ______________________ né ______________________.
5. In una democrazia bisogna assicurare ______________________ tra tutti i cittadini.

GRAMMATICA

A. L'imperfetto del congiuntivo

A. Pregiudizi... Leggi il dialogo e rispondi alle domande.

CINZIA: Non sapevo che tuo padre avesse dei pregiudizi razziali.
IVAN: No, non credo che abbia dei pregiudizi... Il mio fidanzamento con Shamira l'ha solo sorpreso perché non aveva mai pensato che non potessi andare d'accordo con Daniela!
CINZIA: Certo, capisco che sperava che tu finissi per diventare dirigente nell'azienda di suo padre...
IVAN: Mio padre è sempre stato materialista, e poi sentissi mia madre! Ma per lei è stata la sorpresa opposta, non voleva che mi sposassi con Daniela ed è stata contentissima. Non speravo però che le piacesse Shamira. Invece, le piace molto, anche se non capisce la sua cultura. Mi piacerebbe molto se i miei decidessero di fare un bel viaggio in Etiopia.
CINZIA: Regalagli tu il viaggio, allora!

1. Perché il padre di Ivan non è contento del fidanzamento con Shamira?
____
2. Cosa pensa Ivan di suo padre?
____
3. Qual è la posizione della madre?
____

B. Bisognerebbe che... Ci sono tante cose da fare. Riscrivi le seguenti frasi. Comincia con **Bisognerebbe che** e fai tutti gli altri cambiamenti necessari.

ESEMPIO: Dovrei scrivere ai sindacati → Bisognerebbe che io scrivessi ai sindacati.

1. Marco dovrebbe fare amicizia con persone meno materialiste.

____

2. Dovresti deciderti a votare contro quella legge.

____

3. Dovremmo iscriverci a quel seminario sull'immigrazione.

____

4. Silvia e Piera dovrebbero leggere il giornale tutti i giorni.

____

5. Dovrei scegliere la sede (*center*) per la nostra prossima riunione.

____

6. Tu e Gianni dovreste imparare a convivere meglio con gli immigrati.

____

C. Lettera a un'amica. Completa la seguente lettera con le forme corrette del congiuntivo dei verbi tra parentesi.

—... ed ora vorrei che qualcuno del gentile pubblico venisse sul palcoscenico per aiutarmi nel prossimo numero!

Cara Francesca,

come vorrei che tu ____________________[1] (essere) qui! Mi sento molto solo. A dire la verità, ci sono molte persone intorno a (*around*) me, ma preferirei che ____________________[2] (andare) via tutti. Ho cercato tante volte di parlare con loro, ma non c'era nessuno che mi ____________________[3] (capire). Bisognerebbe che io ____________________[4] (cercare) di divertirmi un po'. Come se ____________________[5] (essere) possibile divertirsi senza di te!

Cara, vorrei che noi ____________________[6] (potere) stare insieme sempre, e che non ci ____________________[7] (dovere) essere questi orribili periodi di separazione. Ma, come ti ho detto quando ci siamo lasciati due giorni fa, sarebbe bene che noi ____________________[8] (pensare) di sposarci, e subito. Dicevi che ero pazzo, ma non era possibile che tu ____________________[9] (parlare) sul serio. Carissima Francesca, non vorresti che io ____________________[10] (morire) di dolore (*pain*), vero?

Scrivimi presto,

tuo Paolo

D. Preferenze, voglie, esigenze (*demands*)**...** Completa i dialoghetti con la forma corretta dell'infinito o del congiuntivo, presente o imperfetto. Aggiungi le preposizioni dove è necessario.

1. s1: Simone, era importante che tu ______________________ (fare) quello che ti avevo chiesto.

   s2: Mi dispiace, Nina. Avevo intenzione ______________________ (passare) dai Maffei ma all'ultimo momento sono dovuto ______________________ (restare) in ufficio.

2. s1: Franco preferisce che suo figlio ______________________ (studiare) legge.

   s2: Suo figlio, invece, preferirebbe ______________________ (frequentare) l'Istituto di Belle Arti. Spero che loro ______________________ (riuscire) mettersi d'accordo (*come to an agreement*).

3. s1: Ah, come mi piacerebbe ______________________ (provare) quelle sigarette francesi!

   s2: Ma Valeria, il dottore vuole che tu ______________________ (smettere) fumare.

4. s1: Lina, vorrei che tu non ______________________ (essere) così pignola (*fussy*)!

   s2: Gianni, io voglio solo che tu ______________________ (pulire) la tua camera ogni tanto!

5. s1: Adriana, bisogna che tu mi ______________________ (dare) una mano in cucina.

   s2: Ma Michele, credevo che tu ______________________ (potere) fare tutto da solo.

—Ehi, mamma, credevi che fossi nella vasca da bagno[a]?

[a]vasca... *bathtub*

❖ **E. Opinioni personali.** Completa le frasi secondo i tuoi desideri e le tue opinioni.

ESEMPIO: Bisognerebbe che tu... →
Bisognerebbe che tu fossi più impegnato in questioni sociali.

1. Vorrei che i miei amici...

   ____

2. Preferirei che la mia famiglia...

   ____

3. Quando ero giovane, i miei genitori non volevano che io...

   ____

4. Sarebbe meglio che, nella classe d'italiano, noi...

____

5. Speravo che il nuovo presidente...

____

6. Mi piacerebbe che...

____

B. Il trapassato del congiuntivo

A. Mah! Le tue convinzioni su cosa hanno fatto le seguenti persone sono sbagliate. Di' che ti eri sbagliato. Segui l'esempio.

ESEMPIO: Non vi siete sposati. → Credevo che vi foste già sposati.

1. Non hanno partecipato alla manifestazione contro il razzismo.

____

2. Francesca non è andata alla riunione.

____

3. Non si sono fermati dal meccanico.

____

4. Non abbiamo risolto il problema.

____

5. Non avete imparato ad usare il computer.

____

6. Non ti sei laureata.

____

B. La settimana di Beatrice. Racconta della settimana lavorativa di Beatrice. Unisci le due frasi. Usa **di** + infinito o **che** + congiuntivo. Segui l'esempio.

ESEMPI: Beatrice era contenta. Era riuscita a fare tutto. →
Beatrice era contenta di essere riuscita a fare tutto.

Beatrice era contenta. La sua amica aveva trovato un buon lavoro. →
Beatrice era contenta che la sua amica avesse trovato un buon lavoro.

1. Beatrice era contenta. Aveva ricevuto una lettera da un'azienda di Milano.

____

2. Era sorpresa. Le avevano scritto.

____

3. Era probabile. Qualcuno aveva fatto (*mentioned*) il suo nome.

____

4. Sembrava strano. Avevano deciso di chiamarla per un colloquio alle otto di mattina.

____

5. Aveva paura. L'azienda aveva ricevuto molte domande di lavoro.

____

6. Era contenta. Non era andata in vacanza in quel periodo.

____

C. Correlazione dei tempi nel congiuntivo

A. Trasformazioni. Completa le seguenti frasi con il tempo adeguato del congiuntivo.

ESEMPIO: È meglio che tu torni a casa. → Sarebbe meglio che tu tornassi a casa.

1. L'hanno mandato in Italia affinché imparasse l'italiano.

   Lo mandano in Italia affinché ____________________ l'italiano.

2. Penso che i tuoi genitori abbiano ragione.

   Pensavo che i tuoi genitori ____________________ ragione.

3. Vogliono che io faccia l'ingegnere.

   Volevano che io ____________________ l'ingegnere.

4. Speravano che il nuovo governo eliminasse il problema dei senzatetto.

   Sperano che il nuovo governo ____________________ il problema dei senzatetto.

5. Non c'è nessuno che si fidi di lui.

   Non c'era nessuno che ____________________ di lui.

6. Qualunque sia il problema, bisogna risolverlo.

   Qualunque ____________________ il problema, bisognava risolverlo.

7. Parlano dei tossicodipendenti come se non facciano parte della società.

   Parlavano dei tossicodipendenti come se non ____________________ parte della società.

8. Speriamo che lo sciopero finisca presto.

   Speravamo che lo sciopero ____________________ presto.

9. Vi do il libro perché lo leggiate.

   Vi ho dato il libro perché lo ____________________.

10. Eravamo contenti che fossero ritornati.

    Siamo contenti che ____________________.

B. Problemi sociali. Utilizza ciascun gruppo di parole per formare una frase.

ESEMPIO: Era bene che / Martin Luther King / lottare / contro / l'ingiustizia → Era bene che Martin Luther King lottasse contro l'ingiustizia.

1. Sarebbe bene che / la gente / cercare di / eliminare / l'inquinamento

   ___

2. Bisogna che / i genitori / fidarsi di / i figli

   ___

3. Tutti vorrebbero che / non esistere / il razzismo

   ___

4. È necessario che / il governo / assicurare / la parità di diritti / tra uomini e donne

   ___

5. È bene che / la gente / lottare / per / proteggere / i diritti di ogni cittadino

   ___

—Ma a te piacerebbe che venissimo a curiosare[a] in casa tua?

[a]*to snoop around*

C. Sbagliato! Meno male che c'è Gregorio per dirti come sono le cose! Reagisci alle sue affermazioni. Usa **pensare** o **credere.** Segui l'esempio.

ESEMPIO: Non sono fratelli, sono amici. → Oh, pensavo che fossero fratelli!

1. Non sono contro la legge sull'aborto; sono contro la legge che limita l'assistenza agli immigrati.

   ___

   ___

2. Non si è fermata a fare spese; si è fermata al Centro sociale.

   ___

   ___

3. Non hanno organizzato uno sciopero; hanno organizzato una conferenza sull'Aids.

   ___

   ___

4. Non sono extracomunitari; sono turisti.

   ___

   ___

D. Mini-dialoghi. Completa i dialoghetti con il tempo adeguato del congiuntivo o con l'infinito. Aggiungi le preposizioni, se sono necessarie.

1. s1: Credevo che Marco ____________________ (sapere) che Luisa e Stefano divorziano.

   s2: Tutt'altro. Quando l'ho visto mi ha detto di non ____________________ (saperne) niente.

2. s1: Mi dispiace tanto che il signor De Marco ____________________ (stare) male. Vorrei ____________________ (fare) qualcosa per la famiglia.

   s2: Non ti preoccupare—ho l'impressione che le cose ____________________ (andare) già un po' meglio per loro.

3. s1: Cercano qualcuno che ____________________ (conoscere) il BASIC.

   s2: Davvero? Pensavo che ____________________ già ____________________ (trovare) qualcuno.

4. s1: Questo documentario sull'alcolismo è il più interessante che io ____________________ mai ____________________ (vedere).

   s2: Sarebbe una buona idea che anche gli altri lo ____________________ (vedere).

5. s1: Ho deciso ____________________ (scrivere) una lettera ai Della Corte. Ti ricordi il loro padre?

   s2: Un uomo in gamba! Continuava ____________________ (organizzare) conferenze e ____________________ (lottare) contro i pregiudizi benché ____________________ (avere) più di novant'anni.

PROVA-QUIZ

A. Piccoli dialoghi. Completa i dialoghetti con la forma adeguata di **avere** o **essere** (all'indicativo o al congiuntivo).

1. s1: Mi hanno detto che Massimo si ______________ laureato in fisica. ______________ vero?

   s2: A dire la verità, ho l'impressione che ______________ la laurea in biologia, ma non sono sicuro.

2. s1: Come stanno i signori Ruggieri? Ho l'impressione che ______________ molto stanchi.

   s2: Anch'io lo penso. So che ______________ fatto un lungo viaggio; può darsi che ______________ bisogno di riposarsi.

3. s1: Sono sicura che Mario ______________ partito stamattina.

   s2: E allora dov'è? È possibile che non ______________ ancora arrivato?

4. s1: Sai, Giorgio mi ha detto che Cinzia e Sandro si ______________ lasciati.

   s2: Se te l'ha detto lui, è chiaro che ______________ una bugia!

B. Davvero? Nicola è sempre contento di sentire belle notizie sugli altri. Scrivi le sue reazioni alle seguenti affermazioni. Comincia ogni frase con **Davvero? Sono contento che...** Segui l'esempio.

ESEMPIO: Sai che non ci sono lezioni oggi? →
Davvero? Sono contento che non ci siano lezioni oggi!

1. Sai che Giovanna si sposa?
____
2. Sai che Mario è stato eletto?
____
3. Sai che Maurizio va in America?
____
4. Sai che gli zii si sono trasferiti a Sirmione?
____
5. Sai che Stefania ha avuto una borsa di studio (*scholarship*)?
____
6. Sai che il signor Feltrinelli sta meglio?
____
7. Sai che Guido si è sposato?
____
8. Sai che i Bargellini hanno comprato una casa?
____

C. Mi tengo il mio lavoro! Mimmo ha deciso di non accettare un lavoro che gli è stato offerto. Completa la sua lettera con le adeguate preposizioni (se necessarie) e la forma giusta dei verbi tra parentesi.

Gentile Dottor Perdomini,

dopo ________________[1] (pensare) a lungo alla Sua proposta di lavoro, ho deciso ________________[2] continuare ________________[3] scrivere per il mio giornale. Per quanto allettante (*enticing*) ________________[4] (essere) lo stipendio, mi sembra ________________[5] non trovare le condizioni di lavoro abbastanza soddisfacenti. Sfortunatamente non sono riuscito ________________[6] convincerLa ________________[7] accettare le mie richieste contrattuali, sebbene queste ________________[8] (essere) tutte molto ragionevoli.

Non credo ____________________[9] poter mai ____________________[10] abituarmi ____________________[11] lavorare ottanta ore la settimana; ____________________[12] (viaggiare) ogni week-end mi sembra poi assurdo.

A meno che Lei non ____________________[13] (riconsiderare) questi due punti, non penso ____________________[14] essere il candidato giusto per la Sua ditta.

La prego gentilmente ____________________[15] rispondere alla mia lettera prima che io ____________________[16] (partire) per le vacanze.

Distinti saluti,

Mimmo Celletti

D. Discussioni. Guido, Enrico e Giulia discutono le ultime dichiarazioni politiche del governo. Completa il dialogo con il congiuntivo presente, congiuntivo passato o l'infinito dei verbi dati tra parentesi.

GIULIA: Allora, sembra che (loro) ____________________[1] (volere) tagliare (*cut*) le pensioni...

GUIDO: Sì, pare che (loro) ____________________[2] (ridurre) la percentuale dello stipendio con cui si va in pensione.

ENRICO: Non hanno ancora capito che bisogna che i ricchi ____________________[3] (pagare) più tasse mentre è giusto che gli operai, gli impiegati, gli insegnanti ____________________[4] (avere) la pensione che si sono guadagnati!

GIULIA: Nella riunione di ieri credo che ____________________[5] (decidere) anche di dare più soldi alle scuole private. Così è probabile che le nostre scuole pubbliche, che adesso funzionano molto meglio di quelle private, ____________________[6] (diventare) le scuole dei poveri. Peccato che io non ____________________[7] (essere) ministro!

GUIDO: Mi sembra che (noi) ____________________[8] (essere) tornati indietro di cinquant'anni!

E. Traduzioni. Traduci in italiano. Scrivi su un tuo foglio.

When Fatima and Manuel arrived in Italy, they were hoping to become integrated (**integrarsi**) into the new society without too many problems. They would have preferred to stay in their country, if it had only been possible. . . . It was important for them to find a job right away, but it wasn't easy. They had to fight against the intolerance of many, and sometimes they wished they had never come. Fortunately, they met many people engaged in social causes who were happy to help them.

LETTURA

La società multiculturale

Leggi il brano e rispondi alle domande.

Anche l'Italia, oggi, è una società multiculturale. Deve affrontare i problemi che integrazione, razzismo e disoccupazione portano con se. Prima dell'arrivo dei nordafricani (dalla Tunisia, dall'Algeria e dal Marocco), l'Italia aveva già il problema interno, economico ma anche sociale, della differenza tra Nord e Sud (un Nord più ricco e un Sud meno sviluppato e più povero, che ancora oggi esiste). È uno stereotipo conosciuto bene quello dell'italiano meridionale considerato pigro, magari mafioso, non «italiano». Uno stereotipo che non prende in considerazione come la ricchezza del Nord è stata creata da migliaia di meridionali che sono emigrati dal Sud al Nord in cerca di lavoro e che si sono scontrati con le difficoltà di integrazione. Hanno aiutato l'economia della nazione, negli anni '50 e '60, quando l'Italia ha avuto una forte espansione economica.

Adesso l'Italia, quinta potenza industriale, è un paese ricco. Le crisi internazionali nei paesi a lei vicini hanno costretto grandi masse di uomini, donne e bambini a chiedere asilo in Italia dall'Albania, dalla Croazia, dalla Bosnia e ancora prima dal Marocco, dal Senegal o dall'Etiopia o Somalia (un tempo colonie italiane). Questo ha creato tensioni interne anche perché in Italia c'è una forte disoccupazione tra i giovani, specialmente nel Sud.

Alcuni partiti hanno chiesto di vietare l'ingresso a queste persone, altri hanno chiesto di dividere l'Italia in due o tre nazioni indipendenti, anche per tagliare ogni legame del Nord col Sud. La maggior parte della popolazione italiana ha risposto con la solidarietà, ma i problemi ovviamente continuano ad esistere.

Forse una politica unica europea e l'aiuto all'Italia da parte dell'Europa riusciranno a migliorare la situazione. Ma intanto l'Italia del 2000, da terra da cui si emigrava un secolo fa per andare in America, è diventata terra di immigrazione, una patria promessa per molti popoli e molta gente esiliata dai paesi dell'Est e del Sud del mondo.

1. Qual è uno stereotipo italiano nella divisione tra Sud e Nord? ______________________

   ____

2. Che cosa ha creato tensioni in Italia in anni recenti? ______________________

   ____

3. Che cosa è cambiato nell'Italia di oggi? ______________________

   ____

UN PO' DI SCRITTURA

❖ **A. Problemi sociali.** Violenza, povertà, alcolismo: scegli uno di questi problemi. Come vorresti che fosse risolto? Scrivi una pagina e mezzo. Scrivi su un tuo foglio.

ESEMPIO: Per risolvere il problema della povertà, vorrei che la gente fosse disposta a pagare più tasse. In questo modo, potremmo creare più posti di lavoro, aprire asili economici ed efficienti...

❖ **B. Diversità.** Società multietnica: è possibile la convivenza (*living together*)? Scrivi una pagina e mezzo. Scrivi su un tuo foglio.

ESEMPIO: Secondo me, la convivenza non è solo possibile ma è anche necessaria. Dire che il mondo sta diventando più piccolo è un cliché, ma è un cliché verissimo; se la gente imparasse a rispettare le differenze...

ATTUALITÀ

A. Basta un po' di buona volontà (*will*)! Leggi questo spot pubblicitario e rispondi alle domande che seguono. Scrivi frasi complete.

C'È BISOGNO ANCHE DEL TUO AIUTO PER LOTTARE CONTRO L'AIDS

SOSTIENI LA LILA

PREVENZIONE
INFORMAZIONE
ASSISTENZA
SOLIDARIETÀ
DIFESA DEI DIRITTI

ELFO

Versamenti sul c/c postale N° **12713202** intestato a:
L.I.L.A. Sede di Milano: V.le Tibaldi, 41 - 20136 MILANO
oppure: Cariplo - Agenzia 29 - Milano c/c N° **17350/1** intestato a
L.I.L.A. Nazionale

Per informazioni telefona ai seguenti numeri dove potrai ricevere direttamente risposte alle tue domande o chiedere l'indirizzo delle 25 sedi dislocate su tutto il territorio nazionale per avere informazioni più specifiche sulla tua realtà.

LILA Nazionale 02/58114980 Servizio informazioni 02/58103515

1. Cos'è la Lila?

   ____

2. Secondo te, a chi è diretto questo appello (*appeal*)?

   ____

3. A che numero bisogna telefonare per avere informazioni?

   ____

❖ 4. Ci sono leghe simili a questa in questo paese? Come si chiamano? Le sostieni (*Do you support them*)?

   ____

   ____

❖ **B. Solidarietà.** Alcolismo, tossicodipendenza, razzismo, intolleranza religiosa, malattie incurabili: crea un tuo annuncio pubblicitario che abbia a che fare con uno dei problemi elencati. Specifica di che associazione si tratta, cosa si richiede, dove telefonare, eccètera. Scrivi da 8 a 10 frasi. Scrivi su un tuo foglio.

ESEMPIO: LALC, la Lega Americana per la Lotta contro il Cancro! Preveniamolo (*Let's prevent it*), informiamoci! Molte persone hanno bisogno del tuo aiuto... Per informazioni, telefona a...